Risk Financing

Risk Financing

Michael W. Elliott, MBA, CPCU

Senior Vice President
MMC Enterprise Risk, a unit of
Marsh Inc.

First Edition

American Institute for Chartered Property Casualty Underwriters/
Insurance Institute of America
720 Providence Road, Malvern, Pennsylvania 19355

© 2000

American Institute for Chartered Property Casualty Underwriters/
Insurance Institute of America

First Edition • Fifth Printing • January 2004

Library of Congress Control Number: 134182
ISBN 0-89462-142-4

Foreword

The American Institute for Chartered Property Casualty Underwriters and the Insurance Institute of America are independent, nonprofit organizations serving the educational needs of the risk management, property-casualty, and financial services businesses. The Institutes develop a wide range of curricula, study materials, and examinations in response to the educational needs of various elements of these businesses. The American Institute confers the Chartered Property Casualty Underwriter (CPCU®) professional designation on people who meet its examination, ethics, and experience requirements. The Insurance Institute of America offers associate designations and certificate programs in the following areas:

- Accounting and Finance
- Agent Studies
- Business Writing
- Claims
- Global Risk Management and Insurance
- Information Technology
- Insurance Fundamentals
- Management
- Marine Insurance
- Performance Improvement
- Personal Insurance
- Premium Auditing
- Regulation and Compliance
- Reinsurance
- Risk Management
- Surety Bonds and Crime Insurance
- Surplus Lines
- Underwriting

The American Institute was founded in 1942 through a cooperative effort between property-casualty insurance company executives and insurance professors. Faculty members at The Wharton School of the University of Pennsylvania in Philadelphia led this effort. The CPCU designation arose from the same type of business and academic partnership at Wharton as the Chartered Life Underwriter (CLU) designation did in 1927.

The Insurance Institute of America was founded in 1909 by five educational organizations across the United States. It is the oldest continuously functioning national organization offering educational programs for the property-casualty insurance business. It merged with the American Institute in 1953.

The Insurance Research Council (IRC), founded in 1977, is a division of the Institutes. It is a not-for-profit research organization that examines public policy issues that affect property-casualty insurers and their customers. IRC research reports are distributed widely to insurance-related organizations, public policy authorities, and the media.

The broad knowledge base in property-casualty insurance and financial services created by the Institutes over the years is contained mainly in our textbooks. Although we use electronic technology to enhance our educational materials, communicate with our students, and deliver our examinations, our textbooks are at the heart of our educational activities. They contain the information that you as a student must read, understand, integrate into your existing knowledge, and apply to the tasks you perform as part of your job.

Despite the vast range of subjects and purposes of the more than eighty individual textbook volumes we publish, they all have much in common. First, each book is specifically designed to increase knowledge and develop skills that can improve job performance and help students achieve the educational objectives of the course for which it is assigned. Second, all of the manuscripts for our texts are reviewed widely before publication, by both insurance business practitioners and members of the risk management and insurance academic community. In addition, the revisions of our texts often incorporate improvements that students and course leaders have suggested. We welcome constructive comments that help us to improve the quality of our study materials. Please direct any comments you may have on this text to my personal attention.

We hope what you learn from your study of this text will expand your knowledge, increase your confidence in your skills, and support your career growth. If so, then you and the Institutes will truly be *succeeding together*.

Terrie E. Troxel, Ph.D., CPCU, CLU
President and CEO
American Institute for CPCU
Insurance Institute of America

Preface

This text provides an overview of risk financing and risk financing plans. Risk financing is defined in this text as a means to obtain funds to pay for or offset an organization's losses that arise from risk. Risk is defined in this text as a potential variation in outcomes, so it can result in unexpected losses and, often, unexpected gains for an organization. Therefore, an important concept that is discussed throughout this text is that an organization can use its gains arising from risk to finance some or all of its losses arising from risk.

An organization's losses can arise from many different types of risk, including operating, credit, financial, and hazard (accidental) risk. While this text concentrates on financing losses arising from hazard risk, it also discusses the financing of losses arising from other types of risk, particularly foreign exchange rate risk and interest rate risk. Funds to pay for or offset an organization's losses can arise from internal sources, such as an organization's cash flow or assets, or from external sources such as the organization's insurer, banker, or stockholders. The various types of risk and sources of funds for risk financing are discussed throughout the text. Included is a discussion of enterprise risk management, which is a comprehensive approach to managing all of an organization's risks.

The chapters of this text build on one another. The first two chapters introduce basic risk financing concepts, and later chapters use these concepts to illustrate various types of risk financing plans. Many of the chapters describe traditional risk financing plans, such as guaranteed cost insurance, self-insurance, retrospectively rated insurance, and captive insurance plans. The last two chapters describe nontraditional plans, including finite risk insurance plans, integrated risk insurance plans, and various capital market (non-insurance) products for risk financing.

Most of the plans discussed throughout this text are appropriate for large organizations that retain rather than transfer a significant amount of their losses that arise from risk. Although the plans discussed are mainly used to finance hazard risk, some organizations are using them to finance losses from other types of risk, such as interest rate risk and foreign exchange rate risk.

Risk financing should be viewed from a global perspective. The concepts described and analyzed in this text apply universally. Although most of the examples given are from the United States, where this text originated, we have also included examples from countries outside the U.S.

Reviewers play an important role in the development of a text. I thank the following individuals who reviewed the entire manuscript and provided useful comments.

James D. Blinn

Alan W. Friedlander, CPCU, ARM

Larry L. Klein, CPCU

Michael J. McNamara, Ph.D., CPCU, ARM

In addition, I thank the following individuals who provided useful comments on one or two of the chapters: Robert O. Ball, Jr.; Albert J. Beer, FCAS; C. Zakia Campbell, ARM; Len Churnetski; George L. Head, Ph.D., CPCU, ARM; Doo-Sung Kim, CPCU, ARM, ARe; David S. Laster, Ph.D., ARM; Thomas A. McCarthy; William F. Traester, CPCU, ARM.

Jean-Paul A. Louisot, ARM, manages the ARM program in France and provided helpful comments on five of the chapters.

I hope you enjoy this text. If you have any questions or comments, please contact the Institutes' Customer Service department at (800) 644-2101.

Michael W. Elliott

Contents

Chapter 1

Introduction to Risk Financing

Introduction

Every organization faces risk. Examples are the possibilities of damage by fire, changes in interest rates, and loss of reputation. Although an organization can control most risk to some degree, it must finance its residual, or remaining risk. This text explores contemporary risk financing concepts and applies them to medium-sized and large-sized organizations.

Before this chapter discusses risk financing in detail, it is important to define the terms "risk," "loss," and "loss exposure." The term **risk**, as used in this text, is potential variation in outcomes.[1] Risk can result in unexpected losses and, often, unexpected gains for an organization. A **loss**

> **Risk** is potential variation in outcomes.
>
> A **loss** is an outcome that reduces an organization's financial value.
>
> A **loss exposure** is anything that presents a possibility of loss.

is any outcome that reduces an organization's financial value. Examples are the destruction of an organization's property or a rise in an organization's cost of an input to its production process. A **loss exposure** (sometimes called a risk exposure) is anything that presents a possibility of loss, such as an organization's property that might be destroyed by fire or the potential of a rise in the market price of an input to an organization's production process. Many risk exposures, such as a potential rise or fall in interest rates, present an organization with a possibility of a gain as well as a loss.

Organizations are exposed to risk from many sources. As discussed later in this chapter, these sources arise from an organization's operations and finances and include specific types of risk such as business, credit, hazard (accidental), and foreign exchange risks. An organization that makes a capital investment is also exposed to risk because the cash flow arising from the investment may or may not meet the organization's expectations.

Some types of risk are within an organization's control while others are not. Although subpar financial performance is often attributed to poor management, it can arise from a noncontrollable risk, such as an increase in the market price of an input of production. An example is an increase in the worldwide market price of oil, which increases an oil refiner's costs and reduces its profit margins.

While most losses are a direct expense to an organization, some arise because of a missed opportunity. For example, an organization might delay a decision to modify its product in response to changes in market demand. Therefore, the organization might lose market share and profit that it could have made on that product. An example is the delayed entrance of many retail brokerage firms into on-line trading.

Because losses arise from risk, organizations are uncertain about whether or not losses will occur and about their magnitude. An organization should manage its risk of loss because losses can lower its net income, net worth, and cash flow. Techniques available for managing risk of loss include avoidance, control, diversification, retention, and transfer. This text covers the financial aspects of managing risk and, therefore, focuses on various ways that an organization can retain or transfer its losses.

Many financial instruments, including insurance, allow organizations to transfer their losses that arise from risk. A key consideration for most organizations is not how much risk they *can* transfer but rather how much risk they *should* transfer to maximize their return on capital. For example, financial services firms, such as banks, are in the business of bearing risk for a return.[2] A variety of financial instruments (called "derivatives," which are discussed later) is available that allows a bank to eliminate risk, even all of its risk if it so chooses. However, these instruments have a cost. Therefore, a bank maximizes its value by retaining and managing an appropriate level of risk that provides it with a sufficient return on its capital.

What Is Risk Financing?

Risk financing means to obtain funds to pay for or offset an organization's losses that occur.[3] The funds to pay for or offset an organization's losses can arise from internal

Risk financing means to obtain funds to pay for or offset an organization's losses.

sources, such as the organization's cash flow or assets, or from external sources, such as the organization's insurer, banker, or stockholders (when equity is issued to pay for a loss). The sources of funds can be arranged before (pre-loss financing) or after (post-loss financing) a loss occurs. Also, an organization can use its gains arising from risk to offset some or all of its losses.

Examples of Risk Financing

A machine shop business that owns a building is subject to risk because the building might or might not be damaged by a fire. If a fire occurs, the cost to repair the building (the amount of the loss) can be paid for by the shop if it has sufficient cash flow or assets available for that purpose. Alternatively, the shop can arrange to transfer its risk of loss before a loss occurs (pre-loss financing) by purchasing insurance on the building, thereby using external funds (the insurer's) to repair the building if a loss occurs.

An importer in the United States that negotiates its contracts in foreign currencies is subject to risk because the exchange rate of the foreign currency in terms of the U.S. dollar might rise or fall. If the exchange rate of the foreign currency rises, the importer suffers a loss because it must pay more U.S. dollars than it expected to pay for its imported goods. The importer can pay for its loss out of its own cash flow or assets. Alternatively, it can purchase a financial instrument to hedge against a foreign exchange loss (pre-loss financing).

Sources of Risk for Organizations

The many sources of risk that organizations face have no standard categories. Exhibit 1-1 attempts to categorize risk by breaking it down into operational and financial/market risk, each with its own subcategories. The categories are not intended to be mutually exclusive or exhaustive. Some professionals add categories to the list, such as regulatory, technological, and strategic risk. Others use different terms, such as "accidental risk" in place of "hazard risk" and "operating risk" in place of "operational risk." This text uses the risk categories shown in Exhibit 1-1, which are defined throughout this section.

Exhibit 1-1
Various Sources of Risk for an Organization

Operational Risk

Operational risk is defined in different ways by different organizations because its characteristics are specific to a particular organization. It is often defined by the types of risks it includes, such as business and operating risks. Some organizations also include credit risk and hazard (accidental) risk under operational risk.

> **Operational risk** is specific to a business and is defined by the types of risks it includes, such as business, financial, operating, credit, hazard, and reputation risks.

Business Risk

Business risk arises from changes in economic variables, such as product demand and market competition.[4] For example, a jean manufacturer faces business risk because if the demand for jeans falls, the manufacturer will have lower revenues. Alternatively, the manufacturer will have higher revenues if demand rises. Changes in regulations and technology can also affect business risk.[5]

> **Business risk** is the possibility of loss or gain due to economic variables, such as product demand and market competition.

Risk Management in Practice

Business Risk at Mattel

In the fiercely competitive toy business, hot products can quickly lose their luster, resulting in a loss of revenue for the products' manufacturers. Toy makers seek to offset losses from this business risk by purchasing smaller organizations that have original ideas or unique products. For example, in 1999, Mattel, a toy manufacturer, purchased Learning Company, a leader in children's software.[6]

Financial Risk

Financial risk is the risk that an organization will not be able to meet its fixed financial obligations, such as the principal and interest payments on its debt. A firm is obligated by contract to meet these commitments regardless of its level of gross earnings. Therefore, a firm's level of financial risk increases as it uses higher levels of debt financing.[7]

> **Financial risk** is the risk that a firm will not be able to meet fixed financial obligations, such as the principal and interest payments on its debt.

Operating Risk

Operating risk can be defined as the risk that existing systems may malfunction or break down. An example is a computer malfunction that could disrupt power to an auto assembly plant, resulting in lost sales and profits for the auto manufacturer.

> **Operating risk** is the possibility of loss due to the malfunction or breakdown of existing technology or support systems.

Credit Risk

Credit risk is the risk of loss due to the failure of a borrower or counterparty[8] to fulfill its contractual obligations.[9] For example, credit risk is central to the operations of a financial institution, such as a bank. The *1998 Annual Report* of The Chase Manhattan Corporation contains the following statement: "Chase seeks opportunities to take credit risk prudently and manage it effectively in order to create value for its shareholders."[10] An insurance company takes credit risk when an insured's premium is past due because the insured may or may not pay the premium.

> **Credit risk** is the possibility of loss due to the borrower's failure to fulfill its contractual obligation to pay back funds.

Hazard (Accidental) Risk

Hazard risk, also called **accidental risk**, is the risk of loss resulting from property, liability, net income, and human resource loss exposures. Examples are losses to property due to perils such as fire and explosion, and legal liability for products that cause harm to others. Traditionally, hazard risks have been transferred (wholly or partially) through property-liability insurance.

> **Hazard risk** (also called **accidental risk**) is the possibility of loss arising from property, liability, net income, and human resource loss exposures.

Risk Management in Practice

Hazard Risk at British American Tobacco

In 1998, there was a $206 billion industry-wide settlement between the U.S. State Attorneys General and the tobacco industry over accusations that cigarettes cause disease. In early 1999, British American Tobacco said that losses in its most recent quarter had widened due to costs of the settlement. British American Tobacco's quarterly loss grew to 171 million British pounds from 163 million British pounds a year earlier, with 463 million British pounds of settlement costs recorded in the quarter.[11]

Reputation (Brand-Name) Risk

Reputation risk (or **brand-name risk**) results from a real or perceived loss of reputation or tarnishing of a brand name. For example, Exxon's reputation was harmed after the Exxon Valdez spilled oil and polluted the coast off Alaska.

Reputation risk (brand-name risk) refers to a real or perceived loss of reputation or tarnishing of a brand name.

Financial/Market Risk

Financial/market risk is the second major category of risk mentioned in this section. It should not be confused with financial risk, which was mentioned previously. **Financial/market risk** is defined in this text as the exposure to a change in the value of financial instruments caused by a change in market prices or rates, including changes in interest rates, foreign exchange rates, securities prices, and commodities prices.[12]

Financial/market risk is the possibility of loss or gain in the value of financial instruments caused by a change in market prices or rates. It includes changes in interest rates, foreign exchange rates, securities prices, and commodities prices.

Risk Management in Practice

Financial/Market Risk at Crown Cork & Seal Company

Crown Cork & Seal is a leading manufacturer of packaging products for consumer marketing companies around the world. As such, it is subject to several types of financial/market risk. The 1998 Annual Report of Crown Cork & Seal contains the following statement:

> In the normal course of business, the operations of the Company are exposed to fluctuations in currency values, interest rates, commodity prices, and other market risks. The Company addresses these risks through a program that includes the use of financial instruments.[13]

Interest Rate Risk

Interest rate risk is the chance that interest rates will rise or fall. An organization that depends on debt to finance its operations faces interest rate risk. With variable rate debt, a rise or fall in market interest rates would raise or lower the organization's cost of borrowing. When refinancing debt, an organization might be faced with higher or lower market interest rates than those that existed when it arranged the original debt.

Interest rate risk is the chance that interest rates will rise or fall.

Foreign Exchange Rate Risk

Foreign exchange rate risk is the chance that the value of the currency of one country will change relative to the value of the currency of another country and, as a result, will affect an organization's revenue or costs.

Foreign exchange rate risk is the chance that the value of the currency of one country will change relative to the value of the currency of another country.

Example of Foreign Exchange Rate Risk

A United Kingdom automobile manufacturer that pays for parts from Japan with Japanese yen is exposed to foreign exchange rate risk. The manufacturer will suffer a loss if the exchange rate of the British pound falls relative to the Japanese yen, causing the imported parts to cost more in terms of British pounds. If the exchange rate of the British pound rises relative to the Japanese yen, the manufacturer will experience a gain. The imported parts will cost less in terms of British pounds.

Commodity Price Risk

Commodity price risk is the risk that the price of a commodity, such as crude oil, will rise or fall. In order for this risk to affect an organization, the commodity must be one of the inputs or outputs of its production process.

Commodity price risk is the possibility that the price of a commodity, such as crude oil, will rise or fall.

Speculative Versus Pure Risk

Many of the risks previously defined are **speculative risks** because they can result in either a loss or a gain. For example, there

> **Speculative risk** is a risk that can result in either a loss or a gain.

could be a fall in the demand for a product (a business risk), resulting in a loss, or alternatively, there could be an increase in demand for that same product, resulting in a gain. A rise in interest rates (a financial/market risk) increases an organization's cost of borrowing (a loss); however, a fall in interest rates lowers the organization's cost of borrowing (a gain).

Some of the risks described in this chapter are **pure risks** because they present a possibility of loss only, with no possibility of gain.

> **Pure risk** is a risk that can result only in a loss and no gain.

For example, operating, credit, and hazard risks fall into this category.

Systematic Versus Unsystematic Risk

Risk can be systematic or unsystematic. **Systematic risk (nondiversifiable risk)** means that gains or losses arising from risk exposures in a portfolio tend to occur all at the same time rather than randomly. Because

> **Systematic risk (nondiversifiable risk)** refers to gains or losses on a portfolio of risks that tend to occur at the same time, rather than randomly.

of this characteristic, it is not possible to reduce systematic risk through diversification. Losses arising from general economic conditions present a systematic risk because they tend to affect all firms at the same time. For example, when monetary conditions become tight, interest rates increase for all firms at the same time. Therefore, if an insurance company were to insure firms against increases in interest rates, it would not be able to diversify its portfolio of interest rate risk by underwriting a large number of insureds because all of them would suffer losses at the same time.

Unsystematic risk (diversifiable risk), sometimes called "firm-specific risk," means that gains or losses on a portfolio of risk exposures tend to occur randomly. For example, building fires tend to occur randomly

> **Unsystematic risk (diversifiable risk)** means that gains or losses on a portfolio of risks tend to occur randomly.

and, therefore, a portfolio of fire risk exposures contains unsystematic risk. An insurance company can diversify the risk associated with building fires by insuring a large number of buildings (exposures), each in a different location. Given a sufficient number of fire risk exposures, an insurance company is able to predict its fire losses for any one period with a reasonable degree of accuracy and, therefore, to determine an adequate premium.

Focus of This Text

While this text concentrates on financing losses arising from hazard (accidental) risk, it also discusses the financing of other types of risk, including speculative risk. For example, Chapter 10 discusses how an insurance contract can be used to protect an organization from both hazard losses and financial/market losses.

Characteristics of Losses

Losses have different characteristics depending on the source of risk from which they arise. These characteristics, which have implications for the way in which an organization finances its risk, include frequency and severity as well as the possibility of a delay in discovery and payment.

Frequency and Severity Characteristics of Losses

An organization's losses are characterized by frequency (number) and severity (size). These concepts apply to all types of losses, whether arising from an organization's operational or financial/market risks.

Frequency and Severity of Losses

Frequency of losses is the number of occurrences resulting in loss over a specified time period, such as a year. **Severity** of losses is the size of losses in terms of the dollar amount that must be paid to recover from the losses. Severity can be used to describe the size of an individual loss or of a group of losses.

High-severity/low-frequency losses are severe but infrequent losses that arise from catastrophic occurrences, such as plant explosions or earthquakes. By contrast, low-severity/high-frequency losses are common. An example is physical damage losses to automobiles within a large fleet.

Most large organizations experience a high number of relatively small hazard (accidental) losses. For example, many large manufacturing firms annually experience a large number of minor injuries to their employees. Any organization might suffer a catastrophic loss, such as a large fire or a plant explosion, on—one would hope—an infrequent basis. In between these two loss extremes are medium-sized losses that may or may not occur with some regularity.

Exhibit 1-2 provides a conceptual model that illustrates the general relationships among losses with different frequency-severity characteristics. The width of the triangle illustrates the relative frequency of losses at different severity levels. For most organizations, the higher the severity of a loss, the lower its frequency. The opposite is also true, with the lower the severity of a loss, the higher its frequency.

Some categories of loss are not represented by the triangle. For example, organizations frequently experience losses that are characterized by both low severity and low frequency. Those losses are usually of little financial consequence to an organization. Organizations also could experience losses characterized by both high severity and high frequency. These losses are likely to be difficult to transfer and might bankrupt an organization.

Exhibit 1-2
Frequency and Severity Characteristics of Losses

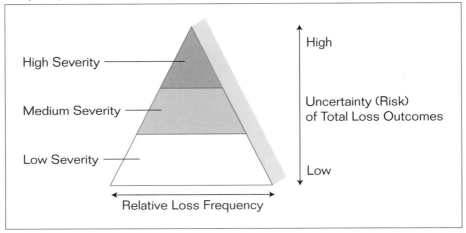

The top segment of the triangle in Exhibit 1-2 represents catastrophic losses that are characterized by both high severity and low frequency. The cost of these losses is unpredictable, regardless of whether they are looked at individually or as a group. Therefore, they present a high risk to organizations. Most organizations arrange to transfer these types of losses before they occur (pre-loss financing).

The bottom segment of the triangle in Exhibit 1-2 represents losses that are characterized by both low severity and high frequency. Organizations with a high frequency of losses find that low-severity losses, taken as a whole, are predictable. Therefore, organizations usually retain them. It follows that organizations with a low frequency of low-severity losses retain them as well.

The middle segment of the triangle in Exhibit 1-2 represents losses that are characterized by medium severity and medium frequency. Organizations might choose to either retain or transfer these losses depending on their tolerance for risk and the cost of risk transfer.

"High," "medium," and "low" are relative terms that vary by organization. For example, "low" loss severity would probably be much smaller for a medium-sized organization than for a Fortune 500 organization. In like manner, "medium" loss severity for an organization that is financially secure with a high risk tolerance would probably be much larger than for an organization that is financially weak with a low risk tolerance. Therefore, the placement of the horizontal lines in the triangle varies by organization.

The concepts of frequency and severity apply to all types of losses faced by organizations, not just hazard (accidental) losses. For example, the cost for inputs of production can rise and fall by various amounts during a specific time period. Increases in the cost of these inputs create losses to an organization because it must pay more than usual for the inputs. Similarly, decreases in the cost of these inputs create gains for the organization. The concepts of frequency and severity also apply to other types of organizational losses such as those arising from business risk and reputation risk.

Frequency and Severity of Losses to an Oil Refiner

Assume crude oil prices rise and fall over time as shown below:

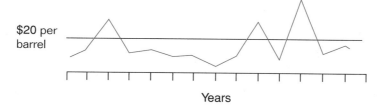

$20 per barrel

Years

Furthermore, assume that an independent oil refiner expects the market price of crude oil, which is an input to its production, to equal $20 per barrel over the next several years. Therefore, the oil refiner realizes a gain when the price of crude oil falls below $20 a barrel and suffers a loss when the price of crude oil rises above $20 a barrel. From the oil refiner's perspective, the frequency and severity with which crude oil prices rise above $20 a barrel represent frequency and severity of loss due to a price upswing in an input of production.[14] In the graph, the frequency of loss over the years is three because the price went above $20 per barrel three times. The severity of loss in each of the three years is the difference between the price of crude oil paid by the refiner and $20 per barrel, multiplied by the number of barrels purchased.

Delayed Discovery and Payment of Hazard Losses

For some types of hazard risks, mainly those arising from liability exposures, a substantial delay can occur between when a loss occurs and when it is discovered and paid. As discussed throughout this text, that loss characteristic has implications for the design of a risk financing plan.

Paid, Reserved, and Incurred Losses

Paid, reserved, and incurred losses are concepts that are usually applied to losses arising from hazard risks. At any point in time, **paid losses** are the amounts already paid for losses that have occurred. **Loss reserves** are estimates of the amounts to be paid in the future for losses that have occurred.

Loss reserves consist of case reserves plus incurred-but-not-reported reserves. **Case reserves** are estimates of the amount to be paid on losses that are known (sometimes called reported losses). **Incurred-but-not-reported (IBNR) loss reserves** are estimates of the amount to be paid on losses that have occurred but have yet to be discovered by (or reported to) the organization suffering the loss. IBNR estimates are usually derived from past loss discovery patterns.

Incurred losses are determined by the following formula:

Incurred Losses = Paid losses + Loss reserves

Incurred losses are usually accumulated on a yearly basis, with individual losses categorized by the year in which they occur. As loss payments are made, a year's total paid losses increase, its total loss reserves decrease by an equal amount, and its total incurred losses remain the same. As losses occur, a year's total incurred losses increase because reserves are established for the estimated future payments on those losses. Depending on the type of losses involved, an incurred loss account is often kept open for several years until all losses that occurred in a single year are discovered and paid.

Even well after a loss year has ended, the total incurred losses for that year can increase because losses that were not reserved for are discovered. Also, reserves for reported losses are frequently revised upward well after the year in which the losses occurred because additional information that justifies an increase in the estimated future payments for those losses is discovered. This tendency for incurred losses to increase over time is known as **loss development**.

Losses arising from liability exposures usually are subject to a substantial delay between when losses occur, are discovered, and are paid. Losses arising from property exposures usually are not. Exhibit 1-3 shows the typical relationships between paid, reserved, and incurred losses arising from a single year for a liability exposure.

Note that over time total paid losses from a single year increase. The total incurred losses also increase, or develop. Several years after the year in which the losses in question occurred, all losses are paid, and total paid losses equal total incurred losses.

Exhibit 1-3
Losses Arising From a Liability Exposure

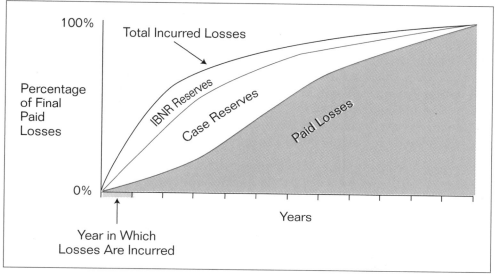

Loss Retention and Transfer

Two basic risk financing techniques used by organizations to finance their losses are retention and transfer. This section compares those techniques.

Retention means that an organization uses its own resources to pay for its losses. Cash to pay for losses can be generated from cash flow, taken from current assets, borrowed, or contributed by stockholders in exchange for an ownership interest in the organization. The amount that an organization will pay for its retained losses is uncertain, so they have the potential to significantly reduce an organization's net income, net worth, and cash flow. An organization that retains losses arising from its speculative risks, as opposed to its pure risks, also retains the benefit of any gains arising from those speculative risks.

> **Retention** means that an organization uses its own resources to pay for its losses.

Mandatory Retention

Although retention is usually chosen by an organization, sometimes it is mandatory. For example, all automobile physical damage insurance policies require a minimum deductible, which forces an insured to pay for its own losses up to the minimum amount. Other types of insurance policies, such as most earthquake policies, mandate that the insured take a fixed percentage of the value of the insured property as a deductible for each loss.

Transfer means that an organization (the transferor) uses another organization's (the transferee's) resources to pay for or offset its losses. The transferee receives compensation in exchange for taking the risk that it might need to pay for a loss. For an orga-

> **Transfer** means that an organization (the transferor) uses another organization's (the transferee's) resources to pay for or offset its losses.

nization that transfers losses arising from its speculative risks, the cost to transfer the losses offsets all or part of any gains that might arise from those risks.

Reimbursement for transferred losses can take many forms. For example, the organization can receive a cash payment directly from the transferee. Alternatively, the organization can use the positive settlement value of a financial instrument that it has invested in to offset its losses.

For hazard risks, a common type of risk transfer technique is insurance. Insurance companies are compensated by a premium in exchange for indemnifying (or paying on behalf of) their insureds for any covered losses that occur.

Organizations often enter into noninsurance contracts in the course of their business to transfer their risk of loss. For example, a retail toy store often requires its suppliers (toy manufacturers) to indemnify it for any liability losses arising from the sale of toys. (In this case determining the exact compensation paid to the transferee is difficult because it is included as part of the transaction between the retailer and the manufacturer.)

Another form of noninsurance contract that organizations use to transfer their risk of loss is a derivative. A **derivative** is a financial instrument that derives its value from another asset, called an underlying asset. To

> A **derivative** is a financial instrument that derives its value from another asset, called an underlying asset.

transfer its risk of loss, an organization might purchase a derivative, the value of which is positively correlated with a specific category of the organization's losses. The organization uses gains in the value of the derivative to offset the cost of its losses. Hedging with derivatives is commonly used by an organization to offset its risk of loss arising from financial/market risks, such as foreign exchange rate risks, interest rate risks, and commodity price risks. It can also be used to offset risk of loss arising from hazard risks. (Hedging hazard risk using derivatives is further discussed in Chapter 3 and Chapter 11.)

Insurance-linked securities are another form of noninsurance contract that organizations use to transfer hazard risk. With an insurance-linked security, investors accept the risk of hazard loss, which is embedded in the security. To date, insurance-linked securities have been mainly in the form of catastrophe bonds used by insurers to transfer their catastrophic risk. (Insurance-linked securities are further discussed in Chapter 3 and Chapter 11.)

Exhibit 1-4 compares retention and transfer.

Exhibit 1-4
Comparison of Retention and Transfer

	Retention	**Transfer**
Where do resources to pay for or offset losses come from?	Resources of the organization that incurs the losses: • Cash flow • Assets • Borrowed funds • Stockholders	Another organization's resources: • Insurance companies • Noninsurance organizations or individual investors
Do losses potentially destabilize earnings, net worth, and cash flows?	Yes	No (If the transfer is properly designed, the loss is largely offset by recoveries and gains.)
Does an outside organization receive compensation for accepting risk of loss?	Not Applicable	Yes • Insurance premium to an insurer • Compensation to a noninsurance organization or an individual investor

Note that borrowing is categorized as a form of retention. Even though the funds to pay for losses come from another organization (such as a bank), the borrower must promise to repay the funds and, therefore, can be viewed as using its own resources to pay for losses.

In practice, most organizations use a combination of retention and transfer to finance their losses. In the machine shop example previously mentioned toward the beginning of this chapter, assume that the organization purchased an insurance policy with a deductible. A deductible is a retention technique, so the machine shop would retain any losses that fall under the deductible and, therefore, would pay for those losses with its own financial resources. Insurance (above the deductible) is a transfer technique, with the machine shop paying a premium and using the insurer's financial resources to pay for the portion of any covered loss that exceeds the deductible.

This text describes various types of retention and transfer plans for risk financing. Although all of the plans discussed throughout this text can be used by large organizations, many of them can be used by medium-sized organizations as well.

Advantages and Disadvantages of Retention

A major advantage of retention is that its long-run cost tends to be lower than the cost of transfer. For hazard risks, an organization usually saves money over the long run by using retention rather than insurance because it does not have to pay for an insurance company's operating expenses and profits, which are included in the expense component of an insurance premium. The organization also does not have to pay an insurance company's **risk charge**, which is a charge over and above the expected loss component of the premium to compensate the insurer for taking the risk that losses might be higher than expected. An additional savings to retention results from the cash flow benefit of maintaining loss reserves for certain types of losses, which are not paid until several years after they occur. Significant savings are also available when an organization retains other (nonhazard) types of risk.

> **Risk charge** is a charge over and above the expected loss component of the premium to compensate the insurer for taking the risk that losses might be higher than expected.

A second major advantage of retention is that it encourages risk control. For example, when an organization pays the cost of its own hazard losses, it has an incentive to prevent and reduce them because, by doing so, the organization saves the loss payments and the expense of adjusting the losses. Also, the organization avoids devoting resources in the aftermath of a loss, such as time it must spend cleaning up after a property loss or tending to workers that are injured. Furthermore, the organization avoids possible major disruptions in its operations, such as a plant's total shutdown following an explosion.

A major disadvantage of retention is the associated uncertainty of loss outcomes, which can negatively affect an organization's earnings, net worth, and cash flow. When an organization decides to finance its losses by retaining rather than transferring them, it faces the possibility that retained losses will be much greater in number (frequency) or size (severity) than initially expected. Because of this uncertainty, an organization should limit its retention for each individual loss to a severity level at which it can tolerate the potential variability of the total retained loss outcomes.

Financial Accounting Treatment of Retained Losses

For financial accounting purposes, organizations recognize their retained losses as they are incurred, just as an insurance company does. Reserves for future loss payments (loss reserves) are posted as a liability on the organization's balance sheet and are charged as an expense on its income statement if the following two conditions apply:

- The loss occurred before the date of the financial statements.

- The amount that will be paid on the loss can be reasonably determined.

Organizations also post a liability and a corresponding expense for incurred-but-not-reported (IBNR) losses as long as they can be reasonably determined. It is likely that a large organization with hundreds of retained losses a year is able to "reasonably determine" its IBNR loss liability.

The above financial accounting rules limit an organization's ability to use reserves for retained losses as a method to help smooth out its reported profits and losses over multiple accounting periods. For example, an organization cannot post retained loss reserves and charge retained losses as expenses on its financial statements for losses that have not yet occurred. If it were able to do this, the organization could smooth out its reported net income by using these excess reserves and prematurely charged expenses to increase its reported net income in a later year when it incurs higher-than-normal losses.

Advantages and Disadvantages of Transfer

In general, the advantages and disadvantages of transfer are the opposite of those for retention. For example, a major advantage of transfer is its ability to reduce the financial uncertainty associated with an organization's losses, which helps the organization stabilize its earnings, net worth, and cash flow. Also, transfer provides a readily available source of reimbursement for losses, so the organization does not need to tie up its assets in liquid investments to make cash available to pay for retained losses.

A disadvantage of transfer is that its long-run cost tends to be higher than the cost of retention because of the previously mentioned expenses, such as the risk charge, that must be paid to the transferee for accepting risk of loss. Another disadvantage is that transfer does not encourage risk control.

Retention as Part of a Risk Financing Strategy

Retention should be a key component of any organization's risk financing strategy. An organization should weigh the estimated cost savings, on average, for retaining losses at various retention (severity) levels against the uncertainty of the cost of losses at each retention level.

In general, the higher an organization's loss retention level, the higher the uncertainty of its cost of retained losses, but the lower its long-term average cost of retained losses and transfer combined. Exhibit 1-5 shows the relationships among loss retention level, uncertainty of the cost of retained losses (risk), and long-term average cost of risk.

Exhibit 1-5
Relationships Among Loss Retention Level, Uncertainty, and Long-Term
Average Cost of Risk

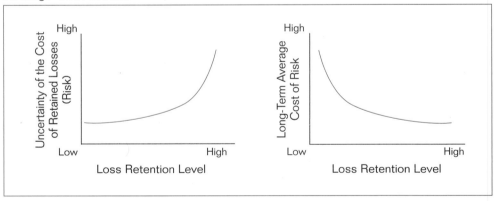

The relationships illustrated in Exhibit 1-5 vary based on a number of factors. Included are the number of independent risk exposures retained, the time period considered, the maximum size of any one retained loss, and the competitive conditions in the risk transfer market (for hazard risk, this is primarily the insurance market). For example, the larger the number of independent risk exposures and the lower the maximum value of any one retained loss, the lower the uncertainty (risk) of retained losses. In a competitive ("soft") insurance market, insurers might accept premiums that are below the long-term expected costs of paying for and adjusting the associated hazard losses. This "buyers' market" situation offsets savings that would otherwise be available from retaining losses.

Independent Risk Exposures

A car-rental agency might own 4,000 vehicles widely dispersed around the United States with values ranging from $11,000 to $30,000, and an average value of $17,000. Because the maximum physical damage loss is $30,000 and the agency has a large number of independent risk exposures, the agency's total automobile physical damage losses for any one year are fairly predictable based on its historical loss data. Therefore, the agency might decide to fully retain physical damage losses arising from the vehicles.

An organization's risk financing program should strike a balance between loss retention and transfer, taking into account specific factors that affect uncertainty of its retained loss outcomes and the long-term cost of its risk. Also, the organization should retain losses only up to a level for which it can tolerate the uncertainty arising from the range of probable loss outcomes.

Determining an Optimal Retention Level

Determining an optimal retention level is usually more of an art than a science. In general, the retention level should be based on several factors, including an organization's

- Tolerance for risk (uncertainty),
- Financial condition,
- Ability to diversify its retained risk,
- Potential gains as well as losses (for example, retaining the exposure to loss because the possibility of gain as well as loss exists),
- Ability to administer a loss retention program,
- Ability to control its losses in a cost-effective manner, and
- Ability to transfer its risk of loss in a cost-effective manner.

For publicly traded organizations, an optimal retention level is one that maximizes the firm's market value, which involves taking a level of risk that maximizes its return on capital. A publicly traded organization should also consider the value that its shareholders place on steady earnings compared with the value that they place on earnings that vary due to the uncertainty (risk) associated with retained losses.

The Evolution of Risk Financing

The financing of losses arising from hazard risks has changed dramatically over the past three decades. Three major changes are

1. Increased loss retentions on the part of large organizations,

2. Increased use of alternatives to traditional insurance, and

3. Inclusion of several types of risk, such as operational and financial/market risk, together with hazard risk in risk financing programs.

In the 1970s, the cost of hazard risk for most large organizations increased dramatically. As a result, their property-liability insurance premiums also increased. In an effort to save costs, large organizations increased the retained loss portion of their risk financing programs. Many realized a cost savings by increasing the deductible levels under their insurance policies. A large percentage of Fortune 500 companies insured their own losses by forming captive insurance companies, which are subsidiaries that exist to insure the loss exposures of their parents and their affiliates. Organizations of all sizes adopted self-insurance programs. (Captive insurance companies are covered in detail in Chapter 9, while self-insurance plans are covered in detail in Chapter 7.)

Alternatives to traditional insurance developed further in the 1980s. In 1986, an availability crisis for liability insurance prompted the further use of captive insurance companies, self-insurance plans, and other alternative risk financing techniques. Also, in 1986 a group of companies formed its own excess liability insurer, called ACE, Ltd., to make insurance available for the owner companies' liability losses in excess of $100 million. By forming this group captive insurer, these companies, in effect, agreed to insure each other rather than to rely on the traditional insurance market. A similar type of group insurer, called X.L. Ltd., formed quickly thereafter to cover liability losses of $50 million in excess of $50 million. These developments were followed by the formation of additional group captive insurers in the late 1980s.

Also, in the late 1980s, organizations began to purchase multi-year, multi-line insurance policies called integrated risk plans. Instead of purchasing separate insurance policies each year for each source of risk, an organization could save premium dollars by purchasing just one insurance policy to cover several sources of risk over several years. These multi-year plans permitted organizations to lock in their premium costs over several years. (Integrated risk plans are covered in detail in Chapter 10.)

Throughout the late 1980s and the 1990s, as organizations became more comfortable with retaining and managing their own losses, insurance premiums fell in relation to overall insurance industry losses. In this so-called soft market, the cost of transferring hazard losses became relatively inexpensive compared with the cost of retaining them. However, despite a prolonged period of falling insurance prices, organizations continued to take substantial loss retentions. Also, alternative risk financing plans, such as captive insurance companies and self-insurance, were used by many organizations and continued to grow.

Today, most large organizations are comfortable retaining substantial amounts of hazard risk and have developed the administrative ability to manage their hazard loss retention programs. The majority of organizations will continue these retention programs and, therefore, probably will never go back to traditional insurance for the retained portion of their losses. Accordingly, much of this text is devoted to risk financing plans that are alternatives to traditional insurance.

A Holistic Approach to Risk Financing

In the mid-1990s, some large organizations began to explore ways to better manage all of the risks faced by their enterprises. Instead of having their insurance department manage only hazard risks and their finance department manage only financial/market risks, organizations began to manage these and other risks together. This comprehensive approach to managing risk is often called **enterprise risk management** or **holistic risk management**.[15] Holistic risk management involves a holistic approach to risk financing.

> **Enterprise risk management** (also called **holistic risk management**) is a comprehensive approach to managing all of an organization's risks.

A holistic approach to risk financing is a logical step for large organizations that take substantial loss retentions because, in general, different types of risk are not correlated with each other. In other words, different types of losses tend to not all occur at the same time, and gains can be used to offset losses. For example, property losses arising from hurricanes do not necessarily occur at the same time as losses due to increases in market interest rates. Therefore, an organization can reduce its costs by analyzing and by managing its portfolio of risks as a whole rather than by managing each source of risk separately.

Exhibit 1-6 illustrates the benefit of a holistic approach to risk financing. It shows possible outcomes for two sources of risk: hazard risk and interest rate risk. Hazard risk is a pure risk, so the outcomes are "no loss," which is "good," or "loss," which is "bad." Interest rate risk (a financial/market risk) is a speculative risk, so the outcomes are "gain," which is "good," or "loss," which is "bad."

Exhibit 1-6

Possible Outcomes From Two Sources of Risk[16]

Interest Rate Risk (Speculative Risk)	Hazard Risk (Pure Risk)	
	No Loss	Loss
Gain	1 good-good	2 good-bad
Loss	3 bad-good	4 bad-bad

An organization that analyzes each type of risk separately might transfer its losses arising in quadrants 2, 3, and 4 because a "bad" outcome is possible in each of these quadrants. However, an organization that takes a holistic approach to risk financing might transfer just its losses in quadrant 4, which has a hazard risk loss and an interest rate risk loss during the same time period. In quadrants 2 and 3, "good" loss outcomes help offset "bad" loss outcomes, so there is less need to transfer the resulting risk.

When analyzing risk financing across their enterprisewide risks, many organizations find inconsistencies in their approach to loss retention. For example, an organization that retains millions of dollars of risk on a daily basis in the foreign exchange market might find that it takes only a $100,000 retention per loss under its property insurance policy. Taking a holistic, or an enterprisewide, approach to risk financing allows an organization to coordinate and possibly raise its combined overall risk retention level, thus saving money in the long run.

The prolonged soft insurance market of the 1990s induced property-liability insurers to offer several new products that cover risks of loss outside the realm of traditional insurance. For example, integrated risk plans were extended to cover not only hazard risks but also selected types of financial/market risks.

Take the case of a United States-based electronics firm that manufactures electronic chips in Japan and imports them to California, where it assembles them into electronic components. The firm faces a risk of loss from an earthquake (a hazard risk) for its properties in both the United States and Japan. In addition, the firm faces a risk of loss from foreign exchange rate movements (a financial/market risk) because if the value of the U.S. dollar falls relative to the value of the Japanese yen, the imported computer chips will cost more in terms of U.S. dollars. If the U.S. dollar rises relative to the value of the Japanese yen, the imported computer chips will cost less in terms of U.S. dollars, resulting in a gain to the organization. An insurance company could underwrite the firm's earthquake risk and foreign exchange risk with a single integrated risk plan that transfers the firm's combined risk of loss above a specified loss retention level.

In the late 1990s, property-liability insurers developed another new product, called a dual-trigger cover, which is a specific type of integrated risk plan. It covers organizations with strong balance sheets that need protection in the unlikely event that large losses arising from two different types of risk occur during the same time period. Consider the case of an airline. Not only does it have property and liability risk from operating its aircraft (hazard risk), but it also stands to lose a great deal of profit if the price of jet fuel suddenly increases (a financial/market risk). A dual-trigger cover would benefit the airline if it suffers a large property or liability loss related to its aircraft and, during the same time period, incurs a significant increase in the price of its jet fuel. The insurer would reimburse the airline for the combined loss to the extent it exceeds specified retention levels for each source of risk. Dual-trigger covers are designed for organizations that are willing to take a substantial retention but want to transfer loss in the unlikely event that two large losses arising from different sources of risk occur during the same time period. (Dual-trigger covers are discussed in more detail in Chapter 10.)

In the late 1990s, property-liability insurers developed an even more comprehensive policy called an earnings insurance policy, which protects an organization's earnings by covering losses arising from "all risks" of the enterprise. The policy covers not only losses arising from hazard risk but also losses arising from operational and financial/market risks as well, such as earnings shortfalls due to recessions, or increased costs due to increases in commodity prices. The policy excludes losses that are within management control. Examples of losses that are considered within management control are those due to strikes, accounting changes, and mergers/acquisitions.

Convergence of Insurance With Other Financial Services

Throughout the history of the United States and, in particular, since the Great Depression, insurance has been a separate business from other financial services, such as banking or stock brokerage. Until recently, insurers have not been allowed to enter other financial service businesses and vice versa.

In the past, insurers were in the business of insuring just hazard risks. Other organizations, such as financial exchanges and banks, were in the business of hedging financial/market risks, such as changes in the prices of commodities or movements in market interest rates.

In recent years, the line between insurance and other financial services has blurred, with convergence taking place among the various financial services. Insurers see opportunities to expand their traditional business by issuing insurance policies to cover not only losses from hazard risk but also losses from various types of operational and financial/market risks. Financial institutions, particularly investment banks, see opportunities to expand their business beyond financial/market risks by using the capacity of the capital markets to cover losses from hazard risk. They can reach this goal by arranging insurance-linked securities and insurance derivatives, whereby investors accept the risk of hazard losses, such as destruction caused by earthquakes or hurricanes. The movement by the capital markets to develop insurance-linked securities to underwrite risks that were traditionally underwritten solely by insurance companies is called insurance securitization. (Insurance-linked securities and insurance derivatives are further explained in Chapter 3 and Chapter 11.)

Risk Management in Practice
Goldman, Sachs & Co. Advises Clients on Hazard Risks

Traditionally, investment banks have advised their clients on financial/market risks. In recent years, some investment banks have formed divisions to advise their clients on hazard risks, which insurance companies traditionally have underwritten. For example, Goldman, Sachs & Co. has a division called Risk Markets that is able to structure, execute, and distribute insurance-linked securities and insurance derivatives.

The convergence of insurance companies with other financial service firms will lead to a variety of new risk financing products. These products will enable organizations to manage their risk portfolios efficiently.

Is Risk Financing Necessary?

Risk financing consumes organizational resources. For example, the risk management professional for an organization must spend time designing, implementing, and administering a risk financing plan. The various bearers of risk and suppliers of services, including insurers, charge an amount sufficient to cover their overheads and profits. Do the benefits of a formal risk financing plan offset these costs?

A risk financing plan is necessary for many types of firms, particularly for small- to medium-sized firms for which many losses are likely to disrupt or even bankrupt the organization. Also, nonprofit organizations, such as the Red Cross, must finance their losses so as to remain financially solvent and provide necessary services to the public.

But what about publicly traded firms? Must they use the resources needed to develop and implement a formal risk financing plan? In theory, shareholders can diversify firm-specific risk of loss (unsystematic risk) on their own by purchasing stock in many different types of firms. Would shareholders and the economy be better served if publicly traded firms did not consume the resources necessary for formal risk financing?

Many publicly traded firms take a conservative approach to risk financing. The management of most publicly traded firms believes it can maximize the market value of the firm's stock by reporting to investors steadily increasing earnings and strong cash flow. The organization's management transfers risk of loss so as to stabilize reported earnings in its effort to maximize the firm's market value. Management's compensation incentives might also explain management's conservative approach to risk financing. Often, management is rewarded financially for a firm's steadily increasing market value.

An economic rationale for organizations to transfer their risk of loss is that transfer provides specific benefits. Avoiding bankruptcy saves expenses for the firm's owners and other stakeholders. Examples are lawyers' fees and court costs incurred in order to deal with a bankruptcy. If a firm is subject to a progressive tax-rate structure, reporting a steady rather than a variable taxable income saves taxes over time. Another rationale is that a firm can take on investment projects with confidence if it has transferred many of its risks.[17]

The late Bob Hedges, Professor Emeritus of Temple University, writing in 1964, made the following observations regarding risk transfer:

> There are critical values; when losses get beyond these, serious trouble follows. Hence the truth in the large loss principle appears: the effects of small damage are limited to the damage itself, and the utility of insurance payments is pretty well limited to the number of dollars received. If the underwriter knows what he is doing, this amount cannot regularly be expected to exceed the premiums. On the other hand, when the direct loss can cause a depletion in assets sufficient to threaten the financial integrity of the business, then the benefits received from insurance payments go beyond the number of dollars actually paid; the benefits can be as great as the going concern value of the business.[18]

The key to a successful risk financing program is to devote an appropriate level of resources to it so as to maximize benefits over costs. The next chapter explores objectives related to the benefits and costs of risk financing in more detail.

Summary

- Risk financing means to raise funds to pay for or offset an organization's losses. The funds can come from internal sources, such as an organization's cash flow, or from external sources, such as an organization's insurer, banker, or stockholders. Through diversification, an organization can use gains arising from some exposures to offset losses arising from other exposures.

- All organizations are exposed to risk and have various sources of risk. Although there is no standard way to categorize an organization's risks, this text divides them into two major categories: operational risk and financial/market risk. Operational risks are specific to an organization and include business risk, financial risk, operating risk, credit risk, hazard risk, and reputation risk. Financial/market risk is the exposure to a change in the value of financial instruments caused by a change in market prices or rates, including changes in interest rates, foreign exchange rates, securities prices, and commodity prices. The categories of risks presented in this text are not meant to be mutually exclusive or exhaustive.

- Depending on the source of risk from which they arise, losses have different characteristics, which have implications for the design of a risk financing program. These characteristics include frequency and severity, as well as the possibility of a delay in the discovery and payment of losses.

- Two basic techniques used by organizations to finance their losses are retention and transfer. With retention, an organization uses its own resources to pay for its losses. Retained losses have the potential to destabilize an organization's earnings, net worth, and cash flow. With transfer, another organization (the transferee) accepts a risk of loss that matches or is closely related to the transferor's risk of loss. The transferor can be reimbursed with a cash payment from the transferee or can receive the positive settlement value of a financial instrument in which it has invested to offset its losses. In practice, most organizations use a combination of retention and transfer to finance their losses.

- For hazard risks, the most common type of transfer technique is insurance. The use of derivatives is a common technique for transferring losses arising from financial/market risks, such as foreign exchange rate risks, interest rate risks, and commodity price risks. Derivatives can also be used to transfer losses arising from hazard risks. Another financial instrument used to transfer hazard risk is an insurance-linked security.

- A major benefit of retention is that its long-run cost tends to be lower than the cost of transfer. An additional benefit of retention is that it encourages loss control. A major drawback to retention is the associated uncertainty of retained loss outcomes. In general, the advantages and disadvantages of transfer are the opposite of those for retention.

- An organization's risk financing program should strike a balance between retention and transfer, taking into account specific factors that can affect uncertainty of its retained loss outcomes and the long-term average cost of its risk. An optimal retention level is one that maximizes the value of the organization, which involves managing the organization's long-term average cost of risk, while keeping the uncertainty of its annual payments for retained losses within acceptable bounds.

- Risk financing has changed dramatically over the past three decades. Many organizations have increased their loss retentions and use alternatives to traditional insurance, such as a captive insurance company or a self-insurance plan. In addition, many large organizations are taking a holistic approach to risk financing by analyzing and managing together all of the risks faced by their enterprises. A holistic approach to risk financing is a logical step for most organizations because, in general, different types of risk are not correlated with each other.

- In recent years, the line between insurance and other financial services has blurred, with convergence taking place among the various financial services. Insurers see opportunities to expand their businesses by covering various types of risk—such as interest rate risk—that other financial institutions traditionally covered. Other financial institutions see opportunities to use the capacity of the capital markets to cover risks traditionally covered by insurers by issuing insurance-linked securities and insurance derivatives. The convergence of financial services firms will result in a stream of new products that will enable organizations to manage their risk portfolios efficiently.

- Transferring risk of loss provides several economic benefits to a firm. The management of most publicly traded firms maintains a conservative loss retention level because it believes it can maximize the value of the firm's stock by reporting to investors steadily increasing earnings and strong cash flows.

Chapter Notes

1. Arthur C. Williams, Jr., Michael L. Smith, and Peter C. Young, *Risk Management and Insurance,* 8th ed. (Burr Ridge, IL: Irwin/McGraw-Hill, 1998), p. 4.
2. For more discussion of this topic, see William H. Beaver and George Parker, eds., *Risk Management: Problems and Solutions* (New York: McGraw-Hill, 1995), p. 15.

3. Scott E. Harrington and Gregory R. Niehaus, *Risk Management and Insurance* (Burr Ridge, IL: Irwin/McGraw-Hill, 1999), p. 12.

4. Some organizations define "business risk" more broadly to include many of the risks that this text includes in operational risk.

5. "A Modern Approach to Operational Risk," *Risk Professional*, May 1999, p. 25.

6. "Takeovers are Part of the Game," *The New York Times*, February 9, 1999, p. C1.

7. David H. Marshall, Wayne W. McManus, Paul M. Kazenski, and Kenneth N. Scoles, Jr., *Accounting and Finance for Insurance Professionals* (Malvern, PA: American Institute for CPCU, 1997), p. 474.

8. A counterparty is the other party to a contract.

9. This definition is taken from *1998 Annual Report*, The Chase Manhattan Corporation, p. 76.

10. The Chase Manhattan Corporation, *1998 Annual Report*, p. 29.

11. "Loss Widens at British American Tobacco," *The New York Times*, March 10, 1999, p. C3.

12. This definition is taken from *1998 Annual Report*, The Chase Manhattan Corporation, p. 36.

13. Crown Cork & Seal, *Annual Report 1998*, p. 19.

14. Of course, when crude oil prices rise, the independent oil refiner has the option of reducing its production, which is often the case.

15. In some countries such as the United Kingdom, this approach is called integrated risk management.

16. Adapted from a lecture given on April 28, 1999, by Neil A. Doherty, Professor of Insurance and Risk Management, The Wharton School of the University of Pennsylvania.

17. For a detailed discussion of these rationales for minimizing uncertainty, see William H. Beaver and George Parker, *Risk Management: Problems and Solutions* (New York: McGraw-Hill, 1995), pp. 152-156.

18. Bob A. Hedges, "The Problem of Principles in Risk Management," *CPCU Annals* (Malvern, PA: The Society of CPCU, 1964), 17:2:182.

References

Beaver, William H., and George Parker. *Risk Management: Problems and Solutions.* New York: McGraw-Hill, 1995.

Harrington, Scott E., and Gregory R. Niehaus. *Risk Management and Insurance.* Burr Ridge, IL: Irwin/McGraw-Hill, 1999.

International Risk Management Institute. *Risk Financing: A Guide to Insurance Cash Flow.* Dallas: International Risk Management Institute, Inc., 2000.

Smithson, Charles W. *Managing Financial Risk.* New York: McGraw-Hill, 1998.

Williams, Arthur C., Jr., Michael L. Smith, and Peter C. Young. *Risk Management and Insurance*, 8th ed. Burr Ridge, IL: Irwin/McGraw-Hill, 1998.

Chapter 2

Risk Financing Objectives

Introduction

Managers of an organization usually have several financial objectives. They plan sources and uses of cash so as to maintain an appropriate level of cash or near-cash assets for the organization. They also strive to keep the organization solvent to avoid bankruptcy. In addition, for publicly traded firms, managers attempt to maximize market value.

The main financial objective of most publicly traded organizations is to increase market value by maximizing the present

> **Cash flow** is cash inflow minus cash outflow.

value[1] of future **cash flow** (cash inflow minus cash outflow). In theory, investors value a publicly traded organization by projecting the size of its future cash flow. They then discount the expected cash flow back to the present time in order to estimate a current market value for the organization. If an organization develops a successful new product, investors are likely to bid up the current market price of the organization's stock on the assumption that cash flow from the product will be strong in the future.

The degree of risk, or variability, associated with future cash flow also influences a publicly traded organization's market value. The higher the degree of risk, the greater the discount rate that investors apply to an organization's projected future cash flow. (This is particularly true for systematic risk, which investors cannot diversify on their own by purchasing stocks in many different types of firms.) The greater the discount rate, the lower the present value of an organization's cash flow, and the lower the current market value that investors place on the organization. Therefore, an inverse relationship exists between the riskiness of cash flow and an organization's market value.

Risk financing is an integral part of an organization's overall financial management, so most risk financing objectives should be derived from and support an organization's financial objectives. To help increase its market value, a publicly traded organization should carefully manage its cost of risk, which involves minimizing its cost per unit of risk transferred and retaining risk when a sufficient return would result. The return from retaining pure risk can be measured in terms of the savings in risk transfer costs (assuming the organization has the option to transfer its risk). Privately held and not-for-profit organizations should also manage their cost of risk, even though their main financial objective is to provide necessary services rather than to increase market value. In all cases, an organization should retain risk at a level at which it can tolerate the potential variability in loss outcomes.

To manage its cost of risk and maintain a tolerable level of uncertainty for retained losses, an organization should manage all the sources of its risk in an integrated manner. As discussed later in this chapter, this approach is superior to other methods in helping an organization meet its risk financing objectives.

Common Risk Financing Objectives

Most organizations adopt several risk financing objectives. They include

- Paying for losses,
- Maintaining an appropriate level of liquidity,
- Managing uncertainty of loss outcomes,
- Managing the cost of risk, and
- Complying with legal requirements.

Paying for Losses

A basic objective of risk financing is to pay for losses. An organization wants to make sure funds are available when it needs to pay for losses. The availability of funds is particularly important in situations that disrupt the functioning of the organization, such as when the organization needs to replace damaged property. However, paying for losses is also important from a public relations perspective. An organization does not want to tarnish its reputation by not paying legal liability losses resulting from the legitimate claims of third parties.

An organization that purchases insurance must carefully evaluate its insurer's financial condition so as to be reasonably certain that the insurer will pay for covered losses. Similarly, an organization that relies on a noninsurance contract to transfer its risk of loss must carefully evaluate the financial condition of the party to which it transfers risk.

An organization that retains its losses must decide which of its financial resources it will use to pay for the losses. The organization might use its current cash flow to pay for retained losses, or it might periodically liquidate current assets to pay for them. Alternatively, the organization might borrow funds to pay retained losses or raise funds from its stockholders. The use of various financial resources to pay for retained losses is discussed in the Appendix to this chapter.

Maintaining Appropriate Level of Liquidity

A second objective of risk financing is to maintain an appropriate level of cash liquidity so as to pay for retained losses. This objective is closely related to the previous objective of paying for losses.

When an organization retains its losses, it must determine the amount of cash it needs to pay the retained losses and the timing of those cash payments. In deciding how to make its financial resources available to pay for its retained losses, an organization must consider its various sources of liquidity—the liquidity of its assets, the strength of its cash flows, its borrowing capacity, and its ability to issue stock (for publicly traded organizations).

A **liquid asset** is one that can easily be converted into cash. For example, market-able securities are liquid because they can

> A **liquid asset** is an asset that can easily be converted into cash.

readily be exchanged for cash by selling them in the stock or bond markets. Some assets are not liquid, such as machinery and equipment that would be difficult to sell quickly.

An organization can increase liquidity by retaining its cash flow rather than using it to fund capital projects or to pay dividends. If necessary, an organization can also raise cash and, therefore, its level of liquidity by borrowing funds, assuming it has the financial capacity to obtain a bank loan or issue notes to others. Publicly traded organizations can raise cash by issuing stock.

An organization's liquidity is measured by its working capital and its current ratio. Those two concepts are explained in the discussion that follows.

Working Capital and Current Ratio

An organization's **working capital** is calculated by using the following formula:

Working capital = Current assets − Current liabilities

Current assets provide an economic benefit to an organization and consist of cash and other items that can or will be converted into cash within one year. Included are marketable securities, accounts receivable, and merchandise inventory. **Current liabilities** are the organization's obligations that will be paid in cash within one year. Included are accounts payable, other expenses payable, and short-term debt. For an organization that retains its losses, current liabilities also include reserves for losses that have occurred and are expected to be paid within one year. [2]

The difference between current assets and current liabilities (working capital) is a measure of a firm's overall liquidity because it is the amount that would be left over if current assets were used to fund all the cash demands of the firm's current liabilities. As long as its working capital is a positive number, an organization has readily available cash to fund losses from unforeseen events, such as higher-than-expected payments for retained losses.

A second liquidity measure is the current ratio, which shows the size of a firm's current assets relative to its current liabilities. The **current ratio** is calculated by using the following formula:

$$\text{Current ratio} = \frac{\text{Current assets}}{\text{Current liabilities}}$$

In general, a current ratio of 2.0 or higher indicates that a firm has a strong level of liquidity.

Working capital is an absolute measure of a firm's liquidity because it is measured with a dollar amount. The current ratio is a relative measure of liquidity because it states the relationship between a firm's current assets and its current liabilities.

Liquidity Example

Liquidity and its importance to risk financing are best illustrated by examining a hypothetical balance sheet. KYZ Technology's balance sheet as of December 31, 2000 is shown in Exhibit 2-1.

Exhibit 2-1
KYZ Technology Balance Sheet

KYZ Technology Balance Sheet (as of 12/31/2000) (All figures are in '000,000s.)	
Assets	
Cash	$ 12.0
Marketable securities	78.5
Accounts receivable	279.5
Inventory	222.5
Other current assets	25.0
Current assets	*$ 617.5*
Noncurrent assets	1,025.9
Total Assets	$1,643.4
Liabilities + Shareholders' Equity	
Short-term debt	$ 16.9
Accounts payable	310.5
Reserves for retained losses	4.5
Other current liabilities	38.6
Current liabilities	*$ 370.5*
Noncurrent liabilities	601.2
Shareholders' equity	671.7
Total	$1,643.4

KYZ Technology's current assets are $617.5 million (cash + marketable securities + accounts receivable + inventory + other current assets), and its current liabilities are $370.5 million (short-term debt + accounts payable + reserves for retained losses + other current liabilities). Therefore, KYZ Technology's working capital and current ratio are calculated as follows:

KYZ working capital = $617.5 million – $370.5 million = $247.0 million

KYZ current ratio = $617.5 million/$370.5 million = 1.67

KYZ Technology seems to have adequate liquidity. It has $247.0 million in working capital available for unforeseen expenditures, including those for unexpected losses. Its working capital and its current assets ($617.5 million)

are many times larger than its reserves to pay for retained losses that are expected to be paid within one year ($4.5 million). Although its current ratio is not at least 2.0 as some guidelines suggest, given its size, KYZ Technology nevertheless has a strong current ratio.

Acid-Test Ratio

For some firms, inventory and some other current assets might not be easy to convert into cash. To account for this possibility, there is a liquidity measure called the **acid-test ratio** (sometimes called the "quick ratio") that is more stringent than the current ratio. The acid-test ratio is similar to the current ratio, except the numerator does not include inventories and some other current assets that may be difficult to convert to cash. The formula for the acid-test ratio is as follows:

$$\text{Acid-test ratio} = \frac{\left(\text{Cash} + \text{Marketable securities} + \text{Accounts receivable}\right)}{\text{Current liabilities}}$$

KYZ Technology's acid-test ratio is calculated as follows:

$$\text{KYZ acid-test ratio} = \frac{\left(\$12.0\text{ million} + \$78.5\text{ million} + \$279.5\text{ million}\right)}{\$370.5\text{ million}}$$

$$\text{KYZ acid-test ratio} = \frac{\$370.0\text{ million}}{\$370.5\text{ million}} = .999,\text{ or approximately }1.0$$

An acid-test ratio of 1.0 is considered to be adequate. It is more stringent than the current ratio because it does not include all current assets, including inventories, in its numerator.

The Relationship Between an Organization's Retention Level and its Liquidity

The higher the level of an organization's risk retention, the greater its need for liquidity. This is due to the relationship between an organization's loss retention level and the uncertainty of the cost of its retained losses. As mentioned in Chapter 1, the higher an organization's loss retention level, the greater the uncertainty of the cost of its retained losses. As an example, assume KYZ Technology does not purchase insurance or use some other means to transfer its risk of loss. If a catastrophe such as a hurricane destroyed one of KYZ's facilities, KYZ would need a great deal of liquidity to raise cash to rebuild the facility.

Managing Uncertainty of Loss Outcomes

A third major objective of risk financing is to manage uncertainty (risk) of loss outcomes. The appropriate level of uncertainty can vary depending on one's tolerance for risk and one's perspective, that is, whether one is a shareholder or a manager.

As previously mentioned, the degree of uncertainty of a publicly traded organization's future cash flow influences the market value that shareholders place on it. In theory, shareholders can eliminate unsystematic (firm-specific) risk by diversifying their holdings into a portfolio of stocks consisting of different firms. However, shareholders cannot eliminate systematic (marketwide) risk, so, all other things being equal, shareholders prefer low systematic risk to high systematic risk. Therefore, the greater an organization's systematic risk, the lower its market value. In theory, risk financing should focus on reducing systematic risk rather than reducing unsystematic risk.

Importance of Systematic and Unsystematic Risk to Shareholders

In theory, shareholders in a publicly traded firm are able to diversify firm-specific, or unsystematic, risk by constructing a portfolio of stocks of different types of firms. Therefore, in theory, only marketwide, or systematic, risk is of importance to well-diversified shareholders. The higher the degree of systematic risk, the greater the discount that shareholders apply to an organization's future cash flow to reflect this uncertainty.

However, in practice, managers of publicly traded organizations usually want to reduce all of an organization's risk, both systematic and unsystematic. They believe that by being able to report steadily growing earnings to their stockholders, they maximize their organizations' market value. Additional reasons for an organization to reduce uncertainty were given in Chapter 1 and include the following:

- Avoiding bankruptcy and its associated costs,
- Reducing taxes due to a progressive tax-rate structure, and
- Making investments with confidence.[3]

Techniques That Reduce Uncertainty

An organization can use several risk control and transfer techniques to reduce the uncertainty arising from its various sources of risk. For example, a manufacturing organization can reduce its business risk through product diversification, which involves manufacturing different types of products that are subject to different sources of risk. A bank can offset uncertainty associ-ated with its credit risk by using financial derivatives. (Derivatives were introduced in Chapter 1.) For hazard risk, an organization can use loss con-trol techniques, such as separation and duplication, and transfer techniques, such as insurance.

Another technique that an organization can use to manage its uncertainty aris-ing from various sources of risk is to manage its degree of financial risk, which is determined by its degree of financial leverage. The higher a firm's degree of financial leverage, the higher its degree of financial risk. New risk financing products are available to reduce an organization's financial leverage in the after-math of a loss.

Financial Leverage

With **financial leverage**, a firm borrows money with the expectation that it can earn an amount on the borrowed funds that is higher than the interest it must pay the lender, resulting in an increased return to the firm's shareholders. However, financial leverage also makes a firm more risky to its shareholders (financial risk) because the firm takes on a fixed obligation to pay interest and repay principal to the lenders. If the firm does not generate sufficient operating profits to cover the interest and principal repayments, it must still pay its lend-ers, possibly placing the firm in a precarious financial position or insolvency. The more money a firm borrows, all other things remaining the same, the higher the firm's degree of financial leverage. The higher its degree of financial leverage, the higher the firm's financial risk.

To illustrate financial leverage, consider the case of two firms that have the same total assets and operating income, but one borrows money while the other does not. To simplify the analysis, assume each firm has no liabilities other than the debt taken on by the one firm that borrows money. The hypothetical balance sheets and income statements for the two firms are shown below:

Firm 1
(No Financial Leverage)

Balance Sheet (All figures are in '000s.)			**Income Statement** (All figures are in '000s.)	
Assets	$20,000	Debt $0	Operating income	$3,600
		Shareholders' equity $20,000	Interest expense	0
	$20,000	$20,000	Profit (loss)	$3,600

Firm 2
(Financial Leverage)

Balance Sheet (All figures are in '000s.)			**Income Statement** (All figures are in '000s.)	
Assets	$20,000	Debt (8%) $8,000	Operating income	$3,600
		Shareholders' equity $12,000	Interest expense	$640
	$20,000	$20,000	Profit (loss)	$2,960

Firm 1 uses no financial leverage and therefore has no debt and no interest expense. Firm 2 uses financial leverage by borrowing $8,000,000 at an interest rate of 8 percent a year. Therefore, Firm 2 must pay $640,000 in interest per year. The return on shareholders' equity for Firm 1 and Firm 2 is calculated below:

$$\text{Return on Shareholders' Equity} = \frac{\text{Profit (loss)}}{\text{Shareholders' equity}}$$

Firm 1

$$= \frac{\$3,600,000}{\$20,000,000}$$
$$= 18.00\%$$

Firm 2

$$= \frac{\$2,960,000}{\$12,000,000}$$
$$= 24.66\%$$

Firm 2 has increased the percentage return on its shareholders' equity by using financial leverage. Whereas Firm 1 made 18.00 percent on its shareholders' $20,000,000 investment, Firm 2 is able to make 24.66 percent on its shareholders' $12,000,000 investment by borrowing $8,000,000 at 8 percent interest.

Financial leverage also increases a firm's financial risk. If the operating profit of Firm 1 and Firm 2 falls to $100,000, then, after paying its interest expense, Firm 1 would have a profit of $100,000, and Firm 2 would have a loss of $540,000. This example illustrates that, because it uses financial leverage, Firm 2's financial risk is greater than Firm 1's financial risk. A firm can lower its financial risk by lowering its debt and, therefore, its degree of financial leverage.

A Portfolio Approach

When assessing the uncertainty of its risks, an organization should assess the combined uncertainty arising from all its various sources of risk. As discussed in Chapter 1, the organization should take a holistic, or an enterprisewide, approach to managing its risk because most risks are not correlated and, there-fore, the organization can benefit by retaining a diverse set of its risks. By retaining additional risk, an organization can save the cost of risk transfer.

For many sources of risk, a possibility of a gain as well as a possibility of a loss exists. For example, an organization that relies on debt to finance its opera-tions can incur a loss if interest rates rise or a gain if interest rates fall. A loss occurs if interest rates rise because the organization must pay more interest than it expected to pay in order to finance its operations. The opposite is true if interest rates fall.

Gains and losses can occur at the same time, whether from a single source of risk or multiple sources of risk. Therefore, an organization can use its gains to offset its losses. For example, an organization might suffer a fire loss (a hazard risk) to one of its warehouses but at the same time receive an offsetting gain (lower borrowing costs) from a decrease in interest rates.

Exhibit 2-2 shows the effect on the risk of a portfolio when the number of risk exposures included in the portfolio increases. The diversifiable unsystematic risk of the portfolio decreases because the risk is spread, or diversified, among a larger number of risk exposures. However, the systematic risk of a portfolio cannot be eliminated through diversification.

Exhibit 2-2
The Effect of Increasing the Number of Risk Exposures in a Portfolio

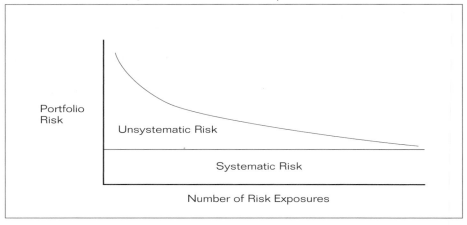

Mixing hazard risk with other types of risk in a portfolio of retained risk is advantageous because hazard risk is not correlated with an organization's other sources of risk. Therefore, adding hazard risk reduces the amount of unsystem-atic risk in a portfolio through diversification.

Determining a Tolerable Level of Uncertainty

An organization often has difficulty determining the maximum level of uncertainty it can tolerate. Its maximum uncertainty level depends on a number of factors, such as the organization's size; its financial strength; and its management's degree of risk tolerance, for example, whether management prefers to accept risk in order to gain a possible benefit or whether management prefers to avoid risk despite the possibility of gain. It also depends on the degree to which an organization's stakeholders are willing to accept risk.

Rules of Thumb for Retaining Hazard Risk

A large, profitable organization with substantial assets is able to withstand a much higher level of uncertainty of loss than a small organization can withstand. For hazard losses, there are financial rules of thumb that are used to recommend a maximum retention capacity based on a percentage of an organization's financial measures, such as working capital, total assets, and earnings. For example, one set of guidelines[4] recommends a risk retention capacity as follows:

- 2 percent to 15 percent of working capital
- 1 percent to 5 percent of total assets
- 1 percent to 8 percent of average pretax earnings over a five-year period

From the previous example, KYZ Technology's risk retention capacity would be as follows:

Based on working capital	$5 million to $37 million
Based on assets	$16 million to $131 million

These measures are general and provide a wide range of estimates; each organization should determine how well these guidelines apply to its specific situation.

Measuring a manager's degree of risk tolerance with precision is challenging. Usually, the best that can be said is that one manager seeks risk while another avoids risk. Measuring the degree of risk tolerance of other stakeholders in the organization is also difficult. A previous section of this chapter stated that, in theory, the greater the degree of systematic risk, the lower the market value that shareholders place on an organization. This relationship between market value and shareholders' tolerance for uncertainty is difficult to quantify. Some industries, such as high technology, have a high degree of systematic risk, so it would seem that shareholders who invest in these stocks have a higher degree of risk tolerance than shareholders who invest in less risky industries. In like manner, determining the degree of risk tolerance of other stakeholders—such as customers, employees, and suppliers—is difficult. Customers and suppliers might avoid dealing with an organization that they view as risky. Employees might demand pay raises or leave organizations that they consider to be risky.

A Quantitative Method for Measuring an Individual's Risk Tolerance[5]

A quantitative method can be used to give some indication of an individual's tolerance for risk. Suppose you were offered a chance to win $1,000 on a coin toss. If the coin lands heads-up you win $1,000, and if the coin lands tails-up you win nothing. Therefore, you have a 50 percent chance that you will win $1,000 and a 50 percent chance that you will win nothing. This risk is shown graphically below:

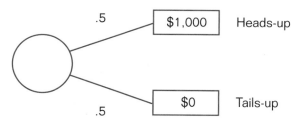

Assume that, as an alternative to the coin toss risk, you are offered various amounts of money. What is the minimum amount of dollars you would accept rather than take the risk that you may win $1,000 or nothing on the coin toss?

Different individuals will have different dollar amounts that they would accept rather than take the risk of the coin toss. Because, with the coin toss, a 50 percent chance of winning $1,000 exists and a 50 percent chance of receiving $0 exists, the expected payoff with the coin toss option is $500, calculated as follows:

$$\text{Expected payoff} = .5(\$1,000) + .5(\$0) = \$500$$

- If you are indifferent to taking $500 or tossing the coin, you are categorized as **risk neutral** because you are indifferent to taking the coin toss risk or taking a certain amount that is equal to the expected payoff from the coin toss option.

- If you would take a minimum amount that is less than $500, you are categorized as **risk averse** because, given the choice, you prefer to take a certain amount that is less than the expected payoff from the coin toss option rather than to take a chance that you might win nothing.

- If you would only take a minimum amount that is greater than $500, you are categorized as a **risk taker** because you are willing to risk more than the expected payoff from the coin toss option for the chance to win $1,000. For example, given the choice, you might be willing to give up a certain amount of $550 for the chance to win $1,000 on the coin toss option.

Managing the Cost of Risk

A fourth major objective of risk financing is to manage an organization's cost of risk. **Cost of risk** is a concept that has historically been applied to pure risks and includes administrative expenses, risk control expenses, retained losses, and transfer costs.

For pure risks, an organization should minimize its cost of risk. However, for speculative risks, an organization should manage its cost of risk because, as mentioned in Chapter 1, organizations are in

> **Cost of risk** includes administrative expenses, risk control expenses, retained losses, and compensation to outside organizations that accept risk.

the business of bearing (retaining) speculative risk in exchange for a return. For example, banks are in the business of managing credit risk. Organizations need a strategy for managing the cost of their various types of risk so as to maximize the amount by which their revenues exceed their expenses.

Risk Management in Practice

"Cost of Risk"

"Cost of risk" is a concept that was developed in 1962 by the Risk and Insurance Management Society (RIMS)[6] to measure the cost of hazard risk. An organization's "cost of risk" consists of

1. Administrative expenses,
2. Risk control expenses,
3. Retained losses, and
4. Insurance premiums.

An organization should minimize its cost of hazard risk because any reduction in expenses for hazard risk leads to a dollar-for-dollar increase in an organization's net income (ignoring taxes).

Following is a discussion of various costs that apply to an organization's risks. Although most of the discussion centers on the cost of hazard risk, the concepts can be applied to all of an organization's risks.

Administrative Expenses

Administrative expenses include an organization's cost of internal administration and its cost of purchased services, such as claim administration, risk management consulting, captive insurance company management, and commissions/fees received by brokers. They also include any premium taxes paid.

An organization should incur administrative expenses to the extent necessary to properly manage its risk financing program. Often an organization has an opportunity to save administrative expenses by modifying procedures or eliminating unnecessary tasks. For example, some firms with a loss retention program save expenses by outsourcing the claim handling function.

Risk Control Expenses

Risk control expenses are devoted to preventing or controlling losses. For hazard risks, an organization can best analyze risk control expenditures by conducting a cost-benefit analysis. Resources should be devoted to risk control as long as the marginal benefit of a risk control measure exceeds its marginal cost. As long as the dollar benefit of a risk control measure exceeds its dollar cost, the firm's value is maximized. However, moral and ethical issues also surround the choice of risk control measures.

Initial dollars that an organization spends on risk control usually provide a large payoff in terms of losses that the organization can prevent or control. (This principle assumes that the organization first devotes risk control expenditures to the measures that have the largest net benefit in terms of cost savings.) Additional dollars spent on risk control also provide a benefit, but the marginal benefit of these additional dollars usually falls as the additional opportunities to control losses have smaller payoffs.

The declining marginal benefit of added risk control measures can be illustrated with an example of a warehouse that stores flammable goods. Installation of sprinklers is a risk control measure that will pay large benefits in terms of controlling fire losses to the goods. But should the warehouse owner go further and spend money on firewalls to compartmentalize the warehouse to contain any fire that occurs? The additional benefit in terms of savings in losses may or may not be worth the additional cost.

Exhibit 2-3 shows the relationship between the marginal benefit and the marginal cost of risk control measures. Assume that as the investment in risk control measures increases, the additional or marginal cost of providing each additional risk control measure also increases. Note that the marginal benefit, in terms of losses that are controlled or prevented, falls as the investment in measures to control risk increases. The optimal level of risk control is the point at which the marginal benefit equals the marginal cost, which is at the intersection of the two curves.

Exhibit 2-3
Marginal Benefit and Marginal Cost of Risk Control Measures

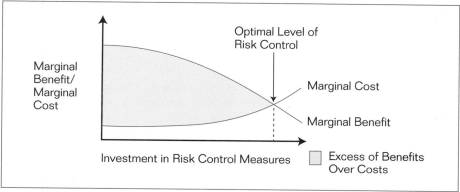

A firm's objective should not be to minimize the amount it spends on risk control. Instead, its objective should be to determine an optimal level of risk control that maximizes its cash flow. A firm can accomplish this objective by spending an amount on risk control until the marginal cost equals the marginal benefit. All risk control measures taken up to that point reduce the cost of a firm's retained losses or insurance premiums more than they add to the cost of loss control measures, thus maximizing cash flow by minimizing the firm's cost of hazard risk. The shaded area in Exhibit 2-3 represents the added cash flow to the firm by adopting risk control measures up to the optimal level.

The preceding analysis did not take into account the timing of both the receipt of the benefits and the payment of the costs. The beginning of this chapter mentioned that the main financial objective of most publicly traded organizations is to maximize the present value of their expected cash flow. Therefore, any analysis of risk control measures must take into account the timing of the associated benefits and costs. For example, installing a sprinkler system generates a current cost that will result in a savings in loss costs and insurance premiums over several future years. In order for the organization to properly assess the benefits and costs of the sprinkler system, it must discount the savings back to the present time by using a discount rate that reflects the organization's cost of capital. When this calculation is performed, the benefits and costs can be compared on an equivalent basis in terms of their present values.

The benefits and costs of a risk control measure are usually difficult to determine. Management makes risk control decisions based partly on solid estimates and partly on educated guesses. For example, the cost of installing and maintaining sprinklers can be easily estimated by consulting a contractor. Also, the savings in current insurance premiums as a result of installing sprinklers can be estimated by consulting one's insurance broker or underwriter. But any savings in retained losses and lowered future insurance premiums are usually based on educated guesses.

When measuring the benefits of risk control, an organization should estimate cost savings that are in addition to premium and loss savings. For example, a property loss involves not only the amount spent to repair damaged property but also lost productivity in terms of lost output and other costs of recovering from the loss.

Moral and ethical issues also influence an organization's choice of risk control measures. How does one measure the benefit of saving a life or preventing sickness or disease? Should some risk control measures be adopted regardless of their costs because of humanitarian concerns? Therefore, an organization should base its decision as to an appropriate level of risk control on ethical issues as well as cash flow considerations.

Retained Losses

Retained losses are a major component of an organization's cost of risk. An organization should control its losses through cost-effective risk control. Organizations should then compare the projected cost of the remaining (residual) losses with the cost of transferring them when deciding on an optimal mix of risk retention and transfer.

Organizations should view retained losses from speculative risks differently from retained losses from pure risks. Speculative risks present the opportunity for gain as well as loss and, therefore, an organization should evaluate potential gains as well as potential losses. An organization that avoids a speculative risk because of the potential for loss incurs an opportunity cost because it is not able to share in any potential gain.

Retaining some types of losses, particularly long-tail losses such as liability losses, offers an additional benefit. Liability and other types of long-tail losses are not paid to claimants immediately but instead are paid over time. The deferred payment of losses benefits the organization retaining them and lowers its cost of risk when the retained losses are measured on a present value basis.

Measuring the Cash Flow Benefit of Retained Losses

Take the case of a large manufacturer that has thousands of workers compensation claims each year. When workers are injured on the job, they do not immediately receive payment for the full amount of their losses. Instead, they are indemnified for loss of wages and other costs over several years. Also, lump sum settlements for loss of limb and other injuries usually are paid many years after the injuries occur. Therefore, workers compensation losses are paid over time, and the organization retaining the losses benefits from the cash flow on the deferred loss payments.

The benefit of deferred payments can be measured quantitatively. Assume that the manufacturer incurs $1 million in retained workers compensation losses in Year 1 and must fund these losses at the beginning of Year 1. Also assume that the losses are paid in the following percentages over five years. (To simplify the analysis, assume all losses are paid at the end of each year.)

	Year 1	Year 2	Year 3	Year 4	Year 5	Total
Incurred Losses	$1,000,000					
Percentage Paid	25	25	20	15	15	
Amount Paid	$250,000	$250,000	$200,000	$150,000	$150,000	$1,000,000

Even though the manufacturer incurs $1 million in losses in Year 1, it pays only $250,000 to claimants in Year 1. The manufacturer pays the balance of the losses in Year 2 through Year 5.

Assume that the manufacturer has a pretax cost of capital of 14 percent yearly. Thus, it values any deferred cash flow benefits at 14 percent yearly because it is able to invest the cash back into its business and, therefore, is able to avoid raising additional capital. What is the present value benefit to the manufacturer of paying the $1 million in retained losses over five years?

The **present value** of an amount paid out one year from now can be thought of as the amount that must be set aside today that will equal the amount to be paid one year from now if invested at the **discount rate**, or the rate of return expected on the funds. Thus, if 88 cents is invested today earning 14 percent per year, it will equal $1.00 one year from now (.88 × 1.14).

Present value factors are used to calculate present values of future dollar amounts. These factors, when multiplied by future dollar amounts, calculate the present values of those amounts. Present value factors can be obtained from a table.

Continued on next page.

The following shows a portion of a present value table:

Factors for Calculating the Present Value of $1

	Discount Rate		
No. of Periods	10%	14%	16%
1	.9091	.8772	.8621
2	.8264	.7695	.7432
3	.7513	.6750	.6407
4	.6830	.5921	.5523
5	.6209	.5194	.4761

From the table, the present value factor for one year from now at a discount rate of 14 percent is .8772. Thus, $1 multiplied by .8772 is 88 cents (rounded to the nearest cent), which is the present value of $1 paid one year from now at a discount rate of 14 percent.

The present value concept can be applied to the deferred paid losses in the manufacturer example. The present value factors are obtained from the present value table. For example, at the end of Year 3 (three years after the beginning of the first period) the present value factor at 14 percent is .6750. When that factor is multiplied by the $200,000 loss payment at the end of Year 3, the present value of the loss payment is $135,000. The present value of the losses that the manufacturer paid for each year is shown below.

	Year 1	Year 2	Year 3	Year 4	Year 5	Total
Amount Paid	$250,000	$250,000	$200,000	$150,000	$150,000	$1,000,000
Present Value Factor (14%)	.8772	.7695	.6750	.5921	.5194	
Present Value	$219,300	$192,375	$135,000	$88,815	$77,910	$713,400

Therefore, $713,400 is the present value cost to the manufacturer of paying the $1 million of incurred losses over five years. The difference between the incurred losses and the present value cost of the loss payments is calculated as follows:

$1,000,000 Incurred losses
  – 713,400 Present value of loss payments
$ 286,600 Present value of cash flow benefit

Therefore, $286,600 is the present value of the manufacturer's before-tax cash flow benefit from paying the $1 million in retained losses over five years.

An organization should measure the value of the deferred loss payments on long-tail losses when analyzing the cost of its loss retention program. Deferring loss payments lowers the organization's cost of risk. An organization could lower its cost of risk even further by intentionally delaying payment to claimants. However, this is not a practical technique because an organization has both an ethical and a legal obligation to treat its claimants fairly.

An organization should also take into account the value of the cash flow benefit from retaining losses when deciding whether to retain or transfer its losses. A premium paid to an insurance company to transfer losses is usually due at the beginning of the policy period, whereas retained losses are paid at later dates, generating a cash flow benefit to the organization and, therefore, lowering its present value costs.

A Note on Taxes

Up to this point, this text has not mentioned income taxes as a consideration in managing an organization's cost of risk. An important tax issue with regard to risk financing is the timing of deductions of expenses from an organization's taxable income.

Although all risk retention and transfer expenses are tax-deductible, an organization maximizes the present value of its cash flow by taking a tax deduction as soon as possible. The organization receives a cash flow benefit by taking a tax deduction sooner rather than later.

Some risk financing plans that involve loss retention allow a tax deduction for the full amount of incurred losses in the year that they occur, while others only allow tax deductions as the losses are paid, usually over several years. An organization should consider this timing difference in tax deductions when deciding on a risk financing plan so as to minimize its cost of risk.

Transfer Costs

As discussed in Chapter 1, transfer means that another organization (the transferee) accepts the uncertainty of the cost of an organization's losses and reimburses the organization for losses or pays losses on its behalf. In general, the transferee receives compensation in exchange for accepting the risk of loss. Insurance companies are compensated with a premium in exchange for accepting their insureds' risks of loss. Other financial institutions receive various forms of compensation for hedging an organization's losses.

An organization should minimize the amount it pays to outside organizations to transfer its risk of loss. It can accomplish this by employing a broker or negotiating directly with insurers and other organizations that accept its risk of loss. Compensation to outside organizations that accept risk of loss is usually a large expense, so minimizing such compensation helps an organization to maximize the net present value of its cash flow.

Complying With Legal Requirements

The last risk financing objective mentioned in this chapter is to comply with legal requirements. Legal requirements are externally imposed.

Organizations often are legally required to purchase insurance for various reasons. For example, an organization that raises funds by issuing bonds may be subject to a covenant imposed by the bond purchasers that requires it to insure its property for a specific amount. The insurance laws of most states require organizations to purchase liability insurance for their vehicles or, alternatively, to qualify as self-insurers.

Toward an Optimal Portfolio of Retained Risk

An organization can manage its enterprisewide risk by retaining a portfolio of its various sources of risk. A major advantage of this approach is that an organization can reduce its aggregate retained risk through diversification. However, an organization should retain only risk for which it receives a sufficient return. To decide on an optimal portfolio of retained risk, an organization should analyze its various risks and their returns in an integrated manner. Even the retention of pure risks can provide a return, as explained below.

Estimating the Return From Retaining Hazard Risk

Chapter 1 mentioned that as an organization increases its loss retention level, it increases its risk of loss (uncertainty) and lowers its long-term cost. For hazard risk, an organization's increase of its loss retention level can be analyzed as an investment that involves risk and return. An organization's return for increasing its loss retention level can be estimated by calculating the organization's expected, or average, net savings (premium savings minus additional expected retained losses) and dividing that amount by the capital that must be made available to support the additional variability in outcomes from the increased retention.[7]

First, determine the amount of additional capital that an organization has at risk ("capital-at-risk") when it increases its retention level. One way to measure this

---

amount is to take a catastrophic loss scenario that will occur infrequently, such as once every 100 years, and determine the amount of capital that the organization would lose under this catastrophic loss scenario because of the increased retention. Then, determine the annual premium savings for the increased retention, and subtract the annual increase in expected, or average, retained losses (a cost) for taking the increased retention. (For long-tail losses, the expected retained loss payouts should be discounted to the present time using the firm's cost of capital.) The formula for calculating the return is as follows:

$$\text{Return} = \frac{\text{Annual premium savings} - \text{Annual increase in expected retained losses}}{\text{Capital-at-risk}}$$

An organization should analyze the risk and return available from taking hazard risk along with the risk and return available for taking other risks, including speculative risks. To conduct a risk and return analysis, an organization can construct a large number of retained risk portfolios based on combinations of various types and sizes of risk, with each portfolio containing its own set of risk and return characteristics. In order for the organization to maximize the net present value of its cash flows, it must select a portfolio of retained risks that maximizes its return at a level of risk it can tolerate.

In constructing portfolios of retained risks, the organization is subject to a number of constraints. It might be required to transfer some risks (purchase insurance) and retain others. Many risks are not transferable. Also, for many types of risk it is difficult to calculate risk and return as well as interdependencies among them.

Exhibit 2-4 shows risk and return portfolios for a hypothetical organization. Notice that the line shows higher returns for increased levels of risk. As a general rule, organizations receive higher returns for taking higher levels of risk; however, the tradeoff between risk and return varies by organization because it depends on the specific risks faced by an organization. It is also subject to the constraints mentioned above.

The sloping line in Exhibit 2-4 represents the efficient frontier of risk portfolios. The **efficient frontier** is a series of portfolios that maximizes the return for each level of risk. Alternatively, the efficient frontier can be viewed as a series of portfolios that minimizes the risk for each level of return. The points B and C represent two of the risk portfolios on the efficient frontier.

> An **efficient frontier** is a series of portfolios that maximizes the return for each level of risk.

Exhibit 2-4
Efficient Frontier of Risk Portfolios

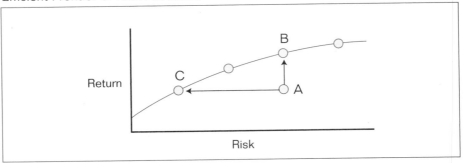

Point A in Exhibit 2-4 represents a risk portfolio that is inefficient because it lies below the efficient frontier. An organization is able to move from point A toward the efficient frontier by changing the composition of its risk portfolio. For example, the composition of the portfolio at point A can be changed so that it increases return with the same degree of risk, as represented by point B. Alternatively, the composition of the portfolio at point A can be changed so that it provides the same return with a lower degree of risk, as represented by point C.

For our hypothetical organization, assume its current portfolio of retained risks is at point A in Exhibit 2-4. Further assume that the organization has a relatively low level of retention for its hazard risks and a relatively high level of retention for its other risks, including interest rate risks and risks from investments in new products. By increasing the retention on its hazard risks, the organization probably will move from point A toward point B on the efficient frontier. This occurs because, in general, hazard risks are not correlated with the organization's other risks, so increasing the amount of hazard risk in the organization's retained risk portfolio is likely to increase portfolio return while adding little or no risk to the overall portfolio.

The point at which an organization's risk portfolio should lie along the efficient frontier depends on the organization's risk tolerance. Notice that as the risk level increases, the return per unit of risk decreases, as evidenced by the shape of the line for the efficient frontier. A risk-averse organization would want its risk portfolio to lie toward the left side along the frontier, while a risk-taker organization would want its risk portfolio to lie toward the right.

Measuring the risk and return for different risk portfolios is difficult, and new tools are being developed that will improve the accuracy of the measurements. By analyzing its risk-return decisions in an integrated manner for its portfolio of risks, an organization can maximize its return at a tolerable level of risk and, therefore, maximize the net present value of its cash flows.

Conflicts Between an Organization's Risk Financing Objectives and Society's Interests

Sometimes an organization's risk financing objectives conflict with society's interests, leading to an inefficient use of an economy's resources. As mentioned at the beginning of this chapter, a key risk financing objective for an organization is to manage its cost of risk. A key economic objective for society is to use its resources efficiently to produce the goods that businesses and consumers desire. In addition, as previously mentioned, ethical and moral issues should be considered in deciding on an optimal allocation of resources.

A conflict arises between an organization's objectives and society's interests when an organization does not incur all of the cost of risk associated with producing its product or delivering its service. For example, a product manufacturer might dump a chemical byproduct that pollutes a stream. The pollution creates a cost to society because people may not be able to fish in the stream, obtain drinking water from it, and enjoy its natural beauty. Unless the organization is taxed or fined for polluting the stream, it does not incur the cost of polluting the stream. Society, rather than the manufacturer, bears the cost of the pollution. When a cost is borne by a party that does not receive the associated benefits, an **externality** exists.

> **Externality** means benefits are transferred to parties that do not incur any of the associated costs, or costs are transferred to parties that do not receive any of the associated benefits.

Externalities can be positive or negative. Industrial pollution creates a negative externality from society's point of view. A positive externality arises when an individual or organization receives a benefit without incurring the associated costs. Take the case of an individual who receives a vaccination against a disease. Obviously the vaccinated individual will benefit from the medical treatment because it prevents the disease. But other people who come in contact with the vaccinated individual will also benefit because they will not contract the disease, even though they did not directly spend time or money to take the vaccine themselves. Therefore, these other people receive a positive externality.

When an externality exists, buyers and sellers do not consider all the costs and benefits associated with a transaction. A manufacturer that pollutes a stream does not consider the cost to society of polluting the stream when it decides on a production level for its product. In this case, the manufacturer's private costs are lower than society's costs, which leads to an overproduction of the product from society's point of view.

The divergence of social and private costs caused by negative externalities is shown in Exhibit 2-5.

Exhibit 2-5
Effects of a Negative Externality on Output and Costs

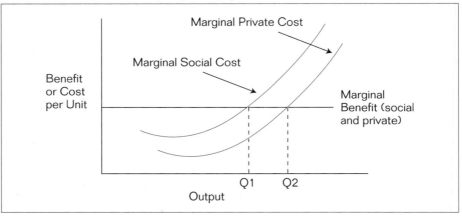

In a competitive market, a firm produces a product until the marginal cost of producing an additional product equals the marginal benefit. The firm's marginal costs include its marginal cost of risk.

Exhibit 2-5 shows two marginal cost lines: one for marginal private cost and the other for marginal social cost. When a third party suffers a negative externality as a result of a firm's production process, the marginal social cost of production is above the firm's marginal private cost. This relationship exists because the marginal private cost to the firm of producing the product does not take into account the cost of the externality. Notice that for marginal benefits, Exhibit 2-5 shows the marginal private benefit of producing the product as equal to the marginal social benefit.

The lower marginal private cost to the firm leads to overproduction of the product from society's point of view. The firm will produce the product at the level Q2, where its marginal private cost equals its marginal private benefit of producing the product. However, society would be better served if the cost of the externality were considered a cost of producing the product. Therefore, from society's viewpoint, the firm should produce Q1 units of the product so that marginal social cost equals the marginal social benefit. The overproduction of the product leads to an inefficient allocation of economic resources from society's viewpoint.

The legal system helps bring the firm's marginal private cost in line with its marginal social cost. It accomplishes this goal by passing laws that make a firm responsible for the cost of its own losses. For example, laws require a firm to clean up any pollution it creates as well as to indemnify third parties that suffer losses as a result of pollution. Firms are responsible for injuries to their employees under the workers compensation statutes. Product liability laws make firms responsible for harm caused by their products.

Occupational Disease and Externalities

Consider production processes that generate high rates of occupational disease for employees. If an employee is covered for occupational disease by social insurance funded by general taxes, the cost of risk for occupational disease is passed on to society (an externality). The employer does not bear the cost of risk associated with occupational disease, so the employer's private cost of production is lower than the social cost of production. From society's point of view, the employer will overproduce its product, and an inefficient allocation of resources will result.

Workers compensation insurance provides a mechanism to include the costs of occupational disease in a firm's private costs of production, thus reducing a negative externality. In theory, a more efficient allocation of resources results because decision makers must incorporate the costs of workers compensation in their production calculations. In countries where taxpayers bear the costs of occupational disease, firms in hazardous industries are more likely to overproduce products than are similar firms in countries with a private workers compensation system.

Not-for-Profit Organizations

In general, not-for-profit organizations and for-profit organizations have similar risk financing objectives. Not-for-profit organizations have a fiduciary responsibility to conserve the resources provided by their donors so as to provide necessary products and services to the public. Therefore, they have a need to manage their cost of risk and their uncertainty of loss outcomes so as to operate efficiently. They also have a need to maintain liquidity and solvency so that they are financially able to perform their missions.

A key difference between not-for-profit and for-profit organizations is that not-for-profit organizations do not pay income taxes. Therefore, tax considerations do not affect their decisions as to an optimal risk financing program.

Another key difference is that not-for-profit organizations usually place greater emphasis on safeguarding their assets and cash flow in order to carry out their missions than do for-profit organizations. Therefore, not-for-profit organizations might place more emphasis on minimizing uncertainty than for-profit organizations would. This might lead a not-for-profit organization to take a lower loss retention level, forsaking potential long-term savings.

Summary

- The following risk financing objectives apply to most organizations: (1) paying for losses, (2) maintaining liquidity, (3) managing uncertainty of loss outcomes, (4) managing the cost of risk, and (5) complying with legal requirements.

- The majority of an organization's risk financing objectives should be derived from and support its financial objectives. The main financial objective of most publicly traded organizations is to increase market value by maximizing the present value of their future cash flow. To help accomplish this financial objective, an organization should manage its cost of risk while maintaining liquidity and keeping uncertainty at a tolerable level.

- The degree of uncertainty of an organization's future cash flow also influences its value. For a publicly traded organization, in theory, the wider the probable range of future cash flow, the greater the discount that investors apply to the cash flow, lowering the organization's current market value. Additional reasons to manage uncertainty are to avoid bankruptcy, to reduce taxes, and to make investments with confidence.

- A major objective of risk financing is to pay for losses. An organization that purchases insurance must carefully evaluate its insurer's financial condition so that it can be reasonably certain that covered losses will be paid by the insurer. When an organization retains its losses, it must decide whether to use its current cash flow, establish an internal fund, liquidate assets, borrow funds, or raise funds from shareholders in order to pay for retained losses.

- A second major objective of risk financing is to maintain a proper level of liquidity to pay losses. An asset is liquid when it can easily be converted to cash. Two measures of an organization's liquidity are its working capital and its current ratio. Working capital (current assets minus current liabilities) is an absolute measure of a firm's liquidity, while the current ratio (current assets divided by current liabilities) is a relative measure because it shows the size of a firm's assets relative to its liabilities. The acid-test ratio is more stringent than the current ratio because the numerator does not include inventories and some other current assets that may be difficult to convert to cash.

- A third major objective of risk financing is to manage uncertainty of loss outcomes. The higher an organization's loss retention level, the greater the uncertainty of its loss outcomes. However, a major benefit of retention is that its long-run cost tends to be lower than the cost of transfer.

- An organization can use several techniques to reduce uncertainty. For example, an organization can reduce business risk through product diversification. For hazard risk, loss control and prevention measures as well as insurance are the traditional tools used by organizations to reduce uncertainty. Another way that an organization can reduce its uncertainty is to reduce its degree of financial leverage.

- When assessing its risk, an organization should assess the uncertainty arising from all of its enterprisewide risks together. Most types of risk are not correlated with each other, and therefore the organization can benefit from retaining a diverse set of risks. As the number of risk exposures in a portfolio increases, the unsystematic risk of the portfolio decreases through diversification.

- A fourth objective of risk financing is to manage an organization's cost of risk. Managing an organization's cost of risk does not necessarily imply that the cost of risk should be minimized because organizations are in the business of bearing risk for a price.

- Administrative expenses should be incurred to the extent necessary to properly manage a risk financing program. Often an organization has an opportunity to save administrative expenses by modifying procedures or eliminating unnecessary tasks.

- Risk control expenses are best analyzed by conducting a cost-benefit analysis. Resources should be devoted to risk control as long as the marginal benefit of a risk control measure exceeds its marginal cost. A firm's objective should not be to minimize the amount it spends on risk control. Instead, its objective should be to determine an optimal level of risk control that maximizes the net present value of its cash flows. In addition, a firm should consider ethical and moral issues.

- Retaining losses allows a firm to realize long-term savings. Retained losses, particularly long-tail losses such as liability losses, have an additional benefit. Because losses are paid over time, an organization is able to invest its loss reserves until it needs them to pay its retained losses.

- The cash flow benefit from retaining losses can be calculated by taking the present value of loss payments and subtracting it from the total amount paid (undiscounted) for losses. A discount rate that reflects a firm's cost of capital is used to calculate the present value of the loss payments. An organization should consider the value of the cash flow benefit from retaining losses when deciding whether to retain or transfer its losses.

- An organization should minimize the amount it pays to transfer its risk to outside organizations. For insurance transactions, an organization can minimize its cost by employing a broker or negotiating directly with insurers.

- The fifth major risk financing objective is to comply with legal requirements. An example of a legal requirement is a state's requirement to purchase liability insurance for automobiles.

- An organization should analyze all of its risks in an integrated manner and retain only risk for which it receives a sufficient return. An organization can construct an efficient frontier of risk portfolios that maximizes its return for each level of risk. The point along the efficient frontier at which the organization's risk portfolio should lie depends on its risk tolerance, for example, whether it is risk averse or a risk taker.

- For hazard risk, the return for retaining risk can be estimated by calculating the net savings (premium minus expected retained losses) and dividing it by the capital ("capital-at-risk") that must be available to support the retention.

- Sometimes an organization's risk financing objectives conflict with society's economic interests and lead to an inefficient use of society's resources. A conflict arises when an organization does not incur all of the cost of risk associated with its operations due to an externality. An example of a negative externality (from society's viewpoint) is the pollution of a stream caused by a manufacturer's chemical byproduct. The manufacturer does not incur the pollution cost when manufacturing its product. A negative externality causes a firm's marginal private cost of production to fall below the marginal social cost, which leads to an overproduction of the product from society's point of view. The legal system helps bring a firm's marginal private cost in line with the marginal social cost.

- In general, not-for-profit organizations have risk financing objectives similar to those of for-profit organizations. Because not-for-profit organizations do not pay income taxes, tax considerations do not affect their decision as to an optimal risk financing program. Also, not-for-profit organizations usually place great emphasis on safeguarding their assets and cash flows in order to carry out their missions. Therefore, they might place relatively more emphasis on minimizing uncertainty than for-profit organizations would.

Chapter Notes

1. The concept of present value is covered in detail later in the chapter.
2. Losses that have occurred and are expected to be paid in more than one year are classified as long-term liabilities.
3. For a detailed discussion of these rationales for minimizing uncertainty, see William H. Beaver and George Parker, *Risk Management: Problems and Solutions* (New York: McGraw-Hill, 1995), pp. 152-156.
4. International Risk Management Institute, Inc., *Risk Financing* (Dallas: International Risk Management Institute, Inc., 2000), vol. I, December 1997, p. II.J.1.
5. For a more detailed discussion of this concept, see Gordon C. A. Dickson, Dan Cassidy, Alan W. Gordon, and Shawn Wilkinson, *Risk Management* (London: The Chartered Insurance Institute, 1995), pp. 313-314.
6. "1998 RIMS Benchmark Survey," p. 5.
7. For a more detailed discussion of this concept, see Scott Sanderson, "Taking Stock of Your Risks," *Financial Executive*, July/August, 1997.

References

Chen, Yung-Ping, and Robert C.A. deVos. *Choices and Constraints: Economic Decisionmaking*, 3d ed. Malvern, PA: American Institute for CPCU, 1994.

Dickson, Gordon C. A., Dan Cassidy, Alan W. Gordon, and Shaun Wilkinson. *Risk Management*. London: The Chartered Insurance Institute, 1994.

Haight, Timothy G., ed. *Insurers Guide to Enterprisewide Risk Management*. Arlington, VA: A. S. Pratt & Sons, 1999.

Harrington, Scott E., and Gregory R. Niehaus. *Risk Management and Insurance*. Burr Ridge, IL: Irwin/McGraw-Hill, 1999

Williams, Arthur C., Jr., Michael L. Smith, and Peter C. Young. *Risk Management and Insurance*, 8th ed. Burr Ridge, IL: Irwin/McGraw-Hill, 1998.

Appendix 2A

Basic Loss Retention Concepts

This chapter mentioned that one of an organization's risk financing objectives is to pay for losses, including those losses it retains. This Appendix examines the various financial resources that an organization can use to pay for its retained losses. It also explains the concepts of planned retention and retention by default. Chapter 3 discusses specific retention plans in detail.

Paying for Retained Losses

An organization that retains its losses uses its own resources to pay for them. These resources can be the organization's cash flow, current assets, borrowed money, or money raised through stock (equity) offerings.

Cash Flow

Some organizations have a sufficient cash flow (cash inflow minus cash outflow) to pay for retained losses as the payments become due. By using its cash flow, an organi-

> An **unfunded loss retention plan** is any retention plan whereby assets are not set aside in order to pay for losses.

zation does not have to tie up assets so as to make them available to pay for retained losses. When an organization relies on cash flow to pay for its retained losses, it has an **unfunded loss retention plan** because assets are not set aside in order to pay for losses.

Organizations with weak or fluctuating cash flow cannot rely on that cash flow to pay for their retained losses. Instead, they usually rely on a combination of cash flow and their other resources to pay for the losses.

Risk Management in Practice

Oil Producers Rely on Cash Flow To Offset Losses

When the market demand for crude oil decreases, an oil producer usually suffers a loss because the market price for its product falls, squeezing its profit margins and reducing its cash flow. Larger oil producers usually depend on the cash flows generated from their other related businesses to maintain solvency during a period of falling market demand.

Current Assets

A firm with an insufficient cash flow might liquidate its current assets to pay for retained losses. This method is viable only if the firm has a positive working capital. (Recall that current assets consist of cash and other liquid assets that can or will be converted into cash within one year. Working capital equals current assets minus current liabilities.) Just as with relying on cash flow, a firm that relies on liquidating its current assets to pay for retained losses has an unfunded loss retention plan.

Take the case of KYZ Technology (KYZ) introduced earlier in this chapter. KYZ's balance sheet in Exhibit 2-1 shows current assets of $617.5 million and reserves for retained losses of $4.5 million. KYZ's working capital is $247.0 million. Therefore, KYZ has a more-than-sufficient amount of current assets that it can liquidate to pay for its retained losses as the payments become due.

Some organizations establish an internal fund to pay for their retained losses. When an organization uses an **internal fund**, it earmarks liquid assets, such as cash or marketable securities, to pay for its retained losses. This type of plan is a **funded loss retention plan** because assets are set aside specifically to pay for retained losses.

> In an **internal fund**, current assets are segregated in a fund to pay for retained losses.
>
> A **funded loss retention plan** is any retention plan whereby assets are set aside specifically to pay for retained losses.

Assets set aside in an internal fund are shown separately on an organization's balance sheet. In some cases, an outside organization, such as an insurance company, holds the funds on behalf of the organization retaining its losses. When this occurs, the fund is external to the organization and, depending on the accounting treatment, might not appear as an

> An **off-balance sheet fund** is a fund held by an outside organization, such as an insurance company, to pay for an organization's retained losses. The value of the fund does not appear on the organization's balance sheet.

asset on its balance sheet. When a loss fund does not appear on an organization's balance sheet, it is referred to as an **off-balance sheet fund**. Off-balance sheet funding is further discussed in later chapters of this text.

When an organization maintains current assets or uses an off-balance sheet fund to pay for retained losses, it incurs an opportunity cost because the funds are tied up; otherwise, the funds could have been used to reduce the organization's capital requirements. This concept is further explained below.

Opportunity Cost of Tying Up Assets To Pay for Retained Losses

An **opportunity cost** is a cost that an organization incurs when it forgoes the opportunity to invest its assets at a higher rate of return than the rate it actually makes on them. A firm that pays for its retained losses by maintaining current (liquid) assets or an off-balance sheet fund incurs an opportunity cost. If the firm could rely on its cash flow instead, it could, in theory, reduce the assets it has tied up to pay for retained losses and invest the assets back into its business, freeing up capital.

Because most organizations' cost of capital is higher than the rate of return they can earn on liquid assets, reducing those assets and freeing up an equal amount of capital results in a savings. This savings is the reduction in an organization's opportunity cost of maintaining current (liquid) assets or an off-balance sheet fund to pay for retained losses.

The savings can be illustrated by examining an organization's balance sheet. Selected portions of the balance sheet for ABC Corporation (ABC) are shown below:

ABC Corporation
Balance Sheet
(as of 12/31/00)
(All figures are in '000,000s.)

Assets	
Loss Fund (4% return)	$ 6.0
*	
*	

Liabilities + Shareholders' Equity	
Reserves for retained losses	$ 6.0
Debt (8% cost)	$300
Shareholders' equity (12% cost)	$600

Continued on next page.

Assume that ABC has set aside $6 million of its current (liquid) assets in an internal loss fund. Also, assume these assets earn 4 percent yearly on average. (Current assets, by definition, are short-term and liquid, so they earn a relatively low rate of return.) ABC's reserves for retained losses of $6 million are equal to the assets in its internal loss fund. Therefore, ABC has a fully funded loss retention plan consisting of an internal fund of $6 million in current assets. The earnings on the $6 million internal loss fund need to be compared with ABC's cost of maintaining an additional $6 million of its capital.

ABC's capital consists of both debt and shareholders' equity. Calculating ABC's cost of capital requires that a weighted average cost of its debt and equity first be calculated. ABC's debt is $300 million and costs 8 percent yearly, and its shareholders' equity is $600 million and costs 12 percent yearly. In this example, tax effects are ignored, even though the interest that ABC pays on its debt is tax-deductible while the cost of its equity is not.

ABC's weighted average cost of capital is calculated as follows:

$$\frac{(\$300 \text{ million} \times 8\%) + (\$600 \text{ million} \times 12\%)}{\$300 \text{ million} + \$600 \text{ million}}$$

$$= \frac{(\$24 + \$72)}{\$900}$$

$$= 10.66\%$$

If ABC did not maintain current assets of $6 million in the internal fund, it would, in theory, be able to reduce its capital by $6 million, saving $639,600 ($6 million times 10.66%), which is the cost of that capital. However, it would also forgo earnings on the current assets in its loss fund. Therefore, the forgone earnings on the current assets must be subtracted from the savings in capital cost. This is shown below:

Reduction in capital cost	$6 million × 10.66% = $639,600
Less: Forgone earnings on current assets	$6 million × 4.00% = $240,000
Estimated annual savings to eliminating loss fund	$399,600

The estimated annual savings of $399,600 from eliminating the $6 million loss fund is the annual opportunity cost to ABC of maintaining the fund.[1]

Borrowing

When an organization uses the technique of borrowing, it arranges a line of credit from a bank to pay for retained losses as the payments become due. Two benefits of borrowing are

1. Funds are readily available to pay for retained losses, and
2. Liquid assets, with their associated opportunity cost, do not need to be maintained to pay for retained losses.

An organization that borrows funds to pay for retained losses as the payments become due has an unfunded loss retention plan.

Borrowing can be expensive, particularly if the line of credit is arranged after a large loss occurs, because the lender might view the firm as posing a higher credit risk as a result of the large loss. Also, when it attempts to arrange a credit line, a firm may have used up its borrowing capacity, placing it in a position whereby it cannot borrow funds to pay for retained losses. Another disadvantage of borrowing is that it increases a firm's financial leverage, which increases the firm's financial risk, raising its cost of issuing equity.

Sometimes an organization is required to fund its loss retention. In such a case, the organization might rely on borrowing to raise cash for the loss fund. Borrowing money for this purpose has a net cost to the organization because the interest rate paid to borrow money is likely to be higher than the rate of return on the liquid assets in the loss fund.

Issuing Equity

One additional technique that an organization can use to raise funds to pay for retained losses is to issue equity, or stock, which is an ownership interest in the organization. When an organization uses this technique, it is using its own resources because it is exchanging an ownership interest for cash to pay for retained losses.

Issuing equity involves substantial costs. In general, only in unusual circumstances, such as when a catastrophic loss is retained, would an organization raise funds to pay for retained losses by issuing equity. Insurance companies have successfully used this technique by prearranging the right to issue equity if a catastrophic loss above a certain size occurs. This is called a catastrophe equity put arrangement and is further discussed in Chapter 11.

Summary of Various Financial Resources To Pay for Retained Losses

Exhibit 2A-1 summarizes the various financial resources available to an organization to pay for its retained losses.

In general, the least expensive way for an organization to pay for retained losses is to rely on its cash flow. This method assumes the firm has a cash flow that is large enough to cover retained losses as payments become due. Relying on cash flow avoids the opportunity cost of tying up liquid assets and avoids the costs of borrowing or raising equity to pay for losses.

Exhibit 2A-1
Financial Resources To Pay for Retained Losses

Financial Resource	Losses Are Funded/Unfunded?	Opportunity Cost From Tying Up Assets?
Cash flow	Unfunded	No
Current (liquid) assets	Unfunded	Yes
Internal fund	Funded	Yes
Off-balance sheet fund	Funded	Yes
Borrowing	Unfunded	No
Issuing equity	Unfunded	No

When deciding between using current assets (whether or not they are set aside in an internal fund) and borrowing to pay for losses, an organization should consider the timing and the amounts of cash it needs to pay for its retained losses. It should also consider the length of time it needs to repay loans using its projected cash flow. After considering these factors, the organization should weigh its estimated cost of borrowing to pay for retained losses against its opportunity cost of maintaining current (liquid) assets for the same purpose. An organization that infrequently needs cash to pay for losses might find that a line of credit (borrowing) is less expensive than tying up current assets in order to make them available to pay for retained losses.

Organizational Perspective on Financing Retained Losses

An organization should examine the methods it uses to pay for retained losses within the context of its entire financing program. Any savings in financing loss payments might generate additional costs in other areas of an organization's financing program.

For example, an organization that uses cash flow to pay for its retained losses could have otherwise used the cash flow to pay for various items, such as inventories. By not having the cash flow available to pay for inventories, the organization might need to borrow funds and incur interest expenses.

Planned Retention and Retention by Default

A characteristic of loss retention is that it can be planned or can occur by default. With **planned loss retention**, the organization identifies and measures its loss exposures, decides to retain them, and decides on a retention plan, such as self-insurance, to pay for any losses that occur. (Self-insurance is explained in the next chapter.) When retention occurs by default (**retention by default**), the organization has not identified and measured its loss exposures and/or has not decided on a plan to retain them. These various characteristics of loss retention are illustrated in Exhibit 2A-2.

Planned loss retention means the organization has identified and measured its loss exposures and has decided on a retention plan.

Retention by default is the result of not identifying and measuring loss exposures and/or not deciding on a plan to retain or transfer them. It also can occur when risk transfer is not available or a third-party payer is unable or unwilling to pay for losses.

Exhibit 2A-2
Planned Retention and Retention by Default

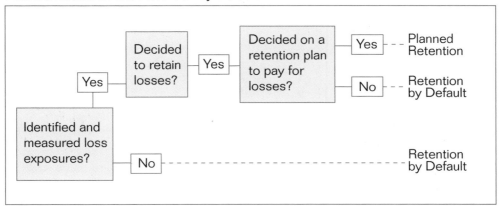

Retention by default can occur for the following reasons:

- An organization has identified and measured its loss exposures and has decided to transfer them but has not decided on a transfer plan to pay for losses;
- An organization is unable to transfer losses it would like to transfer;
- A loss payment is denied for a loss that an organization expected to be covered by its transfer plan; or
- An insurer or another third-party transferee is unable to pay for covered losses.

Losses retained by default can catch an organization by surprise and are potentially severe. Therefore, they can substantially lower an organization's capital and its cash flow. An organization should minimize the number of losses it retains by default by identifying as many of its loss exposures as possible. It should also devise a well-thought-out plan for retaining or transferring the losses.

Deciding Which Losses To Retain

Exhibit 2A-3, which is similar to Exhibit 1-2, shows the relationship between the frequency-severity characteristics of losses and the decision of whether or not to retain them. In general, low-severity losses in the aggregate are predictable and, therefore, should be retained, while high-severity losses should not. An organization must decide whether or not to retain losses that fall between these two extremes. As mentioned in Chapter 1, "high" and "low" are relative terms that vary by organization, usually depending on an organization's size.

Exhibit 2A-3
Loss Characteristics and the Decision To Retain Losses

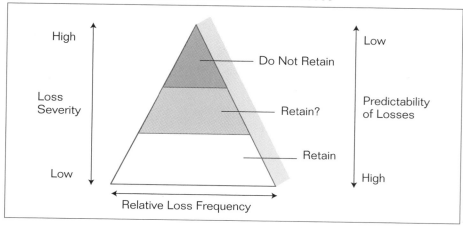

An organization that analyzes its loss exposures and decides to retain losses needs to implement a retention plan. Retention plans, along with other types of risk financing plans, are explained in the next chapter.

Appendix Summary

- An organization that retains its losses uses its own financial resources to pay for them. These resources can be the organization's cash flow, current assets, borrowed money, or money raised through stock (equity) offerings.

- Some organizations can rely on their cash flow (an unfunded loss retention plan) to pay for retained losses. In general, relying on cash flow is the least expensive way for an organization to pay for its retained losses.

- An organization could liquidate current assets to pay for retained losses as they become due. This method can be funded or unfunded. Some organizations establish an internal fund through which they earmark liquid assets to pay for retained losses. An internal fund, by definition, is a funded loss retention plan. Other organizations use an external fund in which an outside organization, such as an insurance company, holds the funds on behalf of the organization retaining losses. This is known as an off-balance sheet fund.

- An organization that pays for its retained losses by maintaining current (liquid) assets or an off-balance sheet fund incurs an opportunity cost. This arises because, in most cases, an organization's cost of capital is higher than the amount it can earn on the liquid assets that are tied up and made available to pay for retained losses.

- Borrowing provides a readily available source of funds to pay for retained losses. However, borrowing can be expensive and increases an organization's financial leverage (financial risk). Unless a loan is prearranged, lenders may not be willing to loan funds at favorable terms after a large loss occurs.

- In general, only in unusual circumstances, such as when a catastrophic loss is retained, would an organization raise funds to pay for retained losses by issuing equity.

- Retention can be planned or can occur by default. When an organization identifies and measures its loss exposures and decides on a retention plan to pay for them, it is practicing planned retention. An organization should avoid retention by default because the associated losses can be severe and substantially lower the organization's capital and its cash flow.

Appendix Note

1. The amount of opportunity cost for maintaining an off-balance sheet loss fund would depend on whether the insurance company gives an investment income credit.

Chapter 3

Introduction to Risk Financing Plans

Introduction

This chapter introduces common types of risk financing plans. The remaining chapters of this text analyze each of the plans in detail.

The plans described in this chapter can be used to finance an organization's hazard (accidental) risk, which arises from property, liability, net income, and human resource loss exposures. Hazard risk is a pure risk, so this text discusses each plan in terms of its ability to finance losses only. As will be discussed in later chapters, some of the plans discussed here can also be used to finance specific types of financial/market risk, such as movements in commodity prices and interest rates.

Risk financing plans consist of retention plans and transfer plans. A **retention plan** is a plan by which an organization uses its own resources to pay for its losses. A **transfer plan** is a plan whereby an organization uses another organization's (the transferee's) resources to pay for or offset its losses. However, most plans cannot be categorized strictly as providing either retention or

> A **retention plan** is a plan by which an organization uses its own resources to pay for its losses.
>
> A **transfer plan** is a plan whereby an organization uses another organization's (the transferee's) resources to pay for or offset its losses.

transfer because they are **hybrid plans** that combine elements of both. For example, an insurance plan that contains a deductible can be considered a hybrid plan be-

Hybrid plans combine elements of both loss retention and loss transfer.

cause the insured organization retains losses that fall under the deductible, while it transfers losses that fall above the deductible. Some of the more complex plans discussed in this chapter are hybrid plans.

Exhibit 3-1 shows the relationships between risk financing plans and the frequency-severity characteristics of losses. In general, retention plans are used for low-severity losses, while transfer plans are used for high-severity losses. Because they combine retention and transfer, hybrid plans can apply to all losses regardless of their severity. For example, a large deductible insurance plan can be designed to cover all losses that fall within the triangle shown in the exhibit.

Exhibit 3-1
Characteristics of Losses and Risk Financing Plans

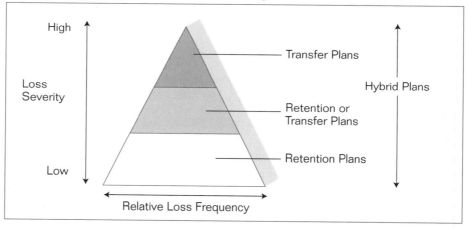

Exhibit 3-2 shows retention, transfer, and hybrid plans that this chapter discusses.

The characteristics of an individual risk financing plan must be examined before categorizing it as a retention, transfer, or hybrid plan. For example, large deductible insurance is usually categorized as a hybrid plan, while guaranteed cost insurance with a modest deductible is usually categorized as a transfer plan. A similar difficulty exists when categorizing a captive insurer plan. When a captive insurer purchases reinsurance, the plan is categorized as a hybrid plan. However, when a captive insurer does not purchase reinsurance, it is categorized as a retention plan. (Captive insurer plans are discussed in detail later in this chapter.) Therefore, keep in mind that the classifications used throughout this chapter for the various types of plans are general and may or may not apply to any given plan, depending on its specific characteristics.

Exhibit 3-2
Categories of Risk Financing Plans

Retention Plans	Transfer Plans	Hybrid Plans
• Informal retention • Self-insurance	• Guaranteed cost insurance • Insurance derivatives and insurance-linked securities	• Large deductible insurance • Retrospectively rated insurance • Captive insurer • Pool • Finite risk insurance

To meet its risk financing needs, an organization often combines several plans into a program. Some of the ways in which an organization can combine retention, transfer, and hybrid plans into a program are discussed in the last section of this chapter.

Retention Plans

Retention plans can be categorized as informal retention or self-insurance. These categories differ in terms of the degree of planning involved.

Informal Retention

With **informal retention**, an organization simply pays for losses with its cash flow and/ or its current (liquid) assets. Therefore, informal retention is an unfunded loss retention plan. A retail clothing store practices informal retention when it absorbs shoplifting losses as part of its normal cost of doing business. An organization that absorbs interest rate increases on its debt (interest rate risk) as a normal cost of doing business is, in a sense, also practicing informal retention.

Informal retention means an organization pays for losses with its cash flow and/or current assets. Generally, no record is kept of losses.

Informal retention has the advantage of low administrative costs. An organization does not need to formally record its losses or have formal loss payment procedures.   *Normal Business operations*

Informal retention is usually applied to low-severity losses that are easily absorbed by the organization's cash flow and/or current assets. The total losses retained for any one period should be minimal or fairly predictable so that they do not severely lower an organization's working capital or disrupt its cash flow.

Using informal retention does not mean that an organization has not consciously planned its retention program. Informal retention is characterized by planned retention; however, it lacks the formality and administrative control involved with self-insurance, which is discussed below.

Self-Insurance

With **self-insurance**, an organization identifies its loss exposures, decides to retain them, and formulates a plan to pay for and handle its retained losses. Self-insurance differs from informal retention in that with self-insurance an organization keeps records of its losses and has a formal system to pay for them. The term "self-insurance" is generally used only in relation to losses arising from hazard (accidental) risk.

> **Self-insurance** is a loss retention plan for which an organization keeps records of its losses and maintains a formal system to pay for them.

The Meaning of "Self-Insurance"

The term "self-insurance" is sometimes used broadly to describe any type of plan for which an organization retains its own losses. This text uses "self-insurance" to refer to those loss retention plans for which an organization keeps records of its losses and has a formal system to pay for them.

Using the latter definition, one could argue that self-insurance includes the retained portion of losses under deductible plans, retrospective rating plans, captive insurance plans, pools, and finite risk plans (all are discussed later in this chapter). However, this text categorizes these other plans separately from self-insurance plans.

Some authors use the term "self-insurance" only when referring to a loss retention plan that is funded. Others discourage the use of the term, claiming that insuring one's self is impossible.

Because self-insurance involves retaining losses, it is best suited for losses that, taken as a whole, are fairly predictable, such as losses that are both low-severity and high-frequency. (Obviously, it is also well suited for losses that are both low-severity and low-frequency.) In order to self-insure just the portion of hazard (accidental) losses that, taken as a whole, is somewhat predictable, a firm usually purchases excess insurance to transfer the high-severity portion of its losses.

Self-insurance is particularly well suited for losses that are paid out long after they occur, thereby providing a cash flow benefit to the organization retaining them. For this reason, workers compensation, general liability, and automobile liability loss exposures are frequently self-insured.

A self-insurance plan can be funded or unfunded. If it is unfunded, the self-insured organization pays for losses out of its cash flow and/or available current assets. With a funded self-insurance plan, the organization establishes an internal fund to pay for its losses. As discussed in the Appendix to Chapter 2, an organization that uses an internal fund incurs an opportunity cost.

One risk financing objective mentioned in Chapter 2 is to comply with legal requirements. Certain legal requirements might apply to a self-insurance plan. To self-insure some types of loss exposures, the various U.S. states require that an organization obtain approval from the state in which the loss exposure is located. For example, approval is typically required to self-insure automobile liability and workers compensation loss exposures. In order to obtain approval, the organization must comply with certain requirements, such as a security requirement (letter of credit or surety bond to guarantee loss payments), mandatory purchase of excess insurance above the self-insurance layer of loss, and an actuarial certification of its self-insured loss reserves. These requirements vary by state, so a multi-state self-insurance plan can be complex to implement and administer.

When a firm self-insures, it must obtain certain services that an insurance company normally provides as part of an insurance plan. Risk control procedures must be developed and implemented; claims must be investigated, defended, and adjusted; and a system of paying, keeping track of, and analyzing claims must be developed. The firm can obtain these services by using its staff or employing outside contractors. Firms often save expenses by outsourcing these services.

Workers Compensation and Self-Insurance

Workers compensation is a mandatory no-fault system in which employees who have work-related illnesses or injuries receive payments for their lost wages, medical expenses, and bodily injuries. In most states an employer is able to meet its workers compensation obligations by self-insuring the exposure.

Transfer Plans

The transfer plans introduced in this chapter are guaranteed cost insurance, insurance derivatives, and insurance-linked securities. In general, insurance is used to transfer the risk of hazard (accidental) losses. However, insurance is increasingly being used to transfer the risk of loss arising from some specific types of financial/market risks, such as movements in commodity prices, foreign exchange rates, and interest rates. This topic is further discussed in Chapter 11.

Derivatives are capital market instruments that an organization can use to offset the cost of its losses, in effect, transferring its risk of loss. Historically, derivatives have been used to transfer financial/market risks; however, in recent years they have been applied to hazard (accidental) risks through a technique called insurance securitization. (Derivatives and insurance securitization are discussed later in this section and throughout this text.)

Insurance in General

Insurance is a mechanism to pool losses. Through insurance, the organization that suffers a loss transfers the financial consequences of that loss to an insurance company in exchange for a premium. Insurance companies, which are in the business of accepting risk of loss, pool the loss exposures of their insureds with the expectation that the total premium they collect and the investment income they earn will be greater than the losses they must pay plus their expenses.

Law of Large Numbers

Insurance is based on the law of large numbers. The **law of large numbers** states that the larger the number of loss exposures, the more predictable the loss outcomes resulting from those loss exposures taken as a whole. An insurance company depends on the law of large numbers to calculate a sufficient premium for its portfolio of loss exposures so that it can pay losses, cover its expenses, and make a profit.

Organizations retaining their losses also usually depend on the law of large numbers. The larger the number of retained losses, the more predictable the total amount of retained losses and the lower the uncertainty for the organization.

For a given set of loss exposures, the predictability of total loss outcomes depends on the potential size of an individual loss. The larger the potential size of an individual loss, the greater the number of loss exposures necessary for total losses to be sufficiently predictable.

When an insurance company purchases insurance from another insurance company, the transaction is called **reinsurance**. An insurer might purchase reinsurance to increase its capacity to underwrite risk of loss or to stabilize its underwriting results. Chapter 6 discusses reinsurance in detail.

> **Reinsurance** is a transaction in which one insurance company transfers insured risk to another insurance company.

Insurance can also be thought of as a contract. An insurance policy is the legal document that defines the losses that are and are not covered, as well as the rights and responsibilities of the insurance company and the insured. (Chapter 4 explains various types of insurance policy coverages.) As a legal document, an insurance policy is an enforceable contract.

When it is incurred, an insurance premium[1] is charged as an expense on an organization's income statement and is tax-deductible. As long as insurance premiums remain fairly steady from year to year, they help to stabilize an organization's reported profits.

Certain legal requirements apply to insurance. In the United States, an organization must purchase insurance from a licensed insurance company or comply with the state regulations for purchasing insurance from unlicensed insurance companies. Also, an organization often is required to purchase insurance. For example, most U.S. states require amusement park owners to purchase liability insurance.

From the insured's point of view, an insurance plan is a funded plan. By accepting a premium, the insurance company agrees to pay for all of the organization's covered losses. The insurance company also agrees to provide necessary services, such as claim handling, loss control, and a system of paying and keeping track of claims.

Use of the Term "Insurance"

The term "insurance," when used in relation to risk financing, can be confusing because it has different meanings, depending on the context.

Often, "insurance" is used to describe a risk financing plan for which the premium is a fixed amount; for example, the premium is not adjusted based on actual losses that occur during the policy period. Therefore, an "insurance" plan transfers to the insurer the risk that an insured's losses will vary from the amount of loss that is expected to occur on average, which is the amount used to calculate the premium. Because the premium is a fixed amount, these types of insurance plans are often referred to as guaranteed cost insurance plans,

---

Continued on next page.

because they "guarantee," or fix, the amount of premium that the insured will pay for the policy, regardless of the amount of losses that fall under the policy.

The term "insurance" is also commonly used in connection with hybrid plans, such as large deductible insurance plans and retrospectively rated insurance plans. With these plans, only part of the risk of loss is transferred to the insurer, with the balance retained by the insured. For example, with a retrospective rating plan, the premium is adjusted based on a portion of the insured's actual losses during the policy period.

Guaranteed Cost Insurance

As previously mentioned, **guaranteed cost insurance** "guarantees," or fixes, the amount of premium that the insured will pay for a policy, regardless of the amount of losses that actually fall under the policy. Therefore, guaranteed cost insurance is a transfer plan.

Guaranteed cost insurance "guarantees," or fixes, the amount of premium the insured will pay for a policy, regardless of the amount of losses that fall under the policy.

Experience Rating and Guaranteed Cost Insurance

The guaranteed cost premium for most large organizations is based on standard industry rates adjusted upward or downward based on an organization's past loss experience. This practice is known as **experience rating**. For example, an organization with higher-than-average past loss experience would pay a higher-than-average guaranteed cost premium.

Guaranteed cost insurance is best suited for high-severity (catastrophic) losses, which are unpredictable. Many large organizations purchase guaranteed cost insurance only for their catastrophic losses, retaining their lower-severity losses. They can accomplish this in several ways, one of which is to purchase guaranteed cost insurance above a high self-insured retention. (In this case, the guaranteed cost insurance is usually called excess insurance.)

An advantage of guaranteed cost insurance is that it helps an organization to reduce the financial uncertainty associated with its losses. As long as an organization's losses are covered by a policy and the insurer is willing and able to pay the losses, the stability of an organization's earnings, net worth, and cash flow is enhanced. For financial accounting and tax purposes, a guaranteed cost premium is charged as an expense when it is incurred.

Although guaranteed cost insurance provides several benefits, it also has costs. Over the long term, guaranteed cost insurance tends to be more expensive than retaining losses and paying separately for the services that an insurance policy covers. Also, guaranteed cost insurance premiums are usually paid at the beginning of or during a policy period, so the insurer rather than the insured organization benefits from the cash flow available on losses until they are paid out, which can take several years in the case of losses arising from liability exposures.

Insurance Derivatives and Insurance-Linked Securities

Derivatives were introduced in Chapter 1. An organization can use derivatives to offset, or hedge, losses that arise from its insurable loss exposures. Therefore, a derivative can perform a similar function to that of traditional insurance (or reinsurance). In order to understand how derivatives can accomplish this, it is important to understand what they are and how they work.

Derivatives

A *derivative* is a financial contract that derives its value from the price of another asset, such as a commodity. The asset from which a derivative derives its value is called an **underlying asset**. A derivative can also derive its value from the level of an index of values, such as the Standard & Poor's 500 stock index or an index of insured catastrophe losses in the Southeastern United States.

A crude oil producer could enter into a derivative contract that increases in value as the market price of crude oil falls. With this contract, crude oil is the underlying asset because the value of the derivative is based on the market price of crude oil. If the market price of crude oil falls, the oil producer can use the increase in the value of its derivative to offset its loss of revenue due to a fall in the price of crude oil.

As another example, a U.S.-based global organization could purchase a derivative to offset any foreign currency translation losses it suffers due to the rise in the value of a foreign currency in relation to U.S. dollars. In this case, the exchange rate of the foreign currency in terms of U.S. dollars is the underlying asset. If the value of the foreign currency rises in relation to U.S. dollars, the value of the organization's derivative increases, offsetting its currency translation loss.

An **insurance derivative** is a financial contract that derives its value from the level of insurable losses that occur during a specific time period. Therefore, insurable losses are the underlying asset. The two major categories of insurance derivatives are

An **insurance derivative** is a financial contract that derives its value from the level of insurable losses that occur over a specific time period.

swaps and options. Insurance derivatives are discussed in detail in Chapter 11.

An Example of an Insurance Derivative

Assume XYZ Manufacturing (XYZ) is able to purchase an insurance derivative to hedge losses from its hurricane exposures in the Southeastern United States. Assume that the cash settlement value of the insurance derivative is based on XYZ's losses from a single hurricane that exceeds a specific threshold. If a hurricane occurs and XYZ's hurricane losses exceed the threshold, the cash settlement value of the insurance derivative to XYZ increases in direct proportion to the extent to which its losses exceed the threshold. XYZ uses this increase in the cash settlement value of the derivative to hedge, or offset, the losses it suffers from the hurricane.

Insurance securitization was also introduced in Chapter 1. It is defined as creating a marketable insurance-linked security based on the cash flow that arises from the transfer of insurable risks. An example is a catastrophe bond, which is specifically designed to transfer to investors insurable ca-

> **Insurance securitization** is a recent phenomenon whereby marketable insurance-linked securities are created based on the cash flow that arises from the transfer of insurable risks.

tastrophe risk, such as losses that arise from earthquakes or hurricanes. If a catastrophe occurs, investors stand to lose interest, principal, or both on the bonds. The investors' loss is used by another organization (the transferor) to offset its losses arising from the catastrophe.

The market for insurance derivatives and insurance-linked securities is not well developed, so their use is very limited. They tend to be expensive when compared with guaranteed cost insurance and require a great deal of planning to implement. However, the price of these products is likely to fall as investors become more comfortable with them. Also, prices for insurance rise and fall over time, so an increase in the price of traditional insurance would make these products more cost competitive. To date, a limited number of these products have been used mainly by insurers (and reinsurers) to offset losses in their portfolio of risk exposures.

A significant disadvantage of many insurance derivatives and insurance-linked securities is that the amount received by an organization to offset its losses may not match the actual losses suffered by it. This risk, called basis risk, can be eliminated if an organization is able to custom-tailor one of these new risk products for its own risk profile. Chapter 11 explains insurance derivatives and insurance-linked securities in more detail.

Hybrid Plans

As mentioned in the beginning of this chapter, hybrid plans combine elements of both retention and transfer. Hybrid plans are popular with large organizations because they allow the organization to benefit from the long-term cost savings available with retention but also provide a level of transfer that helps protect the organization's earnings, assets, and cash flow. The hybrid risk financing plans introduced in this section are large deductible insurance plans, retrospectively rated insurance plans, captive insurer plans, pools, and finite risk plans.

Some hybrid plans incorporate a funded loss retention because they require pre-funding of the retained losses. (Some of the plans that require pre-funding give the insured organization credit for investment income earned on the funds.) Others do not require pre-funding and, therefore, allow the organization to benefit from the cash flow available on the payout of its retained losses.

Large Deductible Insurance Plans

Deductible plans can be applied to most lines of insurance. However, in the United States a **large deductible plan** usually refers to a deductible plan for workers compensation, automobile liability, or general liability in which the per accident/occurrence deductible amount is $100,000 or greater. Most U.S. states permit organizations to use a large deductible plan.

> A **large deductible insurance plan** is a deductible plan for workers compensation, automobile liability, or general liability, in which the per accident/occurrence deductible amount is $100,000 or greater.

The concept of a deductible plan is straightforward. In exchange for a premium reduction, the insured agrees to reimburse the insurer for all losses up to the deductible level. In effect, the insured retains losses under the deductible level and transfers the portion of losses that fall above the deductible level and up to the limit of the insurance policy. Therefore, a deductible plan is a hybrid risk financing plan because it combines elements of both retention and transfer. The insured must usually provide the insurer with a form of financial security, such as a letter of credit, to guarantee payment of any losses that fall within the deductible level.

A large deductible is similar to a **self-insured retention**. A key difference is that, with a self-insured retention, the insurance policy specifies an underlying self-insured retention in place of a deductible. Another difference is that, with a self-insured retention, the insured organization is responsible for adjusting and paying its

> A **self-insured retention** is a formal retention that sits below the attachment point of an insurance policy.

own losses up to the self-insured retention level. The organization frequently outsources this task to an independent claim adjusting organization and pays a fee. With a deductible plan, the insurance company adjusts and pays all claims for loss, even those below the deductible level, and seeks reimbursement from the insured. (In effect, the insurance company is guaranteeing the payment of all claims.) Therefore, a deductible plan gives the insurance company direct control over individual claims that start out small but have the potential to exceed the deductible level. To compensate for a lack of control over individual self-insured claims, a policy with a self-insured retention usually requires strict reporting to the insurer of any claims that have the potential to exceed the self-insured retention level.

With a large deductible plan, the workers compensation deductible can apply on a per person and/or on a per accident basis, while the automobile liability deductible usually applies on a per accident basis and the general liability deductible usually applies on a per occurrence basis. The plan can also include an aggregate deductible, which caps total deductible payments over a period of time, usually a year.

Deductibles Under a Large Deductible Plan

Assume that a large deductible plan applied to workers compensation incorporates the following:

- A deductible of $100,000 for each injured person,
- A deductible of $250,000 per accident, regardless of the number of persons injured, and
- An annual aggregate deductible of $350,000.

Assume six employees are injured in a single year, with four employees injured in a single accident. The table below shows the cost of the losses for each employee.

Accident No.	Employee No.	Amount of Loss	Amount Payable Under Deductible
1	1	$150,000	$100,000
1	2	85,000	85,000
1	3	70,000	65,000
1	4	10,000	0
2	5	50,000	50,000
3	6	60,000	50,000
		$425,000	$350,000

Under the large deductible plan, the insured organization would reimburse the insurance company $100,000 for Employee 1 (subject to the per person deductible) and a total of $250,000 for Employee 1 through Employee 4 because they were involved in a single accident. In addition, the insured organization would reimburse the insurance company for an additional $100,000 for Employee 5 and Employee 6 together, with the annual aggregate deductible capped at $350,000.

With a large deductible plan, the amount that the insurance company incurs to adjust losses, including legal defense costs, can be inside or outside of the deductible. If they are inside, or included, the insurer adds them to the amount of the loss for the purpose of determining the total amount that is subject to the deductible. If they are outside, they are not added to the amount of the loss for the purpose of determining the amount subject to the deductible and are usually prorated between the insured and the insurance company based on the size of the loss.

Large deductible plans became popular in the United States in the late 1980s and early 1990s as more states allowed their use. Usually, an organization's motive for switching to a large deductible plan is to reduce costs compared with other types of plans. Even though most of the premium reduction is offset because the organization must pay for its losses under the deductible, reducing the premium saves costs for two main reasons:

1. Various states impose charges, such as premium taxes and residual market loadings,[2] which are calculated based on a percentage of premium, and

2. Insurance companies often charge insureds a set percentage of premium for overhead costs.

A large deductible plan dramatically reduces the amount of premium compared with other plans, avoiding a substantial amount of insurance company overhead charges, residual market loadings, and premium taxes.[3] (It is important to note that while residual market loadings were a large expense in the 1980s, they were substantially reduced in the 1990s.)

Another advantage of a large deductible plan is that it allows the insured to benefit from the cash flow available on the reserves for retained losses. The insured reimburses the insurance company as it pays losses under the deductible. Therefore, a large deductible plan is an unfunded loss retention plan. Workers compensation, automobile liability, and general liability losses are usually paid over several years after they are incurred, so the insured is able to benefit from the large amount of cash flow involved with these types of losses.

As with any loss retention plan, losses under a large deductible plan might be higher than expected, lowering an organization's net income and cash flow. By keeping its per occurrence (accident) and annual aggregate deductibles at a prudent level, an organization can manage its uncertainty with respect to the cost of its retained losses. The uncertainty level must be balanced against the total cost (retained losses plus premiums) of a large deductible plan at alternative deductible levels.

Retrospectively Rated Insurance Plans

Retrospectively rated insurance plans (also called retrospective rating plans) are insurance plans that are generally used for workers compensation, automobile liability, and general liability (including products liability). The insured pays a premium to the insurance company, which reim-

> A **retrospectively rated insurance plan** is a plan in which the premium rate is adjusted after the end of the policy period based on a portion of the insured's actual losses during the policy period.

burses claimants for losses and pays other expenses such as loss adjustment costs and legal defense fees. The premium also covers the insurer's overhead and profit.

On the surface, a retrospective rating plan appears to be the same as a guaranteed cost insurance plan. However, retrospective rating plans have an element of loss retention, so they differ from guaranteed cost insurance plans in the calculation of the premium rate. With guaranteed cost insurance, the premium rate is fixed for the policy period. With retrospective rating, a deposit premium is paid upfront, and the premium is adjusted after the end of the policy period *based on a portion of the insured's actual losses during the policy period.*

Deposit Premium Under a Retrospectively Rated Plan

Under a retrospective rating plan, the deposit premium is just that—a deposit. The final premium is based on a portion of the insured's actual losses during the policy period. The higher the insured's losses, the higher the retrospective plan premium. Conversely, the lower the insured's losses, the lower the retrospective plan premium.

The premium for a retrospective rating plan is not calculated solely on an insured's losses. The premium formula includes amounts for other costs, such as insurance company overhead and profits, residual market loadings, service bureau charges, premium taxes, and loss adjustment expenses. A portion of the premium is calculated on a guaranteed cost basis to compensate the insurer for accepting the risk that one or both of the following might occur:

- An individual loss exceeds a specific amount (called a **loss limit**), or
- Total losses under the loss limit for the policy period exceed an aggregate amount.

> A **loss limit** is the level at which each individual accident/occurrence is limited for the purpose of calculating a retrospectively rated premium.

Looked at in a different way, the guaranteed cost portion of the premium limits the extent to which an insured's actual losses are included in the retrospective premium formula. Therefore, it limits the extent to which an insured's actual losses can increase the retrospective plan premium, in effect providing risk transfer protection to the insured. When total losses under the loss limit reach a specified aggregate dollar amount, the maximum premium level is reached, and the insured pays no additional premium regardless of how much higher the losses go for that policy period. Exhibit 3-3 shows the relationship between losses below the loss limit and the adjusted premium for a typical retrospective rating plan.

Exhibit 3-3
Relationship Between Losses and Adjusted Premium for a Typical Retrospective Rating Plan

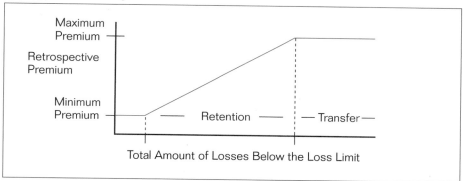

Based on the characteristics described above, it is clear that a retrospective rating plan is a hybrid risk financing plan because it combines elements of retention and transfer. Up to the loss limit, an insured, in effect, retains individual losses because they are used to raise or lower its retrospectively rated premium, subject to a maximum premium amount. The insured pays a portion of the premium on a guaranteed cost basis to transfer (1) the portion of individual losses that exceeds the loss limit and (2) annual losses under the loss limit to the extent that they exceed a specified aggregate dollar amount. Note that lower loss levels are subject to a minimum premium amount. The retained and transferred losses under a retrospective rating plan are also illustrated using a bar chart in Exhibit 3-4.

The dollar amount of aggregate retained losses is not directly specified in a retrospective rating plan. Instead, a retrospective rating plan specifies a maximum premium, which limits the premium an insured would be required to pay for a policy period. The maximum amount of aggregate retained losses can be calculated by working backwards using the maximum premium and the retrospective rating premium formula. Chapter 8 covers retrospective rating plans in more detail, including the formula for calculating the retrospective premium.

Exhibit 3-4
Retained and Transferred Losses Under a Retrospective Rating Plan

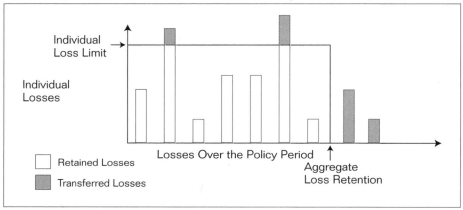

As with all plans that have an element of retention, retrospective rating plans allow an insured to retain a substantial portion of its losses and are well suited for retaining low-to-medium-severity losses. An insured that successfully controls its losses under a retrospective rating plan is able to lower its premium.

Retrospective rating plans may or may not provide the insured with cash flow benefits on the reserved portion of retained losses. With one type of plan, called a paid loss retrospective rating plan, the insured obtains the cash flow benefits, while with another type of plan, called an incurred loss retrospective rating plan, the insured does not obtain the cash flow benefits.

With a **paid loss retrospective rating plan**, the insured pays a small deposit premium at the beginning of the policy period and reimburses the insurer for a portion of its losses as the insurer pays for them. Therefore, the

A **paid loss retrospective rating plan** is a retrospective rating plan whereby the insured pays a small deposit premium at the beginning of the policy period and reimburses the insurer for its losses as the insurer pays for them. The total amount paid is subject to minimum and maximum amounts.

insured benefits from the cash flow available on the loss reserves for the retained portion of its losses, which might not be paid out for several years. A loss limit applies, and the total amount paid is subject to minimum and maximum amounts.

A paid loss retrospective rating plan is an unfunded plan for the retained portion of losses. However, the insured must provide the insurer with a letter of credit or some other form of security to guarantee the future payments for the retained portion of losses.

With an **incurred loss retrospective rating plan**, the insured pays a deposit premium based on its projected average incurred losses (paid plus reserved amounts) for the policy period. Shortly after the end of the policy period, the insurer adjusts the premium by using a formula that is based on the insured's actual incurred losses during the policy period. At that time, depending on the direction of the adjustment, the insured pays an additional premium or receives a return premium. A loss limit applies, and the adjusted premium is subject to minimum and maximum amounts.

> With an **incurred loss retrospective rating plan**, the insured pays a deposit premium during the policy period. After the end of the policy period, the insurer adjusts the premium based on the insured's actual incurred losses.

Incurred Losses Under a Retrospective Rating Plan

Incurred losses are paid losses plus reserves for future payments on losses that have already occurred. As soon as a loss occurs and a reserve is posted for that loss, it becomes part of the insured's "incurred loss" experience. Therefore, for the purpose of adjusting premium under a retrospective rating plan, incurred losses are recognized sooner than paid losses. Because the premium for an incurred loss retrospective rating plan is based on incurred losses, it offers less cash flow advantage than a retrospective rating plan based on paid losses.

With an incurred loss retrospective rating plan, because the insured pays a premium based on its retained incurred losses, it funds not only the paid amounts but also the reserves for its retained losses. By funding its reserves for retained losses with the insurance company, the insured is not able to benefit from the cash flow available on those reserves. This disadvantage can be offset somewhat if the insurance company provides a premium credit for its anticipated or actual investment income on the loss reserves.

An incurred loss retrospective rating plan is a funded plan for the retained portion of losses, with the insurer holding the insured's loss reserve funds until they are used by the insurer to pay for the retained portion of losses. The reserves for retained losses are an off-balance sheet fund from the insured's point of view because the funds are not shown as an asset and loss reserves are not shown as a liability on the insured's balance sheet.

A possible disadvantage of retrospective rating plans is that the insurance company might impose a very high maximum premium. By doing so, the insurance company exposes the insured to substantial uncertainty as to premium adjustments in the event that losses are higher than expected. Another disadvantage is that retained losses under a retrospective rating plan are paid for as a "premium," which means that they attract premium taxes and residual market loadings. As explained previously, these costs can be avoided by using a large deductible plan.

Retrospective rating plans, particularly paid loss retrospective rating plans, are effective in providing many of the benefits of loss retention and, depending on the terms, they can be effective in protecting the insured from the financial uncertainty involved with retaining its losses. Chapter 8 covers retrospective rating plans in more detail.

Captive Insurer Plans

A **captive insurance company** is a subsidiary formed to insure the risks of its parent company and its affiliates, although a captive is sometimes owned by and insures more than one parent. A captive insurer with one parent is called a **single-parent captive**, or **pure captive**. When a captive insurer is owned by multiple parents, usually from the same industry, it is called a **group captive**. A group captive sponsored by an association is often called an **association captive**.

A **captive insurance company** is a subsidiary formed to insure the risks of its parent and its affiliates.

A **single-parent captive (pure captive)** is a captive insurer with one parent.

A **group captive** is a captive insurer owned by multiple parents, usually from the same industry.

An **association captive** is a group captive sponsored by an association.

This text classifies a captive insurer as a hybrid risk financing plan because most captives combine elements of retention and transfer. In general, a captive insurer retains its parent's low-to-medium-severity losses and purchases reinsurance to transfer its parent's high-severity losses. To the extent its captive subsidiary retains risk of loss, the parent organization is, in effect, practicing retention because it owns and is insured by the captive. For the same reason, to the extent its captive insurance subsidiary transfers risk of loss to a reinsurer, the parent organization is, in effect, practicing transfer.

A captive insurer is usually not licensed, or admitted, to transact insurance business in the states, provinces, and territories where its parent's loss exposures are located. Obtaining licenses is time-consuming and expensive. Therefore, most captive insurers reinsure a licensed insurance company that issues insurance policies to the parent and its other subsidiaries. The licensed insurance company usually does not retain any of the losses and, therefore, in effect "fronts" for the captive insurer in exchange for a fee. The licensed insurance company is called a **fronting company**. In effect, the captive rents the license of the fronting company.

> A **fronting company** is an insurance company that issues policies and reinsures all of the risk to another insurance company.

A captive insurer can be used for any type of its parent's or its affiliates' loss exposures, but a captive insurer is commonly used for loss exposures that offer substantial cash flow, such as those covered by workers compensation, general liability, and automobile liability policies. The captive usually operates as a reinsurance company by receiving premiums from the fronting company and reimbursing it for covered losses. The captive itself usually purchases reinsurance for a portion of the losses it has agreed to cover. It pays reinsurance premiums and obtains reimbursement from its reinsurers for losses covered under its reinsurance contracts. Services provided to the captive's parent and affiliates, such as claim handling and loss control, usually are handled by the fronting company, an insurance broker, or a third-party vendor.

Exhibit 3-5 shows the relationships among the insured, the fronting company, the captive insurer, reinsurers, and third-party claimants for a typical captive insurer plan. Premiums are paid by the captive's parent and its affiliates (the insured) to the fronting company. The fronting company subtracts its fee and passes on the balance of the premium and the risk of loss to the captive insurer (which is acting as a reinsurer). The captive insurer transfers some of its risk of loss by passing a portion of the premium and risk of loss to its reinsurers. Because the fronting company issued the insurance policy, it is responsible for paying the losses, both first-party losses to the parent and its affiliates and third-party losses to other claimants. The fronting company is reimbursed for losses by the captive insurer, which, in turn, is reimbursed by the reinsurers for the reinsured portion of its losses.

As with other plans that involve loss retention, a captive insurance company allows the insured to benefit from the cash flow available on losses that are paid out over time because the captive earns investment income on its loss reserves. The captive also earns investment income on its unearned premium reserves.

Exhibit 3-5

Typical Captive Insurer Relationships

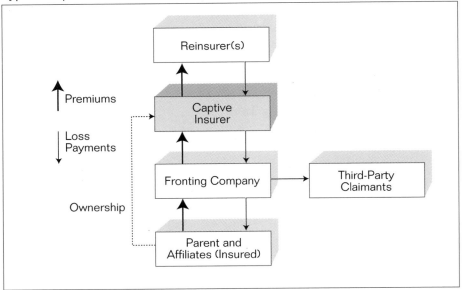

However, there is an opportunity cost to a captive arrangement because the investment income earned by the captive is likely to be less than the parent's cost of capital. In other words, the parent would realize a net savings if it could use the cash tied up in the captive to reduce its capital needs. Because a captive usually holds cash to pay for its retained losses, a captive insurer plan is usually a funded plan.

Captive insurance plans are well suited for retaining low and low-to-medium-severity losses. Because a captive insurer involves retention, an insured that successfully controls its losses is able to save payments for losses and loss expenses.

Through the purchase of reinsurance, a captive insurer can help its parent reduce the uncertainty of its retained losses to a tolerable level. For a single-parent captive, the captive insurer is a wholly owned subsidiary. Therefore, its financial statements are consolidated with those of its parent. Any volatility in the underwriting results of the captive insurer creates volatility in the parent's financial results. However, if the captive purchases reinsurance sufficient to stabilize its underwriting results, the parent's financial uncertainty is similarly reduced.

Captive insurance plans share similarities with retrospective rating plans. In both cases the insured obtains an insurance policy that covers the entire amount of its losses but retains a portion of its losses. A major difference between the two is that, with a captive insurer plan, the portion of premium that funds retained losses is held by an insurance subsidiary owned by the parent. With an incurred loss retrospective rating plan, the portion of premium that funds retained losses is held by an independent insurance company.

Two possible disadvantages of captive insurer plans are that the fronting company may charge an unreasonably high amount and that reinsurance might not be available at a level that sufficiently reduces the uncertainty of the parent's retained losses in the captive. Also, as with retrospective rating plans, the losses that a captive insurer retains are paid for by the insured as a "premium," which attracts premium taxes and residual market loadings. These costs can be avoided by using a large deductible plan.

A captive insurer plan provides a means for a global corporation to coordinate and consolidate its worldwide insurance program. The parent company can use its captive insurer to take an organizationwide retention for its worldwide risks. A licensed (admitted) fronting company usually issues policies in various countries and reinsures the risks back to the parent's captive insurer. Chapter 9 further discusses captive insurers.

Pools

A **pool** is a group of insureds that band together to insure each other's risk of loss. Each insured member of the pool contributes premium based on its loss exposures

> A **pool** is a group of insureds that band together to insure each other's risk.

and, in exchange, the pool pays for each insured's covered losses. In certain types of pools, the members also contribute capital.

The pool can be a stock insurance company or a not-for-profit unincorporated association governed by its members. The pool operates just like an insurance company by collecting premiums, paying losses, purchasing excess insurance or reinsurance, and providing other services such as risk control consulting. In addition, for certain types of coverage a pool might use a fronting company. Technically, group and association captives (mentioned in the previous section) are pools.

A pool can cover many types of loss exposures. In the United States, workers compensation pools are common and are permitted by most states. The various states regulate the formation and operation of pools, with workers compensation pools subject to the most regulation. U.S. public entities use pools extensively to insure their risk of loss.

There are many ways to design a pool. Some pools offer a combination of loss retention for individual members and loss transfer among the members, so they are categorized as hybrid plans. Others transfer all losses among the members, so they are categorized as transfer plans. (Another way to transfer losses is for the pool to purchase reinsurance.) Still other pools are designed so that the members borrow funds from the pool to pay their own losses, and they must pay the funds back to the pool. These pools are retention plans and function as standby credit facilities.

Pools are well suited for organizations that are too small to use a captive insurance company or to self-insure their own losses. Savings are achieved by the pool through economies of scale in administration, claim handling, and the purchase of excess insurance or reinsurance. Each pool member might realize a savings in premium compared with that for traditional insurance. A properly designed pool can reduce an organization's cost of risk and keep the uncertainty of the cost associated with its retained losses at a tolerable level.

Exhibit 3-6 shows typical relationships among a pool, its members (insureds), reinsurers, and claimants.

Exhibit 3-6
Typical Pool Relationships

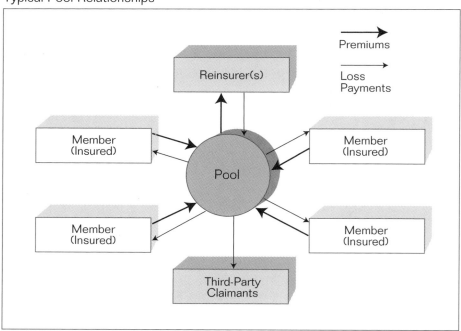

Finite Risk Insurance Plans

A finite risk insurance plan is difficult to define and is best described by its characteristics. In general, a **finite risk insurance plan** transfers a limited amount of risk of loss to an insurer and usually includes a profit-sharing arrangement. The word "finite" refers to the fact that all finite risk insurance agreements transfer a limited amount of risk of loss to the insurer. "Risk," in this context, is defined as the chance that losses and other expenses covered by an insurance agreement will be greater than the premium plus investment income earned by the insurer, requiring that the insurer use additional funds to pay for losses.

> A **finite risk insurance plan** transfers a limited amount of risk of loss to an insurer and usually includes a profit-sharing arrangement.

Most insurance agreements limit the amount of risk transferred to an insurer by imposing policy limits. Finite risk insurance differs from guaranteed cost insurance because a large part of the insured's premium under a finite risk insurance agreement creates a fund for the insured's own losses, and the remaining amount of the premium is used to transfer a limited corridor of risk of loss to the insurer. Because it combines retention and transfer, a finite risk plan is classified as a hybrid plan.

A finite risk insurance plan is flexible and usually has the following characteristics:

- It is often applied to the more hazardous coverages, such as coverage for environmental liability and earthquake damage, in which risk-transfer capacity is limited. It can also be applied to coverages traditionally not covered by an insurance company.

- It is usually applied to high-severity and low-frequency losses.

- The insurer usually shares a large percentage of its profit with the insured.

- It can be used to cover known losses as well as future losses that arise from loss exposures, as with traditional insurance.

- The premium is a very high percentage of the policy limits, which usually apply on an aggregate basis. For example, an insurer might provide an aggregate limit of $10 million for a $7 million premium. The insurer's risk is limited because the most it would ever have to pay is $10 million, and it has the opportunity to earn investment income on the $7 million premium until losses are paid.

The last characteristic enables an insurer to limit the amount of risk it takes under a finite risk plan. By charging a substantial premium for the risk and applying an aggregate to the limit, the insurer has a small chance that its losses and expenses will exceed its premium and earned investment income.

Finite risk plans are sometimes written on an integrated risk basis, meaning that they apply to more than one line of coverage, usually for more than one year. For this reason, they are sometimes referred to as *finite/integrated risk plans*. Applying a finite risk plan to more than one line of coverage over more than one year substantially reduces risk for the insurer through diversification. For example, in any one year losses might be higher than expected for an insured's automobile liability line of coverage but lower than expected for its general liability line of coverage. Also, while an insured's total losses might be higher than expected in one year, they might be lower than expected in the following year.

The finite risk insurance plan that follows can be analyzed in terms of the risk accepted by the insurer. The maximum amount of loss that the insurer could pay for the five-year term is $50 million, and the premium collected is $35 million (5 years × $7 million per year). The insurer earns investment income on this premium, so the insurer's maximum risk is the difference between its $50 million exposure to loss and the $35 million premium plus the investment income earned on the premium before it is used to pay for any losses. For losses that are paid out over a long period of time, the investment income could be substantial. Therefore, the insurer's risk is limited, or finite, when viewed in terms of the entire transaction. For taking this risk, the insurer receives a margin of 10 percent of the premium, or $3.5 million.

	Finite Risk Insurance Example
Exposure Covered	Excess liability (including products)
Term	5 years
Limit	$50 million per occurrence/aggregate in excess of $50 million per occurrence (a single limit applies to the five-year term)
Premium	$7 million per year for the five-year term
Margin	10 percent of premium
Profit Sharing	If premium plus investment income is greater than losses plus the margin, the difference is returned to the insured. At the insured's option, any profit sharing can be rolled over and used to purchase additional limits.

> **Note:** If a large loss exhausts the limits during the first year, the insured is still obligated to pay the annual premium for the next four years even though no further limits are available.

The formula for calculating the profit sharing amount is as follows:

Profit sharing = Premium + Investment income – Margin – Losses

In the example given above, profit sharing is calculated as follows:

Profit sharing = $35,000,000 + Investment income – $3,500,000 – Losses

Exhibit 3-7 shows the relationship between losses and premium (net of profit sharing) for the finite risk insurance example given above. (Note: investment income is not included in the analysis.)

If there are no losses, the insured receives, as profit sharing, all of the premium plus investment income minus the $3,500,000 margin charged by the insurer. If losses equal $31,500,000, the insured pays $35 million ($31,500,000 in losses plus the $3,500,000 margin). When losses exceed $31,500,000, the insured's premium cost is capped at $35 million.

A finite risk plan can be used to transfer a limited number of high-severity losses to an insurer. It provides a predictable cost over the term of the coverage. Finite risk plans are covered in more detail in Chapter 10.

Exhibit 3-7
Finite Risk Plan
Relationship Between Losses and Premium (Net of Profit Sharing)*

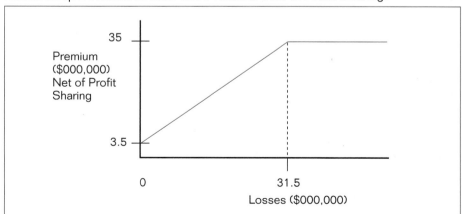

*Note: Investment income credits are not included in this analysis.

Comparison of Risk Financing Plans

This chapter has described various loss retention, loss transfer, and hybrid plans. Each of these plans must be evaluated in terms of its ability to meet a firm's risk financing objectives.

The characteristics of the various plans are summarized in Exhibit 3-8. The purpose of the matrix is to give a general idea of some of the characteristics of the various plans. However, any individual plan could vary from the characteristics mentioned. For example, a self-insurance plan can be applied to high-severity losses (although this is not usually the case).

To be economically feasible, many of the risk financing plans introduced in this chapter require that an organization have a substantial amount of losses to finance. The remaining chapters of this text explain these requirements.

Exhibit 3-8
Characteristics of Various Risk Financing Plans

Type of Plan	Best Suited for Losses of the Following Severity	Degree of Risk Transfer	Degree of Planning Required
Retention			
Informal Retention	Low	None	Low
Self-Insurance	Low to Medium	None	Moderate
Transfer			
Guaranteed Cost Insurance	High	High	Moderate
Insurance Derivatives and Insurance-Linked Securities	High	High	Very High
Hybrid			
Large Deductible Insurance	Low to Medium	Varies	Moderate
Retrospectively Rated Insurance	Low to Medium	Varies	Moderate
Captive Insurer	Low to Medium	Varies	High
Pools	Medium to High	Varies	Very High
Finite Risk Insurance	High	Limited	High

Combining Retention, Transfer, and Hybrid Plans

The risk financing plans described in this chapter are often combined in order to meet a firm's risk financing objectives. Many combinations can be used, but frequently a transfer plan sits above a retention or a hybrid plan.

For example, a firm might self-insure its low-to-medium-severity losses and purchase guaranteed cost insurance for its high-severity losses. (In this case, the layer of insurance purchased is called excess insurance because it sits above another layer.) Exhibit 3-9 shows a combination of self-insurance and excess insurance in which a firm self-insures the first $100,000 per accident/occurrence and purchases excess insurance with a limit of $10 million per accident/occurrence. Therefore, the total amount of loss addressed by the combined plan is $10,100,000 per accident/occurrence.

Exhibit 3-9
Combination of Self-Insurance and Excess Insurance

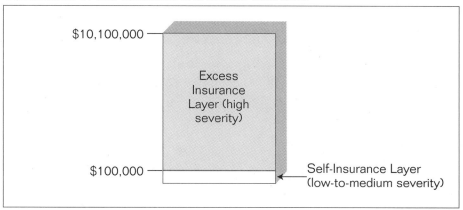

As another example, an organization might use a captive insurer to cover the first layer of its liability insurance, with a finite risk plan above that layer. Exhibit 3-10 shows an arrangement whereby an organization uses its captive to insure the first $5 million per accident/occurrence and a finite risk plan to insure its layer of loss from $5 million up to $25 million per accident/occurrence. The insurance plan between the organization and its captive (using a fronting company) is an incurred loss retrospective rating plan with a limit of $5 million per accident/occurrence and a $100,000 loss limit per accident/occurrence. The captive purchases reinsurance for its layer of loss from $100,000 up to $5 million per accident/occurrence.

Exhibit 3-10
Combination of Captive Insurance and Finite Risk

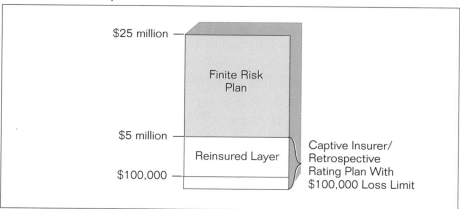

In Exhibit 3-10, the insured organization (which is the parent of the captive insurer) retains $100,000 per accident/occurrence through the retrospective rating plan and, through its captive, transfers the portion of losses from $100,000 up to $5 million per accident/occurrence to a reinsurer. The insured also transfers a limited amount of the risk related to its high-severity losses ($5 million to $25 million) through a finite risk plan.

Many possible plan combinations are available to meet a firm's risk financing objectives. The combinations are limited only by the imagination of a firm, its broker, its consultant, and its insurer.

Summary

- This chapter introduced various types of retention, transfer, and hybrid risk financing plans. Later chapters will describe many of them in more detail.

- In general, retention plans are used for low-severity losses, while transfer plans are used for high-severity losses. Because they combine retention and transfer, hybrid plans apply to losses at all severity levels.

- The characteristics of an individual plan must be examined before categorizing it as a retention, transfer, or hybrid plan.

- To meet its risk financing needs, an organization often combines several plans into a program.

- With informal retention, an organization simply pays for losses with its cash flow and/or available current assets. With self-insurance, an organization identifies its loss exposures, decides to retain them, and formulates a well-developed plan to pay for and handle the losses. Self-insurance differs from informal retention in that an organization keeps records of its losses and has a formal system to pay for them.

• The loss transfer plans introduced in this chapter are (1) guaranteed cost insurance and (2) insurance derivatives and insurance-linked securities. In general, insurance is a mechanism to pool losses and is based on the law of large numbers. With guaranteed cost insurance the premium is a fixed amount regardless of the level of losses that occur. An insurance derivative is a contract that derives its value from the level of insurable losses that occur during a specific time period. An organization can use insurance derivatives to offset, or hedge, its insurable losses. An insurance-linked security is a marketable security, such as a bond, that has insurable risk embedded in it.

• This chapter introduced the following hybrid plans: large deductible insurance plans, retrospectively rated insurance plans, captive insurer plans, pools, and finite risk insurance plans. Each of these hybrid plans has unique characteristics and allows an organization to retain and transfer losses with different severity levels.

Chapter Notes

1. This assumes that the premium is for true "insurance," meaning that there is risk transfer and distribution. Risk transfer means that the insurer bears the risk of loss, and risk distribution means that the insured's premium is available as part of a fund to pay other insureds' losses.

2. A residual market loading is an amount charged to make up for losses in a state-sponsored plan to insure high-risk exposures, such as an assigned risk plan for automobile insurance.

3. Recently, some states have taken steps to impose premium taxes and residual market loadings on the retained-loss portion of large deductible plans.

Reference

International Risk Management Institute. *Risk Financing: A Guide to Insurance Cash Flow.* Dallas: International Risk Management Institute, Inc., 2000.

Chapter 4

Insurance as a Risk Financing Technique

Introduction

Insurance is the predominant technique that organizations use to transfer hazard risk. In exchange for a premium, an insurance company agrees to indemnify an insured for specific types of losses as defined by an insurance policy.

Insurance policies are issued for risk financing plans that involve transfer, including hybrid plans. For example, insurance policies are issued for guaranteed cost plans, retrospectively rated plans, and large deductible plans. A fronting company for a captive insurer issues an insurance policy to the parent of the captive and its affiliates. An insurance policy is also issued under a finite risk insurance plan.

This chapter describes the coverage that standard insurance policies provide. Insurance policies are available to cover property, liability, net income, and human resource losses. In recent years, some insurance companies have expanded the scope of their business by covering additional types of losses, such as losses arising from financial/market risk. For example, insurance policies have been tailored to cover an increase in newsprint prices for a newspaper publisher and an increase in the cost of purchased electric power for a public utility.[1]

Most insurance policies contain a **limit**, which is the maximum amount that the insurer will pay for each loss or, in some cases, all losses over the policy period (called an **aggregate limit**). The limit can apply from the first dollar, meaning that it covers the full amount of the loss up to the limit, or it can apply in excess of a dollar attachment point, below which there is another insurance policy or a self-insured retention. Insurance that covers losses above an attachment point is called **excess insurance**. Insurance that falls below excess insurance and covers from the first dollar is sometimes referred to as **primary insurance** or **underlying insurance**. Exhibit 4-1 shows the relationship between primary and excess insurance.

A **limit** is the maximum amount that the insurer will pay for each loss.

An **aggregate limit** is the maximum amount that the insurer will pay for all losses over the policy period.

Excess insurance covers losses above an attachment point, below which there is usually another insurance policy or a self-insured retention.

Primary insurance (underlying insurance) falls below excess insurance and covers from the first dollar.

Exhibit 4-1
Relationship Between Primary Insurance and Excess Insurance

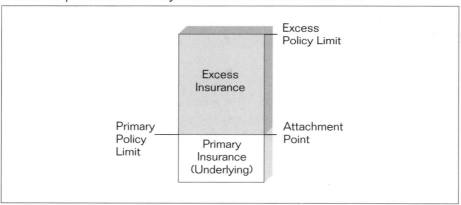

"Insurance" Defined

"Insurance" can be defined in several ways. Some definitions focus on the economic aspects of insurance, while others focus on the legal aspects.

Economic definitions of insurance mention the concepts of risk pooling and transfer. One classic and widely recognized economic definition of insurance describes it as follows:

> Insurance is a social device for accumulating capital to meet uncertain losses. Insurance is carried out by a transferring of the risks of many individuals to one entity or group that functions as the insurer.[2]

Legal definitions of insurance also mention risk pooling and transfer, with an emphasis on insurance as a contract. The following types of questions are often asked to determine whether a transaction legally is insurance:

- Does the insured or the beneficiary have a risk of economic loss that is independent of the contract itself?
- Does the insurer or the promisor assume the risk?
- Does the transaction incorporate a plan to distribute the costs of the loss among members of a group exposed to risk?

This chapter focuses on insurance as a risk transfer technique, so the term "insurance" is used throughout this chapter to refer to guaranteed cost insurance plans and the risk transfer component of hybrid plans. This usage is consistent with the definitions of insurance mentioned above. This chapter discusses primary insurance, and the next chapter discusses excess insurance.

Insurance as Part of a Risk Financing Program

Two key risk financing objectives, mentioned in Chapter 2, are to manage the uncertainty of loss outcomes and to manage the cost of risk. Meeting risk financing objectives involves minimizing the cost per unit of risk transferred and retaining risk when there is a sufficient return, subject to an organization's tolerance for risk.

Insurance is a key technique for a risk financing program. Not only do insurers accept an organization's risk of loss, but they also provide the organization with services in areas such as loss control, claim processing, and legal advice. To some organizations, these specialized services may be more important than the risk transfer aspect of insurance.

Services can often be purchased separately from either an insurer or a third-party vendor. For example, many insurers sell loss control and claim administration services to organizations that self-insure their losses.

Loss Control Services

Because they handle the losses of many different policyholders, insurers develop expertise in recognizing and controlling exposures to loss. This expertise is especially important for exposures that might result in employee injury as well as high-severity losses. Insurers provide assistance both in identifying loss exposures and in recommending ways to control the associated risk of loss.

Under guaranteed cost insurance, insurers bear the cost of losses, so they have a strong financial incentive to identify and implement measures that control their insureds' losses. Insurers provide loss control services to organizations both to complement insurance coverage and as a separate fee-based service. Insured organizations have an incentive to control their losses because the premium for the next coverage period may be based, in part, on current loss experience.

Claim and Legal Services

Because they handle claims made by many different policyholders, insurers develop expertise in claim handling. Settling claims, administering claim payments, and preventing fraud are among the specialized areas of expertise necessary to handle claims. As mentioned above, under guaranteed cost insurance, an insurer has a financial incentive to control claim costs because of its contractual obligation to pay for losses, regardless of their severity.

Insurers have other specialized areas of expertise, such as the management of medical and disability claims. In addition, insurers have knowledge of systems to report, track, and pay for claims.

Many claims, especially liability claims, require attorneys with special expertise. Insurers not only develop staff attorneys with such expertise, but they also develop a network of legal resources over a large geographic area, which benefits policyholders with widespread operations.

With liability insurance, insurers are often viewed as a third party by the claimant and the insured. This sometimes is advantageous in that it reduces stress on other relationships between two parties that may need to cooperate in other matters. An example involves workers compensation claims and the potential for conflict between worker and employer. The conflict is usually buffered when an insurer, rather than the employer, negotiates issues involving the claim.

Ideal Characteristics of an Insurable Exposure[4]

For some types of loss exposures, determining both when losses occur and the cost of recovering from them is difficult, which complicates the process of drafting a contract to transfer the risk of loss. However, certain characteristics of loss exposures enable the insurance mechanism to work efficiently.

Private insurance companies are willing to insure some loss exposures but not others. Therefore, in order to analyze why an insurer might or might not accept a particular risk of loss, it is helpful to consider the ideal characteristics of a commercially insurable loss exposure. Those characteristics are listed below.

- Uncertainty exists as to whether, when, and how often a loss might occur.
- The happening, time, and cost of an insured loss can clearly be determined.
- A large number of exposures is insured.
- A loss will not simultaneously affect many insureds.
- Insurance is economically feasible.

It must be emphasized that the above characteristics are *ideal*. Insurers routinely cover exposures that do not meet all of these criteria. For example, insurers cover satellites, even though there is a small number of satellites worldwide in relation to the high risk of loss.

Uncertainty as to Loss

When there is no uncertainty regarding loss, there is no risk of loss, and insurance would serve no purpose. Uncertainty is absent when a loss cannot possibly happen. By definition, a loss cannot occur when an exposure is avoided, so there is no risk of loss to transfer to an insurer.

Uncertainty also is absent when the insured has complete control over whether or not a loss occurs. A chance of loss exists, but the insured faces no uncertainty.

An insurer would be unwise to knowingly provide insurance against losses that can be caused at will by the party who, in turn, will receive payment from the insurer. Otherwise, an insured that owns a building that is no longer needed could profit by burning it down. Insurance policies normally exclude coverage for losses that are expected or intended by the insured.

Losses Must Be Outside the Insured's Control

To be insurable, losses must be outside the insured's control. Chapter 1 mentioned a comprehensive insurance policy that covers "all risks" of an enterprise, called an earnings insurance policy. It covers not only losses from hazard risks but also losses arising from operational and financial/market risks. A key exclusion in an earnings insurance policy is for losses that are within the control of an insured's management. Examples of losses that are considered within management's control are those attributable to strikes, accounting changes, and mergers or acquisitions.

Uncertainty as to Occurrence of Loss

From the insurance buyer's viewpoint, the main reason for purchasing insurance usually is the uncertainty of whether, or how often, a particular type of loss will occur. Insurance companies handle those kinds of uncertainty by pooling many different insureds' exposures. Although losses are uncertain from the insurance buyer's viewpoint, from the insurer's viewpoint, it is desirable that the losses of a large number of insureds be somewhat predictable. Otherwise, the insurer would find it difficult to determine an appropriate premium to charge.

Some liability exposures are difficult or impossible to insure because loss frequency and severity cannot satisfactorily be predicted. Changing legal standards and large jury awards have, at times, made insurers reluctant to provide certain types of liability coverage such as products liability insurance or medical professional liability insurance. The huge costs of pollution cleanups combined with severe and changing legal standards of liability have tended to make pollution liability insurance difficult to obtain. Risks arising from e-commerce are difficult to identify and quantify, so insurers offer limited products to cover this type of risk.

Uncertainty as to Time of Loss

Insurance deals not only with uncertainty as to whether a loss will occur but also with when it will occur. In some cases, timing is the key element of uncertainty. For example, with life insurance, there is no question that the insured will die and, therefore, that a loss will occur. However, there is uncertainty as to when death will occur.

Risk Management in Practice
Insuring Timing Risk
In a well-known liability case, timing risk was the key uncertainty that was insured by a coverage known as retroactive insurance. (*Timing risk* is the risk that losses will be paid out sooner or later than they are expected to be paid out.) The case involved the MGM Grand Hotel fire in Las Vegas in 1979, in which a number of people were killed or injured. MGM purchased a retroactive insurance policy after the fire to cover known losses. The insurer was to pay for the losses over an indeterminate period of years as they were settled. Since the premium was based on an assumption as to when the losses would be paid out, a key risk taken by the insurer was the uncertainty in the amount of investment income it could earn before the losses were actually paid out.

Definite Happening, Time, and Cost

Ideally, whether or not an insured event has occurred should be obvious, and insurers should draft insurance policies that leave little doubt as to what events they cover. Insurance is best suited for covering potential losses that can later be determined to have happened at a specific time. Insurance policies typically provide coverage for a specific time period, and the insurer is not obligated to pay for losses taking place outside that period.

In practice, "definite time" does not often present a problem with property insurance because most losses involve a dramatic event that is immediately apparent. Even so, questions sometimes do develop for property losses resulting from employee theft, gradual contamination or pollution, or other perils that occur over a period of time. In liability insurance, questions often develop regarding the timing of the event that triggers coverage because an injury may manifest itself many years after the accident that caused the injury.

Establishing a Definite Happening and Cost May Be Difficult
Some of the risks of an enterprise meet the ideal characteristics of an insurable exposure, and others do not. Many hazard risks have the appropriate characteristics. Losses from financial/market risks, such as foreign exchange rate reversals, happen at a specific point in time and can be measured; therefore, they can be insured. However, it is difficult to establish a definite happening and to measure losses from other enterprisewide risks, such as reputational risks, so they are difficult to insure.

It would be difficult for insurance to function unless some method is established, before any loss occurs, to determine how much the insurer would pay if a loss occurs. Insurance policies include many provisions intended to address that specific need.

Large Number of Insured Exposures

An ideally insurable exposure is one for which there are homogeneous exposure units. This type of exposure allows the insurance company to maintain loss statistics over time and to predict losses with a high degree of accuracy.

In practice, few exposure units are identical, but those with similar characteristics can be grouped, and the losses to the group can be analyzed, predicted, and insured. Auto insurance typically is handled by classifying each policyholder into a group that also includes a large number of other drivers with similar characteristics.

Even with auto insurance, few insurance companies insure such a large number of exposure units that their past loss experience is entirely reliable as a predictor of future losses. Statistical organizations accumulate information on the losses experienced by many different insurance companies and use this information to predict expected, or average, loss costs for an insured that falls into a particular category. Insurers can then use this information to set premium rates.

Loss Not Simultaneously Affecting Many Insureds

Insurance is based on the premise that many insureds will pay premiums but that only a few will have losses. Insurance is not well suited for losses that are likely to affect many insureds at the same time. Losses resulting from war or a nuclear accident are excluded from almost all insurance policies for this reason.

Unemployment is another example of a loss exposure that is not well suited for treatment by private insurance. Although involuntary unemployment (the threat of being laid off) is a pure risk faced by large numbers of people, and the exposure might be definite in time and amount, unemployment often occurs as a result of a widespread economic downturn affecting many businesses. Unemployment insurance is, however, provided by government agencies, which are in a position to manage the exposure as a social insurance program.

Another example is the risk that individual bank depositors could lose money in their bank accounts because of a bank insolvency. This exposure is insured, not by private insurers, but through a federal program. This program had to raise huge sums of money to cover losses in the early 1990s, when economic conditions adversely affected many different banks across the country.

Hurricane Risk

Losses arising from hurricanes simultaneously affect many insureds. However, insurance companies often are willing to accept hurricane risk if they are able to purchase catastrophe reinsurance to transfer some of their risk of loss in the event of a large hurricane. Also, insurers carefully manage the concentration of risks they underwrite in a geographical area subject to hurricanes.

There are several ways in which insurers hedge the risk that they will have to pay a loss that simultaneously affects many insureds. They limit the amount of property insurance provided at a single location or within a limited geographic area, and they purchase reinsurance to protect against large losses. Large multinational insurance companies also achieve a spread of risk by writing many different lines of insurance on individuals and businesses facing differing risk exposures. Even if only one group of insureds—for example, a group that manufactured a product using asbestos—sustains large unforeseen losses, premiums collected from insureds in other classes can help offset those losses.

Economic Feasibility

Insurance companies sell insurance and organizations buy insurance only when it makes good economic sense to do so. Exposures involving high loss frequency or low loss severity often fail to meet that criterion.

As Chapter 2 mentioned, high-frequency losses often are predictable enough to be funded using retention, which avoids the overhead expenses of insurance. For example, an organization that ships a large number of low-value packages can usually predict the total losses to the packages.

Most low-severity losses are inconsequential, so they can readily be managed with one's own resources. For example, a large organization can easily pay for a physical damage loss to one of its vehicles.

Although insurance works well for many low-frequency loss exposures, insurance may not be economically feasible for losses with a very low frequency because there is no demand for protection against something that is highly unlikely (or is considered highly unlikely) to occur. Until Mt. Saint Helens erupted in Washington, most people thought that the possibility of a volcanic eruption was practically nonexistent in the continental United States. Many property insurance policies made no specific reference to damage originating from volcanoes, and there was no demand for insurance against volcanic eruption. Likewise, people in many areas of the United States where earthquakes are possible but unlikely to occur do not purchase earthquake insurance.

Loss exposures involving very high severity and very low frequency do not tend to be sound subjects for insurance by private insurance companies. An example might be the possibility of liability for radioactive contamination resulting from a nuclear power plant. Although loss frequency has been extremely low, the potential severity of contamination losses is so high that the resources of the entire worldwide insurance industry might be inadequate to pay the damages that might result from a single incident. The exposure is, however, handled through a complex mechanism that draws on worldwide insurance resources combined with statutory limits on an organization's maximum liability in a nuclear disaster.

Types of Commercial Insurance[5]

The various types of commercial insurance sold by insurance companies define the types of hazard risk that an organization can transfer using insurance. This section describes the standard types of commercial property and liability insurance available for this purpose.[6] As previously mentioned, these insurance policies can be used with all risk financing plans that involve transfer, including hybrid plans.

Manuscript Insurance Policies

This section discusses only standard policies. It does not cover **manuscript policies**, which are negotiated between an insurer and an applicant (or the applicant's representative, such as a broker). Each provision in a manuscript policy is specifically drafted or selected for that one contract. Although some provisions might be taken verbatim from printed or standardized policies, each manuscript policy as a whole is a unique document. Manuscript policies are typically used for insureds with unusual exposures or exposures not routinely covered by insurers, such as the risk of an increase in newsprint prices.

Property Insurance

Commercial property[7] insurance covers an organization's risk of loss to its buildings and personal property. The following are usually covered:

- Buildings,
- Personal property of the insured,
- Personal property of others (applies to personal property on premises in the insured's custody, such as customer-owned appliances that are being repaired), and

- Loss of income and/or extra expense to continue operations resulting from damaged real or personal property.

Coverage applies only if the property is damaged by specific **perils**, which are causes that might lead to loss, damage, or destruction of property. For example, fire, windstorm, and explosion are covered by

---
Perils are causes, such as fire, windstorm, or explosion, that might lead to loss, damage, or destruction of property.

---

virtually all commercial property policies. Some commercial property policies take a comprehensive approach to covering perils by agreeing to cover "risks of direct physical loss" not specifically excluded or limited by the policy (these are sometimes referred to as "all-risks" policies).

Most commercial property policies specifically exclude damage caused by earth movement (earthquake) and flood. Coverage for earth movement can sometimes be obtained for an additional premium. In the United States, flood coverage is available under a separate government-sponsored program.

Loss of Income and Extra Expenses To Operate

A commercial property policy often extends to cover loss of income and/or extra expense to operate. **Loss of income coverage** (often called **business income coverage**) reimburses the organization for the loss of its net income plus expenses that continue during a period the business is shut down.

Extra expense coverage is best illustrated with an example. Suppose fire destroys an auto dealership's business offices. The dealership might continue its operations by renting trailers to serve as temporary offices. Therefore, the dealership would continue to operate and produce income, but it would incur the extra expense of renting the trailers.

A commercial property policy extended to cover loss of income and/or extra expense would reimburse the dealership for its loss of net income plus continuing expenses due to the fire. It would also cover the cost of leasing the trailers under its extra expense coverage.

Boiler and Machinery Insurance

Boiler and machinery insurance covers an organization's steam boilers, other pressure vessels, electrical devices, mechanical devices, and a wide variety of production equipment. Boilers and other pressure vessels can explode, and electrical and mechanical devices can break down in various ways. These occurrences can result in damage to the boiler or machinery, the building housing the equipment, personal property, and other nearby buildings and their contents.

Without a boiler or a critical machine, a business may be interrupted, resulting in a loss of income or extra expenses to continue in operation.

Boiler and machinery insurance dovetails with commercial property insurance. Although commercial property insurance provides coverage for damage to property including boilers and machinery by windstorm, fire, and other perils, it excludes coverage for certain causes of loss that boiler and machinery insurance covers. These causes of loss are boiler explosions and sudden breakdowns of machinery, including electrical arcing and centrifugal force. In general, boiler and machinery insurance covers damage to boilers, buildings, personal property, and any associated loss of business income.

Loss control is vitally important to a business that depends on the operation of its boilers and machinery. In fact, most boiler and machinery losses are prevented because insurers' periodic inspections uncover and correct problems before they lead to a loss. Therefore, boiler and machinery insurance tends to be first a loss control service and, second, insurance for those unusual situations in which a loss occurs despite preventive measures. The bulk of the insurance premium goes to pay the cost of the loss control service.

Most states have laws requiring periodic inspections of boilers and pressure vessels by a licensed inspector. In many states, boiler insurers' loss control representatives are licensed as deputy inspectors for the state, and their inspections meet the requirements of the law.

Commercial Crime Insurance

Commercial property insurance provides limited coverage for crime losses. For example, it excludes or severely restricts coverage for loss of money and securities. Property subject to loss by crime includes all kinds of real and personal property—with money, securities, and jewels especially susceptible to loss.

Over a dozen different commercial crime coverages are available on forms promulgated by Insurance Services Office (ISO). The coverages vary in terms of the covered property (for example, money and securities, or property other than money and securities), covered locations of property, or covered perils. The perils covered by crime insurance include employee dishonesty, forgery, robbery, burglary, theft, computer fraud, and extortion.

Ocean Marine Insurance

Many organizations import and export goods that are transported across the oceans of the world. In addition, organizations ship materials on inland waterways, lakes, rivers, and canals. Waterborne vessels perform many activities such as drilling for oil and gas and helping to build and maintain marine facilities. Tugboats provide essential assistance to larger vessels and move barges on waterways. Yachts are used for pleasure trips. Property and liability exposures arising out of activities such as those described above can be insured with ocean marine insurance.

Some of the same perils that threaten property on land also threaten waterborne commerce. For example, vessels and cargoes are subject to loss by perils such as fire, lightning, and windstorm. However, the hazards to waterborne shipping go well beyond those affecting land transportation. For a ship, there is the complex interaction between the wind and the water, and the ship may strike rocks or shoals. Physical damage or machinery malfunction that would be minor ashore could be disastrous to a ship. For example, a hole in the side of a building may be a minor problem, while a hole in the side of a ship could very well mean the total loss of the ship. Goods shipped by water are subject to loss due to perils such as corrosion, moisture, and the pitching and rolling of ships.

Ocean Marine Policies

Ocean marine insurance policies are classified as hull, cargo, and protection and indemnity (P&I).

Hull—A hull policy provides coverage for the hull of the ship, materials and equipment, and stores and provisions for the officers and crew. Also included are the machinery, boilers, and fuel supplies owned by the insured. A hull insurance policy also contains an important liability insurance coverage, referred to as the "collision" or "running down" clause. This covers liability for damage to other ships and their cargoes from collision involving the insured vessel.

Cargo—Cargo can be covered for specified perils or on an "all risks" basis. Protection can apply to only a single voyage or all voyages of a particular shipper.

P&I—A P&I policy provides liability coverage. Damage to shore and waterway installations and bodily injury to persons, including employees and passengers, are covered, as well as cargo being carried. The P&I policy also covers the insured shipowner's or operator's liability for fines that may be imposed for violation of laws. If the ship is sunk and constitutes a hazard to navigation, the cost of raising, destroying, or removing the wreck is also covered by P&I insurance.

Inland Marine Insurance

Inland marine insurance covers various specific types of property, including those that are typically mobile. Ocean marine underwriters, accustomed to insuring transportation loss exposures, were the first underwriters willing to insure the types of property eligible for inland (non-ocean) marine insurance.

Inland marine policies cover property while in transit or in the custody of bailees, "floating" property, dealer stock, property sold on a deferred-payment basis, instrumentalities of transportation and communication, and electronic data processing equipment.

Major Categories of Inland Marine Insurance

Property in Transit—Coverage for property in transit (such as goods aboard a truck) is available to the property owner. Coverage is also available for a carrier to cover its liability to the property owner if the property is lost, damaged, or destroyed.

Bailee Coverage—A bailee (such as a dry cleaner) is liable under common law for loss to property in the bailee's custody only when the loss is caused by the bailee's negligence. However, to preserve customer goodwill, many businesses purchase insurance for their customers' benefit, and it applies regardless of who is responsible for the loss. This is referred to as **bailees' customer insurance**.

Contractor's Equipment Floaters—Contractor's equipment floaters cover mobile equipment, including equipment used by contractors when constructing such things as buildings, highways, and dams.

Installation Floaters—Installation floaters are used to cover loss to material and equipment that (1) are in transit to a construction site, (2) are at the construction site before being incorporated into the building or structure, or (3) have been installed in a structure until the installation is complete and has been accepted by the property owner.

Dealers' Policies—Dealers policies, such as jewelers block policies, cover stock while on a dealer's premises, in transit, or otherwise off a dealer's premises.

Property Sold on a Deferred-Payment Basis—Inland marine insurance can be written to cover property purchased on a deferred-payment basis, such as a piece of machinery leased or purchased on an installment basis.

Instrumentalities of Transportation or Communication—Inland marine policies can also cover fixed property that is an instrument of transportation or communication, such as bridges, tunnels, or communication towers.

Electronic Data Processing Equipment—Some inland marine forms cover losses related to electronic data processing equipment, including physical loss to hardware, extra expenses to operate, and loss of income. Although electronic data processing equipment is not excluded under commercial property insurance, inland marine forms are usually better suited to provide coverage and can cover perils not covered by commercial property insurance, such as mechanical breakdown.

Inland marine insurance is very flexible. An insured and an insurer can often negotiate coverage and pricing terms to suit their specific needs. The perils covered can be either specified or of the "all risks" type.

Aviation Insurance

An aviation insurance policy usually provides both property and liability coverages. Aircraft physical damage insurance, also called aircraft hull insurance, protects the insured against loss involving physical damage to the insured aircraft. It is written on an "all-risks" basis and may apply only while the aircraft is on the ground, or it may apply both while the aircraft is on the ground and in flight. Aircraft liability insurance is designed to cover the liability exposures of aircraft owners and operators. It provides protection against third-party claims alleging bodily injury or property damage arising out of an insured's ownership, maintenance, or use of aircraft.

General Liability Insurance

Organizations are exposed to potential liability in many ways, including liability arising from their premises, operations, and products. Organizations also assume liability exposures under written contracts or agreements.

Commercial General Liability[8] Policy

A Commercial General Liability (CGL) policy covers liability exposures by providing the following three coverages:

Bodily injury and property damage liability. This covers situations in which the insured is legally liable to others for bodily injury or property damage. The liability can arise from the insured's premises, operations, products, or completed operations. Various related coverages are included, such as liability under contract and liability for small, nonowned watercraft.

Personal injury and advertising injury liability. This covers liability for such offenses as libel, slander, false arrest, malicious prosecution, and some advertising offenses.

Medical payments. This is a no-fault type of accident coverage that applies to medical expenses incurred by others as a result of accidental bodily injury on the insured's premises or arising out of the insured's off-premises operations.

The CGL policy excludes coverage for many exposures that other types of policies cover, such as those for aircraft, autos, owned watercraft, and certain types of professional activities. An example of a professional activity is an architect's design error or a physician's error in patient care. Other exclusions eliminate coverage for workers compensation and employers liability (this type of coverage is discussed later). One other significant exclusion of the CGL is for pollution exposures, including any liability for cleanup mandated by the government. Insurance for this exposure is usually available on a separate pollution liability coverage form.

Business Auto Insurance

Business auto insurance covers exposures related to the business use of autos, such as reduction in value, loss of use, and liability to others. The unendorsed business auto coverage form fits the basic needs of most businesses by offering only two coverages: liability and physical damage. If other coverages are either required by law, such as personal injury protection (no-fault), or selected voluntarily, such as medical payments or uninsured motorists coverage (which also can be mandatory), endorsements must be attached to the business auto coverage form.

Garage and Truckers Insurance

Both garages (including sales and service stations) and trucking companies face auto-related loss exposures similar to those that business auto insurance covers. However, certain exposures are unique to garages.

Because of the nature of their operations, distinguishing between a garage's auto liability and general liability exposures is difficult. The garage policy combines auto and general liability insurance into a single coverage form that also may include auto physical damage to customers' autos in the garage's care, custody, or control.

Truckers (those in the business of transporting goods for others) are subject to many regulations for which they have special insurance needs. In addition, practices such as interchanging trailers with other truckers lead to special coverage needs not adequately addressed by the business auto insurance.

Workers Compensation and Employers Liability Insurance

State workers compensation statutes make an employer liable for the payment of medical expenses, lost wages, and other benefits to a worker disabled by a work-related illness or injury. The employer is responsible whether or not the injury or illness was caused by the employer's negligence—in other words, the employer's obligation applies on a no-fault basis. To finance this exposure, most employers purchase workers compensation insurance.

> ### Workers Compensation and Employers Liability Policy
>
> The Workers Compensation and Employers Liability policy includes two coverages:
>
> *Workers compensation* coverage is governed by the applicable state statutes and pays those amounts that the employer is required to pay for medical expenses, lost wages, and other benefits such as lump sum amounts for specific injuries as well as for rehabilitation expenses and death.
>
> *Employers liability* coverage protects employers from employment-related suits separate and distinct from claims for workers compensation benefits. Although, in general, workers compensation provides the sole remedy for most claims resulting from employee injuries, there are exceptions, the details of which are beyond the scope of this chapter.[9]

Professional Liability Insurance

Doctors, accountants, architects, engineers, attorneys, insurance agents/brokers, and many other professionals face liability exposures because, as professionals, they have certain duties to their customers. Institutions, such as hospitals, also face professional liability exposures. Professional liability claims typically allege an error or omission in rendering, or failing to render, professional services.

Professional liability insurance policies cover defense costs and professional liability imposed on insureds because of acts, errors, or omissions in the conduct of their profession. Coverage does not apply to losses arising out of hazards that general liability insurance usually covers.

Directors and Officers Liability Insurance

Directors and officers may be sued for a breach of their duties to the organization. Directors and officers' liability exposures are based on both common and statutory law. For example, under common law, directors and officers have a duty to exercise reasonable care in the performance of their organizational functions. Under the Securities and Exchange Act of 1934, they have a duty to disclose facts that are material to stockholders, bondholders, and potential investors. In addition, employees, former employees, customers, and suppliers may sue directors and officers.

Directors and officers may be individually liable for their own torts or jointly and severally liable for the tortious acts or omissions of any agent of the organization, including another director or officer. When a director or an officer is a defendant in a lawsuit, most states permit or require that the organization provide indemnification for costs incurred in the suit.

Directors and Officers Liability Policy

A directors and officers legal liability insurance policy, commonly referred to as a "D&O policy," provides coverage for wrongful acts of any individual director or officer or a group of directors and officers. It is divided into two parts: The first covers directors' and officers' individual liability when they are not indemnified by the corporation, while the second part indemnifies the corporation if it has paid money to directors and officers for expenses associated with a claim.

Businessowners Policies

Because most small businesses have similar types of property and liability exposures, they have similar insurance needs. For these businesses, businessowners policies are available that use an approach under which the insured purchases a set of prearranged property and liability coverages on virtually an all-or-nothing basis, with relatively few options or alternatives. The process involves relatively few risk management decisions.

Employment Practices Liability Insurance

Lawsuits by employees against their employers for various employment-related wrongful acts have increased greatly over the past twenty years. These so-called employment practices liability (EPL) claims generally allege wrongful acts in three major categories: (1) wrongful termination, (2) discrimination, and (3) sexual harassment. Employment practices liability insurance is designed to cover these loss exposures.

Insurance Policy Provisions[10]

An insurance policy, like any written document, contains headings, words, phrases, sentences, and paragraphs. These components are called **policy provisions** and constitute the distinctive agreements that collectively form an insurance contract.

Policy provisions are components of an insurance policy that constitute the distinctive agreements that collectively make up an insurance contract.

Every property-liability insurance policy provision can be placed in one or more of the following categories:

- Declarations
- Definitions
- Insuring agreements
- Exclusions
- Conditions
- Miscellaneous provisions

These categories are discussed below.

Declarations

Declarations, the first section of a policy, contains information that is "declared" by both the insured and the insurer. The insured declares information on the application for insurance, and the insurance company declares details of the coverage it provides.

> **Declarations** is the section of a policy that contains information that is "declared" by both the insured and the insurer.

Information Typically Found in the Declarations

- Policy number
- Inception and expiration dates and times of the policy
- Name of the insurance company
- Name of the insurance agent
- Name(s) of the insured(s)
- Mailing address of the insured
- Physical address and description of the covered property or operations
- Numbers and edition dates of all attached forms and endorsements
- Dollar amounts of applicable policy limits
- Dollar amounts of applicable deductibles
- Names of persons or organizations whose additional interests are covered (for example, a mortgagee, a loss payee, or an additional insured)
- Premium amount

Definitions

Many coverage forms[11] contain a section titled "Definitions," which defines the terms used. However, definitions often appear in other sections of a form, such as within exclusions or in the Preamble.

Definitions in the Commercial General Liability Coverage Form

The Commercial General Liability (CGL) coverage form[12] provides an example of how definitions can appear in various sections of a policy.

Preamble

The preamble to the CGL form defines the words "you" and "your":

> Throughout this policy the words "you" and "your" refer to the Named Insured shown in the Declarations, and any other person or organization qualifying as a Named Insured under this policy.

Exclusions

The pollution exclusion defines "pollutants":

> "Pollutants" means any solid, liquid, gaseous or thermal irritant or contaminant, including smoke, vapor, soot, fumes, acids, alkalis, chemicals and waste.

Definitions Section

The Definitions section contains fifteen definitions. It defines "occurrence" as follows:

> "Occurrence" means an accident, including continuous or repeated exposure to substantially the same general harmful conditions.[13]

If a policy does not define a word or phrase, the word or phrase is interpreted according to the following rules:

- Everyday language is given its ordinary meaning.
- Technical words are given their technical meanings.
- Words with an established legal meaning are given their legal meanings.
- Where applicable, consideration is also given to local, cultural, and trade usage meanings.

In general, it is important from the insurer's perspective that definitions be included in the policy. Because the insurer drafted the policy, disputes over the meaning of terms are usually decided in favor of insureds.

Insuring Agreements

An **insuring agreement** is any policy statement in which the insurer agrees to make a payment or provide a service under certain circumstances. The body of most insurance policies begins with the insuring agreement.

An **insuring agreement** is any policy statement in which the insurer agrees to make a payment or provide a service under certain circumstances.

Some policies provide more than one coverage, each based on a separate insuring agreement. For example, a commercial auto policy typically provides liability and physical damage coverage, each with its own insuring agreement. The insuring agreement for the liability coverage provided by the Business Auto Coverage Form[14] reads as follows:

> We will pay all sums an "insured" legally must pay as damages because of "bodily injury" or "property damage" to which this insurance applies, caused by an "accident" and resulting from the ownership, maintenance or use of a covered "auto."

A policy might grant coverage in sections other than the insuring agreement, such as within a definition or as an exception to an exclusion.

How a Definition Can Grant Coverage

The Commercial General Liability (CGL) coverage form excludes coverage for liability arising from "autos," but the definition of "autos" in the CGL states that "mobile equipment" is not an auto. (Mobile equipment has a longstanding definition in the CGL and includes such things as bulldozers and farm tractors.) Therefore, the definition of "auto" in the CGL grants coverage for liability arising from mobile equipment.

How an Exception to an Exclusion Can Grant Coverage

The CGL coverage form grants liquor liability coverage for most businesses through an exception to the liquor liability exclusion. The exclusion reads as follows:

> [This insurance does not apply to:] "Bodily injury" or "property damage" for which any insured may be held liable by reason of:
>
> 1. Causing or contributing to the intoxication of any person;
> 2. The furnishing of alcoholic beverages to a person under the legal drinking age or under the influence of alcohol; or
> 3. Any statute, ordinance or regulation relating to the sale, gift, distribution or use of alcoholic beverages.
>
> This exclusion applies only if you are in the business of manufacturing, distributing, selling, serving or furnishing alcoholic beverages.

Because the final sentence provides an exception, coverage applies to office parties and other liquor-related situations for businesses that are not in the alcoholic beverage business. This provision is frequently referred to as "host liquor liability coverage."

Exclusions

Provisions that exclude coverage can appear in various sections of a policy, not just the section labeled "Exclusions." A policy's exclusions serve several purposes, and any single exclusion may serve more than one purpose. For example, an exclusion that eliminates unnecessary coverages for typical purchasers also assists in keeping premiums at a reasonable level.

Purposes of Policy Exclusions

1. Eliminating coverage for uninsurable loss exposures

2. Assisting the insurer in managing moral and morale hazards

3. Reducing the likelihood of coverage duplications

4. Eliminating coverages that the typical purchaser does not need

5. Eliminating coverages requiring special treatment, and

6. Assisting in keeping premiums at a reasonable level

Each of the purposes of policy exclusions is discussed below.

Eliminating Coverage for Uninsurable Loss Exposures

One purpose of exclusions is to eliminate coverage for exposures that private insurers consider uninsurable. For example, most property and liability insurance policies exclude losses arising out of war as it is considered uninsurable because of its catastrophic nature. Other common exclusions in this category are losses due to the insured's intentional acts, nuclear radiation, earthquake, flood, normal wear and tear, and "inherent vice." (*Inherent vice* is a quality inherent in an object that tends to destroy it, as when iron rusts or wood rots.)

Assisting the Insurer in Managing Moral and Morale Hazards

A second purpose of exclusions is to assist in managing moral and morale hazards.

Moral and Morale Hazards

A **moral hazard** is a condition that increases the chance that some insureds or other persons will intentionally cause a loss. A moral hazard exists when an insured is able to profit by collecting loss payments from its insurer.

A **morale hazard** is a condition that causes insureds to be less careful than they would otherwise be. Some persons, because they have insurance, might engage in more risky behavior than they would engage in if they had no insurance.

Exclusions help an insurer manage moral hazards by eliminating coverage for the insured's intentional acts. For example, crime insurance policies exclude coverage for the insured's fraudulent, dishonest, or criminal acts.

An insurer can manage morale hazards by making insureds bear a financial penalty for their carelessness. For example, under some contracts that provide broad coverage on personal property, breakage of fragile articles is excluded unless caused by some specified peril such as fire, wind, or explosion. The intent is to eliminate coverage for breakage caused by careless handling or misuse.

Reducing the Likelihood of Coverage Duplications

A third purpose of exclusions is to reduce the likelihood of coverage duplications. A policy usually eliminates coverage provided when another type of policy is better suited to the task. For example, commercial property insurance policies eliminate coverage for autos because auto physical damage insurance is readily available and better suited for covering auto property exposures. In general, different types of standard insurance policies are designed to dovetail with each other.

Eliminating Coverages That the Typical Purchaser Does Not Need

A fourth purpose of exclusions is to eliminate coverages that the typical purchaser of a particular type of insurance does not need. For example, the operations of most businesses do not involve the ownership or operation of aircraft, so a general liability policy usually excludes this exposure, which an aircraft insurance policy covers. It would be inequitable to require all insureds to share the cost to cover the aircraft liability exposures faced by only some insureds.

Eliminating Coverages Requiring Special Treatment

A fifth purpose of exclusions is to eliminate coverages requiring special treatment. As used here, the term "special treatment" means rating, underwriting, or loss control that is substantially different from what is normally applied. Examples include the following:

- Commercial liability insurance covering product liability typically excludes coverage for the expense of recalling products. Products recall insurance is sometimes available from excess and surplus lines insurers, which carefully analyze and price this exposure.

- Commercial property insurance policies typically exclude coverage for steam boiler explosions. Steam boilers require a special form of loss control not available to every insurance company and insured.

Assisting in Keeping Premiums at a Reasonable Level

A sixth purpose of exclusions is to assist in keeping premiums at a level that most insurance buyers would consider reasonable. Insurers and rate regulators also share that goal.

To some extent, all exclusions serve to keep premiums reasonable. However, it is the sole purpose of some exclusions. For example, consider the following exclusions from the physical damage section of a Business Auto Coverage Form:[15]

> We will not pay for "loss" caused by or resulting from any of the following unless caused by other "loss" that is covered by this insurance:
>
> a. Wear and tear, freezing, mechanical or electrical breakdown.
>
> b. Blowouts, punctures or other road damage to tires.

The excluded losses are insurable. Auto dealers, tire shops, and various other organizations offer insurance-like service warranties covering just such losses. However, few organizations would be willing to pay the premiums necessary to include in their auto insurance policies coverage for such predictable minor losses.

Conditions

As previously mentioned, an insuring agreement obligates an insurer to make a payment or provide a service under certain circumstances. The insurer's promises are invariably subject to several conditions. **Conditions** can be thought of as qualifications that an insurer attaches to its promises.

> **Conditions** are qualifications that an insurer attaches to its promises.

Common policy conditions obligate the insured to

- Pay premiums,
- Report losses promptly,
- Protect damaged property from further harm,
- Provide appropriate documentation for losses,
- Cooperate with the insurer in legal proceedings, and
- Refrain from jeopardizing an insurer's rights to recover from responsible third parties (subrogation actions).

Miscellaneous Provisions

Insurance policies often contain various provisions that do not strictly qualify as declarations, definitions, insuring agreements, exclusions, or conditions.

These provisions may deal with the relationship between the insured and the insurer, or they may help establish working procedures for carrying out the terms of the contract, but they do not have the force of conditions. An example of a miscellaneous provision is a cancellation provision that explains each party's rights and obligations in canceling the policy. Another example is the appraisal clause that specifies how loss valuation disputes between the insurer and insured will be settled.

Surety

A contract of suretyship is an agreement whereby one party agrees to be answerable for another's default. Such a contract involves three parties: the principal, the obligee, and the surety. The **principal**, also known as the **obligor**, is obligated to perform in some way for the benefit of the **obligee**. The **surety** guarantees to the obligee that the principal will fulfill its obligations. In most cases, the party making the guarantee—the surety—is an insurance company that also writes property-liability insurance. However, a contract of suretyship is not considered an insurance contract.

> The **principal (obligor)** is the party that is obligated to perform in some way for the obligee's benefit.
>
> The **obligee** is the individual or organization for whose benefit the principal is obligated to perform in some way.
>
> A **surety** is the party that guarantees that the principal will fulfill its obligations to the obligee.

To enhance the practical value to others of a principal's legal obligation to perform, an insurer guarantees the performance of the obligation and backs its guarantee with its own name, reputation, and financial resources under an enforceable written instrument called a surety bond. In return, the insurer is compensated by the premium it charges the principal for the bond.

The exposures covered by a surety bond are different from those covered by a commercial insurance policy. The surety exposures consist of the possibility that one party will fail to do something, such as complete a work contract or pay taxes to the government.

The obligee that has the loss exposure does not purchase insurance but instead requires the principal (obligor) to purchase a surety bond. This requirement can be thought of as a form of loss control. The surety will not issue the surety bond until it is comfortable that the principal is in a position to meet its obligations. From the obligee's point of view, requiring the principal to purchase a surety bond is a form of noninsurance contractual transfer of its loss exposures.

As an example, a party that hires a general contractor to construct a building requires the contractor to obtain a surety bond to guarantee completion of the building. If the contractor does not complete the building, the surety steps in and pays the cost of hiring another firm to finish the project.

Summary

- Insurance is the predominant technique that organizations use to transfer hazard risk. In exchange for a premium, an insurance company agrees to indemnify an insured for specific types of losses as defined by an insurance policy.
- "Insurance" can be defined in a number of ways. Both the economic and legal definitions of insurance mention the concepts of risk pooling and transfer. The term "insurance" is used in this chapter to refer to guaranteed cost plans and the risk transfer component of hybrid plans.
- Not only do insurers accept risk, but they also provide loss control, claim, and legal services. These services can also be purchased separately from third-party vendors.
- The ideal characteristics of an insurable exposure are (1) uncertainty exists as to whether, when, and how often a loss might occur, (2) the happening, time, and cost of an insured loss can clearly be determined, (3) a large number of exposures is insured, (4) a loss will not simultaneously affect many insureds, and (5) insurance is economically feasible. However, insurers routinely cover exposures that do not meet all of these criteria.
- The major types of commercial insurance are provided by standard policies. An alternative to a standard policy is a manuscript policy, whereby each provision is specifically drafted or selected for that one contract.
- Policy provisions fall into one or more of the following categories: (1) declarations, (2) definitions, (3) insuring agreements, (4) exclusions, (5) conditions, and (6) miscellaneous provisions. Exclusions can serve one or more of the following purposes: (1) eliminating coverage for uninsurable loss exposures, (2) assisting the insurer in managing moral and morale hazards, (3) reducing the likelihood of coverage duplications, (4) eliminating coverages that the typical purchaser does not need, (5) eliminating coverages requiring special treatment, and (6) assisting in keeping premiums at a reasonable level.
- A contract of suretyship is an agreement whereby one party agrees to be answerable for another's default. Such a contract involves three parties: the principal, the obligee, and the surety.

Chapter Notes

1. Presentation at the 1999 Risk and Insurance Management Society (RIMS) Annual Conference in Dallas on April 15, 1999, by Dennis P. Kane, then President, CIGNA Special Risk Facilities.

2. Alan H. Willett, *The Economic Theory of Risk and Insurance* (Philadelphia: University of Pennsylvania Press, 1951), p. 72.

3. Presentation at the 1999 RIMS Annual Conference in Dallas on April 12, 1999, by Ronald B. Loizzo, Global Insurance Manager, Colgate-Palmolive Company. Used with permission.

4. This section is based in part on material in the text for CPCU 1: Robert J. Gibbons, George E. Rejda, and Michael W. Elliott, *Insurance Perspectives* (Malvern, PA: American Institute for CPCU, 1992).

5. This section is based in part on material in the text for CPCU 1: Robert J. Gibbons, George E. Rejda, and Michael W. Elliott, *Insurance Perspectives* (Malvern, PA: American Institute for CPCU, 1992).

6. The policy forms referred to in this section are those developed by Insurance Services Office (ISO).

7. "Commercial Property" is the label that ISO uses for its series of property forms.

8. "Commercial General Liability" is the label that ISO uses for its general liability form.

9. A common example in which employers liability might apply is in the case of an employer that is operating in a dual capacity. For example, a worker injured by a product manufactured by his employer would have both a workers compensation claim and a liability claim against his or her employer.

10. This section is based in part on material in *The CPCU Handbook of Insurance Policies*, 3d ed. (Malvern, PA: American Institute for CPCU, 1998).

11. A coverage form is a component of an insurance policy.

12. The Commercial General Liability form is a product of ISO.

13. This particular definition has been the subject of extended discussion and litigation over the years. It is not always easy to agree on whether a specific act or series of acts constitutes one or more "occurrences," and large sums of money sometimes depend on the ultimate outcome of a dispute over the definition of this term. Policy limits often apply "per occurrence," and multiples of a policy's limit may be available to cover a loss related to multiple "occurrences."

14. This is an ISO form.

15. This is an ISO form.

Chapter 5

Excess and Umbrella Liability Insurance[1]

Introduction

Excess and umbrella liability policies are used to insure liability loss exposures with the potential to generate high-severity losses.[2] These types of policies sit above other liability policies, called underlying policies, or a self-insured retention.

Differences Between Excess and Umbrella Policies

An **excess liability policy** is designed to provide coverage above, or in excess of, underlying coverage. The coverage that an excess policy provides is no broader than the underlying policies and, in fact, may be even more restrictive. For example, many excess policies do not provide legal defense coverage.

An **umbrella liability policy** provides coverage above underlying policies but also offers coverage not available in the underlying policies. This additional coverage is subject to a self-insured retention, or retained limit, by the insured. Coverage provided by the umbrella and not available in the underlying policies is said to drop down over the self-insured retention. An umbrella policy also usually drops down over the aggregate limits of the underlying policies.

Continued on next page.

In actual practice, the distinction between excess and umbrella coverage is often blurred, especially because the courts and many insurance professionals use the terms interchangeably. Moreover, insurers providing excess and umbrella liability insurance do not use standardized policies. Rather, they develop their own policies, which vary considerably in terms of coverage and format. What one insurer calls an excess liability policy may in reality be an umbrella policy (as defined in this text), and what another insurer calls an umbrella policy may actually be an excess liability policy (as defined in this text).

Exhibit 5-1 shows the relationships among excess, umbrella, and underlying liability policies. In this case the underlying policies are primary policies because they cover losses from the first dollar. The excess liability policy sits directly above the primary policies. The shaded areas, which include the exposures covered by the excess liability policy and exposures not covered by the primary policies, represent the coverage provided by the umbrella policy.

Exhibit 5-1
Relationships Among Excess, Umbrella, and Primary (Underlying)
Liability Policies

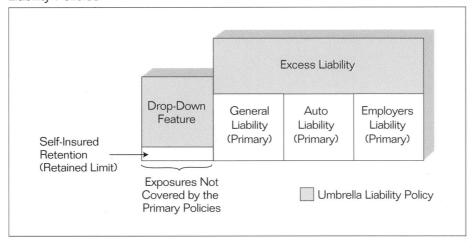

An excess or an umbrella policy is a contract separate from the underlying policies. Therefore, it might have provisions and conditions that relieve the insurer of liability for a loss, regardless of whether the underlying insurer provides coverage for a loss. For example, an excess liability insurer might deny a claim because the insured reports a loss late, even though the underlying insurer has not denied the claim.

Excess Liability Insurance

Although excess policy provisions vary among insurers, they generally perform the following two basic functions:

1. Providing additional limits above the each occurrence/accident limits of the insured's underlying policies, and

2. Taking the place of the underlying insurance when underlying aggregate limits are exhausted.

An excess liability policy that sits above an underlying policy may take any of three basic forms:

1. A following form subject to the same provisions as the underlying policy

2. A self-contained policy subject to its own provisions

3. A combination of the two types

When excess liability insurance sits above a self-insured retention instead of an underlying policy, two types of excess insurance are commonly used. They are

1. Specific excess insurance, and

2. Aggregate excess insurance.

Each of the types of excess policy is discussed below.

Following-Form Excess Policies

A **following-form excess policy** covers a liability loss that exceeds the underlying policy limits *only if the underlying insurance covers the loss.* As an illustration, assume

> A **following-form excess policy** covers a loss only if it is covered by the underlying insurance.

that an insured has an underlying liability policy with a per occurrence limit of $1 million and a following-form excess policy with a per occurrence limit of $1 million. If a claimant obtains a judgment of $1,250,000 against the insured for bodily injury that the underlying policy covers, the underlying policy would pay its per occurrence limit of $1 million, and the excess policy would pay the remaining $250,000.

A True Following-Form Excess Policy

A true following-form excess policy would state that, except for the policy limits, all of the provisions and conditions of the designated underlying policy are incorporated into and adopted by the excess policy. The policy would contain no other provisions.

Although many excess policies are called following-form policies, most contain endorsements that limit coverage. For example, an excess policy might follow the provisions of the underlying policies only to the extent that they do not conflict with the provisions of the excess policy. The result is that the excess policy might cover less than the underlying policy covers.

Self-Contained Excess Policies

A **self-contained excess policy** is subject to its own provisions only, so coverage applies only to the extent described in the policy. The policy does not depend on the provisions of the underlying policies for determining the scope of the coverage (with one exception, noted below). Because self-contained excess policies are in-dependent of the underlying policies, coverage gaps between the excess and underlying policies can occur.

A **self-contained excess policy** is subject to its own specific provisions, so coverage applies only to the extent that the policy describes. It does not depend on the provisions of the underlying policies for determining the scope of the coverage.

A self-contained excess policy applies to a loss that exceeds the underlying limits *only if the loss is also covered under the provisions of the excess policy*. For example, the excess policy may not cover injury within the products-completed operations hazard, even though the underlying policy does cover this hazard. In that case, the excess policy would not pay for a products liability loss, even though the loss was covered by the underlying policy and exceeded the per occurrence limit of the underlying policy.

One exception to the usual approach of a self-contained policy occurs when the excess policy provides coverage in excess of a reduced or an exhausted underlying aggregate limit. Some excess policies provide this coverage on their own provisions, but others specifically state that they will provide this coverage based on the conditions of the underlying policy that they are replacing. This approach can work to the insured's benefit when the excess policy contains exclusions or other restrictions that are not present in the underlying policy.

Combination Excess Policies

An excess policy may combine the following-form and self-contained approaches by incorporating the provisions of the underlying policy and then modifying those provisions with additional conditions or exclusions in the excess policy. This is called a **combination excess policy**.

A **combination excess policy** combines the following-form and self-contained approaches for excess policies.

One type of combination form is an excess policy that provides the broader coverages typically found in an umbrella liability policy, but without any obligation to drop down (provide primary coverage) when a claim is excluded by the primary policy but covered by the excess policy. Because many professionals in the insurance industry do not distinguish between excess and umbrella policies, insureds might not be aware that combination excess policies do not drop down (except to replace depleted aggregate limits). One distinguishing feature of an umbrella policy is a provision stating that the policy drops down and applies over a self-insured retention if the underlying policy does not cover a loss that the umbrella covers. In the absence of this provision, the policy is probably not an umbrella liability policy.

Specific and Aggregate Excess Insurance

Specific excess insurance and aggregate excess insurance are commonly used in connection with self-insured plans. Because these types of policies are designed to apply over a self-insured layer instead of a primary (underlying) layer of commercial insurance, they are structured differently from the excess policies previously described.

Specific and Aggregate Excess Policies

A **specific excess policy** requires the insured to retain a stipulated amount of liability loss from the first dollar *for all losses resulting from a single occurrence or accident.* The excess insurer pays losses above the per occurrence/accident retention, subject to the policy limit. For example, if the specific excess policy required a retention of $100,000 per occurrence, the excess insurer would pay for all losses resulting from a single occurrence in excess of $100,000 up to the policy limit.

An **aggregate excess policy** (also called a **stop-loss excess policy**) requires the insured to retain a total amount of liability loss (regardless of the number of occurrences or accidents) from the first dollar *during a specified period of time*, usually one year. The total amount of losses to be retained during a period of time is called an aggregate retention. The excess insurer then pays for, up to the policy limit, all losses for that period that exceed the aggregate retention.

The specific excess and aggregate excess approaches are illustrated in Exhibit 5-2. Note the similarities between specific/aggregate excess and the transferred losses under a retrospective rating plan as shown in Exhibit 3-4.

Some policies combine the specific and aggregate excess approaches. Such policies provide the insured with the benefits of both approaches. For example, an insured might incur several moderate losses during a policy period, none of which exceeds the per occurrence or per accident retention. Under a specific excess policy, the insured would not be able to collect any insurance proceeds. With a combined specific/aggregate excess policy, however, if the total of losses for the policy period exceeded the aggregate retention, the insured could collect insurance proceeds for the amount of loss in excess of the aggregate retention.

Exhibit 5-2
Specific and Aggregate Excess Insurance

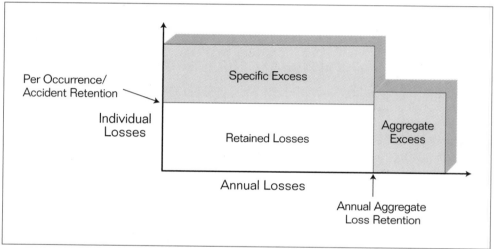

Umbrella Liability Insurance

As previously mentioned, the term "umbrella liability" is used to describe a type of excess insurance that is broader than ordinary excess liability policies. Although ordinary excess policies may apply in excess of only one underlying policy, an umbrella liability policy provides excess coverage over several primary policies, such as general liability, auto liability, and employers liability. As mentioned earlier, the distinguishing feature of umbrella liability policies is coverage that is broader in some respects than that of the underlying policies, thus providing drop-down coverage for certain occurrences that would not be covered by any of the underlying policies. In contrast, ordinary excess liability policies tend to incorporate the same provisions as the underlying policies or narrower provisions in some cases.

Basic Functions of Umbrella Policies

Although umbrella policy provisions vary among insurers, they generally perform three basic functions. Like an ordinary excess liability policy, they

1. Provide additional limits above the per occurrence limits of the insured's underlying policies, and

2. Take the place of the underlying insurance when underlying aggregate limits are exhausted.

In addition, they

3. Cover some claims that the insured's underlying policies do not cover.

The latter two functions are frequently referred to as **drop-down coverage**.

> **Drop-down coverage** is an umbrella policy provision that states the policy takes the place of the underlying insurance when underlying aggregate limits are exhausted and also states the policy covers some claims that the underlying policies do not cover.

Self-Insured Retention

The claims not covered by the insured's underlying policies are subject to a **self-insured retention**, which is an amount of loss that the insured retains (see Exhibit 5-1). The retention normally does not apply when

> A **self-insured retention** in an umbrella policy is the amount of loss that the insured retains when claims are covered by the umbrella policy but not by the underlying policies.

- Paying the excess amount of a loss that the primary policy covers, and
- Dropping down to pay a loss because the primary policy's aggregate limit has been exhausted.

Self-insured retentions vary in amount, from as low as $500 for small businesses to $1 million or more for the largest businesses. Many policies do not apply the self-insured retention to defense costs.

Importance of Certain Definitions

Some umbrella liability policies agree to pay for damages because of bodily injury, personal injury,[3] advertising injury, and property damage, and they define those terms to correspond, in many or most respects, to the definitions of those terms in the Commercial General Liability policy. Other umbrella liability policies agree to pay only for personal injury, advertising injury, or property damage but define "personal injury" to include both bodily injury and personal injury, much as those terms are defined in the Commercial General Liability policy. Still other umbrella policies phrase the insuring agreement in

---

Continued on next page.

terms of "injury" and define that single term to include bodily injury, property damage, and various personal injury and advertising injury offenses.

The umbrella policy's definitions of the above terms can be important. If, for example, the umbrella policy has a narrower definition of personal injury or advertising injury than that in the underlying general liability policy, the umbrella policy might not cover a claim that the general liability policy covers.

Umbrella policies usually contain definitions of personal injury that are broader than the definition of that term in the Commercial General Liability policy. For example, the personal injury definitions in some umbrella policies include discrimination based on race, color, religion, sex, and national origin. If the umbrella policy's definition of personal injury (or another key term) includes some exposure that is not included in the personal injury definition in the underlying policies, the umbrella policy will (assuming no other restrictions apply) provide drop-down coverage for that exposure.

Exclusions Omitted From an Umbrella

Insurers omit some underlying policy exclusions from an umbrella policy in order to broaden the coverage. For example, an umbrella policy often has no exclusion of liability assumed under contract. If the insured becomes legally obligated to pay damages because of a hold harmless agreement or an indemnity agreement under circumstances that the other policy provisions of the umbrella do not exclude, it will cover the insured's contractual liability. If the insured's underlying insurance does not cover the contractual liability, the umbrella will provide drop-down coverage, subject to a self-insured retention.

Other underlying policy exclusions that are frequently omitted from umbrella policies in order to provide umbrella coverage that is broader than the underlying policies include the following:

- The liquor liability exclusion of a general liability policy
- The employers liability exclusion of accidents occurring outside the United States or Canada
- The employers liability exclusion of injury to persons subject to the Federal Employers' Liability Act, the Jones Act, and similar laws permitting employees to sue their employers
- The employers liability exclusion of injury to persons knowingly employed in violation of law

Umbrella Exclusions Less Restrictive Than the Underlying Coverage

In many cases, an umbrella insurer is willing to broaden coverage for a particular exposure without covering it entirely. Thus, instead of omitting an exclusion in the underlying insurance from its umbrella policy, the insurer uses an exclusion that is similar to an exclusion in the underlying policy but is less restrictive. When an umbrella exclusion has a narrower scope of application than a comparable exclusion in the underlying policy, the umbrella policy has the potential for providing drop-down coverage for some claims not insured by the underlying policy. Two examples of umbrella liability exclusions that commonly allow broader coverage than the underlying policies are

1. The watercraft and aircraft exclusion, and
2. The care, custody, or control exclusion.

Watercraft and Aircraft

The Commercial General Liability policy contains an exclusion of liability arising out of the use of autos, watercraft, and aircraft. In most umbrella liability policies, the exclusion is limited to watercraft and aircraft liability because umbrella policies ordinarily cover auto liability exposures in excess of underlying auto liability coverage. In addition, many umbrella liability policies narrow the scope of the watercraft/aircraft exclusion to provide broader coverage than the underlying policy provides.

Example of Drop-Down Watercraft Coverage Provided by an Umbrella

The watercraft exclusion in an umbrella policy might exclude liability arising out of the use of any watercraft over fifty feet in length, if such watercraft is owned or bareboat chartered (chartered without a crew) by the insured. This exclusion would leave coverage intact for the following:

- Watercraft fifty feet or less in length if owned or bareboat chartered by the insured

- Watercraft of any length if not owned and not bareboat chartered by the insured

The Commercial General Liability coverage form, in contrast, excludes the use of watercraft unless they are not owned by the named insured *and* are less than twenty-six feet long.

An umbrella policy with the language shown above would provide considerably broader watercraft coverage than the Commercial General Liability policy

---

Continued on next page.

would provide. The umbrella policy would not only provide excess coverage for watercraft covered under the Commercial General Liability policy but would also provide drop-down coverage for watercraft excluded by the Commercial General Liability policy but covered by the umbrella.

In practice, if the insured owns any small watercraft at policy inception that would qualify for coverage under the named insured's umbrella policy, the umbrella insurer will require the insured to carry underlying insurance on such watercraft. Therefore, the coverage provided by the umbrella policy on owned watercraft is likely to apply as excess insurance over an underlying policy.

Umbrella liability coverage for aircraft is usually more restrictive than the coverage provided for watercraft. A typical approach is to exclude liability arising out of any aircraft owned, or hired without pilot or crew, by or on behalf of the insured. This type of exclusion could, for example, allow coverage for a claim against the insured for injury resulting from a charter pilot's operation of an airplane on the named insured's behalf.

Care, Custody, or Control

Many umbrella liability policies exclude damage to property in the insured's care, custody, or control. These exclusions vary considerably from policy to policy. In some umbrella policies, the exclusion applies to any property in the insured's care, custody, or control. In other policies, the exclusion applies only to watercraft or aircraft or both while in the insured's care, custody, or control. In still other policies, the exclusion applies only to extent that the insured is contractually obligated to pay for damage to the property or to insure it.

**Example of Drop-Down Care, Custody, or Control Coverage
Provided by an Umbrella Policy**

Assume that ABC Manufacturing (ABC) purchases an umbrella policy that contains a care, custody, or control exclusion that applies only to the extent that ABC is contractually obligated to pay for damage to the property or to insure it. If, for example, ABC rented or borrowed an electrical generator or some other piece of mobile equipment without any obligation to insure it, then ABC's umbrella policy would cover its liability for damaging the equipment while in its care, custody, or control. This type of loss is excluded under an underlying Commercial General Liability policy because of the exclusion contained in that policy of damage to property rented or borrowed by the insured.

Umbrella Exclusions More Restrictive Than the Underlying Coverage

Because they provide drop-down coverage for claims not covered by the under-lying insurance, umbrella liability policies are usually thought of as being broader than the underlying policies in all respects. Nevertheless, most umbrella policies contain some exclusions that are broader than those in the underlying policies. Therefore, these umbrella exclusions restrict coverage to a greater extent than do the exclusions in the underlying policies. To accomplish this effect, the insurer may use modified versions of exclusions found in underlying policies or may add exclusions that have no counterparts in underlying policies. A common example of an underlying policy exclusion that is modified in the umbrella to restrict coverage even further is the pollution exclusion. An example of an exclusion that is added to many umbrella liability policies to restrict coverage is a punitive damages exclusion.

Structuring a Liability Insurance Program

Liability insurance is usually arranged in layers. The primary (first) layer of a layered liability insurance program consists of one or more primary (underly-ing) policies (such as general liability, auto liability, and employers liability), with per accident/occurrence limits typically ranging between $500,000 and $2 million. Large organizations usually retain all or part of the primary layer by using one of the retention or hybrid plans that Chapter 3 mentioned. The primary layer is sometimes referred to as a **working layer**, because it is the layer most often called on to pay losses.

> A **working layer** is the layer of insurance most often called on to pay losses.

Many organizations have only one layer in excess of the primary layer. Typically, an organization in this category has an umbrella liability policy above its primary general liability, commercial auto, and employers liability policies. It may also have one or more separate excess liability policies providing a layer of coverage above other primary policies that the umbrella policy does not cover.

In some cases, an insured must purchase a **buffer layer** of excess insurance between the primary layer and the umbrella policy. This approach is used when the umbrella insurer will only provide coverage with underlying coverage limits that are higher than those that the primary insurer is willing to provide.

> A **buffer layer** is a layer of excess insurance between a primary layer and an umbrella policy.

Example of a Buffer Layer

An umbrella liability insurer may require minimum limits of $1 million for all underlying coverages. One of the primary insurers, however, may be willing to provide limits of only $500,000. To qualify for the umbrella policy, the insured will have to obtain additional limits of $500,000 to fill the buffer layer. This can be best accomplished by purchasing an excess liability policy with its own limits of $500,000, which, when combined with the primary policy limits of $500,000, would provide $1 million of coverage beneath the umbrella policy. Insureds that purchase buffer-layer coverage should try to obtain a policy that follows the provisions of the underlying policy as closely as possible.

Insureds who want higher limits of liability than those offered by a primary policy and an umbrella policy usually do so through one or more additional layers of excess coverage. (It is difficult to obtain a true umbrella policy in the higher layers of excess coverage.) The number of layers varies, depending on the limits desired by the insured and the limits available from insurers. The premium per $1 million of limits usually falls for each successively higher layer because there is a lower probability that losses will fall into each successively higher layer. Exhibit 5-3 shows an example of a multilayered liability insurance program that includes a buffer-layer policy for automobile liability. Note the similarities between Exhibit 5-3 and Exhibit 5-1.

Exhibit 5-3

Multilayered Liability Insurance Program That Includes a Buffer Layer

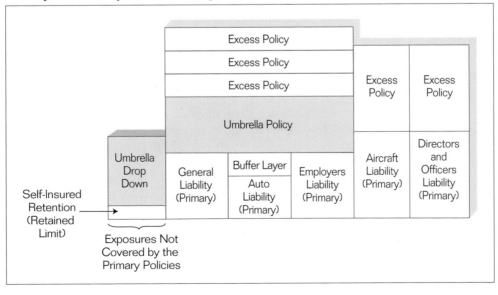

Problems in Layering Coverage

When an excess liability program is layered, each excess liability policy should follow as closely as possible the coverage provisions of the policy beneath it. However, as explained earlier in this chapter, excess policies are seldom true following-form contracts. Even when an excess liability policy states that it is following-form, it should be compared with the policy directly beneath it to reveal any areas in which the excess policy's coverage is more restrictive. The majority of the excess policies currently in use contain wording to the effect that "except as otherwise provided by this policy, the insurance shall follow all of the terms, conditions, definitions and exclusions of the underlying designated policies."

The application of aggregate limits vary with umbrella and excess policies. For example, an umbrella policy may be subject to an aggregate limit on a specific coverage, such as products-completed operations, whereas an excess policy may be subject to a so-called basket aggregate limit, which applies to all coverages. This inconsistency in the treatment of aggregate limits can create a coverage gap when an excess policy sits directly above an umbrella policy, unless the wording of the excess policy clearly states that it will drop down when the umbrella's aggregate limit is exhausted.

Excess policies may differ as to obligations concerning legal defense costs. For example, some excess policies may include coverage for legal defense costs within policy limits and, therefore, recognize such costs in determining whether underlying limits have been exhausted. Others may not provide legal defense coverage.

Adequacy of Excess Limits

The layering of excess policies allows many insureds to secure higher levels of liability protection than they could obtain from one insurer. However, determining the point at which liability limits are "adequate" is subjective. Many risk managers decide on their excess liability limits by comparing information on limits with their peers in the same industry.

How High Should Liability Limits Be?

Consider a corporation with $1 million in net worth. If it carries $1 million in liability insurance, a $2 million court judgment could bankrupt it. If it carries $2 million in liability insurance, a $3 million judgment could bankrupt it. Moreover, even a smaller uninsured verdict of, say, $500,000 could bankrupt or seriously impair the firm's financial condition, particularly when there is the

---

Continued on next page.

possibility of several such losses in a single fiscal period. Therefore, it is difficult to determine how high liability limits should be. The answer depends on the cost and availability of excess liability insurance as well as the maximum possible loss that an organization could face.

Firms must make their insurance-purchasing decisions carefully and consider noninsurance alternatives. For example, if a firm retains smaller losses and implements effective loss control, it should be in a position to obtain economical insurance protection for its larger losses. A firm can get the most from insurance when the insurance is properly combined with noninsurance techniques.

Relationship of Insurance to an Organization's Risk Financing Objectives

Chapter 4 discussed insurance in general, while this chapter discusses excess and umbrella liability insurance. When this text uses the term "insurance" in relation to risk financing, it is referring to guaranteed cost insurance whereby the insurer accepts risk of loss in exchange for a fixed premium. The concept of guaranteed cost insurance applies to both a guaranteed cost insurance plan and the risk transfer component of hybrid plans. A guaranteed cost insurance plan can be applied to a primary layer of insurance, an excess layer, or both.

Exhibit 5-4 discusses guaranteed cost insurance in relation to each of the risk financing objectives introduced in Chapter 2. Properly using guaranteed cost insurance can help an organization meet its risk financing objectives.

Exhibit 5-4
Guaranteed Cost Insurance and Risk Financing Objectives

Risk Financing Objective	Relationship to Guaranteed Cost Insurance
Paying for Losses	Guaranteed cost insurance meets this objective if the policy provides broad coverage and it is purchased from a financially secure insurance company.
Maintaining Liquidity	Guaranteed cost insurance helps meet this objective because the insured does not need to use its liquid assets to pay for losses.

Managing Uncertainty of Loss Outcomes	Guaranteed cost insurance meets this objective if the policy provides broad coverage because the insurer accepts the risk of loss.
Managing the Cost of Risk	As a transfer plan, guaranteed cost insurance is more expensive than retention over the long term. However, guaranteed cost insurance is well suited for managing the cost of high-severity losses.
Complying With Legal Requirements	In cases in which insurance is legally required, guaranteed cost insurance meets the objective of complying with legal requirements as long as the insurance is purchased from a financially secure insurance company.

Summary

- Excess and umbrella liability policies are used to insure liability loss exposures with the potential to generate high-severity losses. These types of policies can sit above other liability policies, called underlying (primary) policies, or a self-insured retention. An umbrella liability policy is a type of excess policy that provides coverage above underlying policies but also offers coverage not available in the underlying policies subject to a self-insured retention, or retained limit, by the insured. An umbrella policy also usually drops down over the aggregate limits of the underlying policies.

- Excess liability policies may take any of three basic forms: a following-form policy subject to the same provisions as the underlying policy, a self-contained policy subject to its own provisions, or a combination of the other two types.

- Specific excess and aggregate excess insurance policies usually sit above a self-insurance layer. A specific excess policy requires the insured to retain a stipulated amount of loss from the first dollar for all losses resulting from a single occurrence/accident. An aggregate excess policy requires the insured to retain a specified amount of loss from the first dollar during a specified period of time, usually one year.

- Liability insurance is usually arranged in layers. The primary layer is sometimes referred to as a working layer because it is the layer most often called on to pay losses. In some cases, an insured must purchase a buffer layer of excess insurance between a primary policy and an umbrella policy.

Insureds who want higher limits of liability than limits offered by a primary and umbrella policy usually purchase the coverage through one or more additional layers of excess coverage.

- A properly designed guaranteed cost insurance plan can help an organization to meet its risk financing objectives.

Chapter Notes

1. This chapter is based in part on material in the text for CPCU 4: Donald S. Malecki, Ronald C. Horn, Eric A. Wiening, and Arthur L. Flitner, *Commercial Liability Insurance and Risk Management* (Malvern, PA: American Institute for CPCU, 1996).
2. Although excess insurance can be used to cover property losses, it is more commonly used for liability losses. Umbrella insurance is used exclusively for liability losses. Therefore, this chapter discusses excess and umbrella insurance for liability losses.
3. "Personal injury" is usually defined to include injuries other than "bodily injury." Included in the usual definition of personal injury are injuries such as false arrest, malicious prosecution, slander, libel, and violation of a person's right of privacy.

Chapter 6

Reinsurance and its Importance to a Risk Financing Program

Introduction[1]

Losses incurred by policyholders can negatively affect an insurance company's financial results. To mitigate the potentially adverse financial effect of a single large loss or a large number of smaller losses, Insurance Company A might pay a premium to Insurance Company B, and, in exchange, Insurance Company B indemnifies Insurance Company A for some or all of its loss payments. Insurance Company A remains responsible to the insureds for all losses. This transaction between two insurance companies is called reinsurance. By purchasing reinsurance, an insurance company can increase its capacity to underwrite risk of loss and can better control its underwriting results.

Reinsurance can be thought of as "insurance for an insurance company." A company that "insures" an insurer is called a reinsurer. A reinsurer may even "insure" another reinsurer.

Reinsurance can be more formally defined as follows:

> The transaction whereby the reinsurer, for a consideration, agrees to indemnify the reinsured company against all or part of the loss that the company may sustain under the policy or policies that it has issued.[2]

Reinsurance is the transaction whereby the reinsurer, for a consideration, agrees to indemnify the reinsured company against all or part of the loss that the company may sustain under the policy or policies that it has issued.[3]

A **ceding company** is an insurance company that **cedes**, or transfers, premiums and losses to a reinsurer. Therefore, an insurer that purchases reinsurance usually is referred to as a ceding company.

A **ceding company** is an insurance company that purchases reinsurance and **cedes**, or transfers, premiums and losses to a reinsurer.

The reinsurance business enables an insurer to share large losses with many reinsurers throughout the world. For example, insurers that accept a large single risk of loss, such as the potential destruction of a commercial office building or a jumbo jet, usually find that they must cede reinsurance to several reinsurers located in various countries in order to protect themselves in the event of a large loss. The same situation applies to insurers that accept the risk that a single catastrophe, such as a hurricane, will destroy many homes and/or businesses.

A reinsurer itself might purchase reinsurance to spread the cost of the losses it has agreed to cover. An arrangement to share risk between two reinsurers is referred to as a **retrocession**, with the reinsurer that transfers the risk of loss retroceding premium to a **retrocessionaire**, which is the term used for the reinsurer that accepts risk of loss in a retrocession.

Retrocession is an arrangement to share risk between two reinsurers.

A **retrocessionaire** is the reinsurer that receives premium and pays losses under a retrocession.

Through a series of reinsurance and retrocession arrangements, losses can be shared by many reinsurers and retrocessionaires worldwide. For example, assume a hurricane strikes the southeastern United States and destroys many buildings covered by an insurer. Depending on the reinsurance and retrocessional arrangements in place, the insurer could be indemnified by reinsurers located in various countries and, in turn, those reinsurers could be reimbursed by retrocessionaires located in various other countries. Exhibit 6-1 illustrates possible relationships between an insurer, reinsurers, and retrocessionaires.

As insurers and reinsurers cede and retrocede coverages to spread their risk, they become interdependent. Insurance Company A might serve as a reinsured in a transaction with Insurance Company B and as a reinsurer in a separate transaction with Insurance Company B. Both Insurance Company A and Insurance Company B might serve as retrocessionaires in a transaction with Insurance Company C. Consequently, through reinsurance, the fortunes of many insurers and reinsurers become mutually dependent as each one relies on the others' good faith and financial strength.

Exhibit 6-1
Worldwide Risk Sharing Through Reinsurance and Retrocessional Arrangements

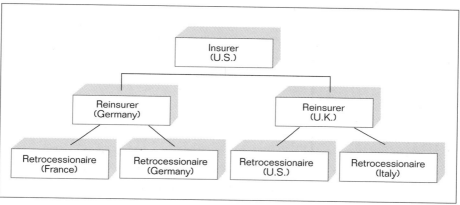

Importance of Reinsurance to a Risk Financing Program

An organization's risk manager should evaluate the financial soundness of the organization's insurers. Because most insurers purchase reinsurance, a risk manager should also evaluate the soundness of the insurers' reinsurers. For some insurance transactions, a risk manager needs only to confirm the claim-paying ability ratings of its insurers' reinsurers. For others, especially insurance transactions involving substantial policy limits, a risk manager should obtain more information, including the types and limits of reinsurance purchased by its insurers.

The reinsurance purchased by an organization's insurers should be appropriate for the insured organization's coverages. For example, an organization that purchases very high excess products liability limits from one insurer should make sure that the insurer, depending on its size, has adequate reinsurance for the exposure. In certain cases, as a condition of purchasing insurance, a risk manager might specify the types and amounts of reinsurance that the insurer must purchase.

Interdependent risk-sharing relationships through reinsurance and retrocessions are efficient and increase the types and amounts of insurance available. However, any disruption to this reinsurance network, such as the bankruptcy of a major insurer or reinsurer, can threaten an insured's risk financing program. A risk manager can do little to avert systematic disturbances in the insurance/reinsurance market. However, a risk manager can avoid some of the effects of systematic disturbances by making sure his or her insurers purchase reinsurance from large, financially sound reinsurers that are not overly dependent on retrocessional arrangements.

Although an insured is not normally a party to a reinsurance contract, in certain situations a risk manager might deal directly with a reinsurer. Those situations are covered later in this chapter.

The Reinsurance Transaction

A reinsurance transaction involves premiums and losses that are exchanged between an insurer and a reinsurer. In many cases more than one reinsurer is used. Often, a reinsurance intermediary (broker) is involved; however, some major reinsurers deal directly with insurers and are called **direct writers**. Exhibit 6-2 shows the parties to a reinsurance transaction that involves an intermediary.

> **Direct writers** are reinsurers that usually do not use intermediaries and, therefore, deal directly with insurers.

Exhibit 6-2
The Reinsurance Transaction (With an Intermediary)

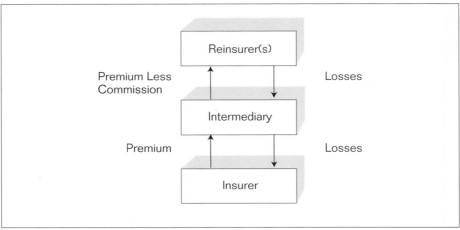

The reinsurance market is divided into direct-writer reinsurers and intermediary reinsurers (reinsurers that use intermediaries). An insurer either negotiates directly with direct-writer reinsurers or uses an intermediary that negotiates on its behalf with intermediary reinsurers. However, under certain market conditions, an insurer might use both intermediary reinsurers and direct-writer reinsurers in order to obtain sufficient capacity for its reinsurance placement. In that situation, the intermediary usually negotiates on the insurer's behalf with both the intermediary reinsurers and the direct-writer reinsurers. This placement arrangement enables an insurer to tap the capacity of the entire reinsurance market.

Reinsurance Intermediaries

Reinsurance intermediaries, sometimes called reinsurance brokers, provide services to both insurers and reinsurers, including coverage and premium negotiation, claim handling, accounting, and underwriting advice. They also investigate, on the insurer's behalf, the financial strength of reinsurers. Reinsurance intermediaries also provide similar services for retrocessional arrangements.

As compensation for their services, reinsurance intermediaries receive a commission from the reinsurance company. They sometimes receive a fee from the insurer in place of the commission, which is then netted out of the reinsurance premium charged by the reinsurer.

Major Types of Reinsurance

Reinsurance transactions fall into one of two major categories: facultative and treaty. Each of these categories is further divided into pro rata and excess of loss reinsurance, as shown in Exhibit 6-3.

Exhibit 6-3
Major Types of Reinsurance

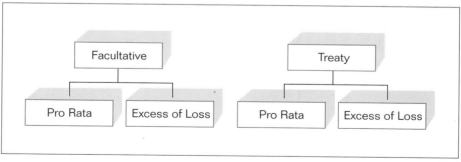

Facultative and Treaty Reinsurance

When an insurer and a reinsurer agree to share all or part of the losses arising from only one of the insurer's policies, the agreement is known as **facultative reinsurance**. There must be an offer and acceptance for each policy, with the reinsurer retaining the "faculty" to accept or reject reinsurance of each policy. When the insurer and reinsurer agree to share losses arising from more than one policy, usually a whole line or book of the insurer's business, the agreement is known as **treaty reinsurance**. Under treaty reinsurance, the ceding of losses arising from an individual policy is usually automatic and does not require the policy to be specifically accepted by the reinsurer as long as it falls within the policy categories covered by the treaty reinsurance agreement (the treaty).

With **facultative reinsurance**, an insurer and a reinsurer agree to share all or part of the losses arising from one of the insurer's policies. There must be an offer and acceptance to reinsure each policy.

In **treaty reinsurance**, an insurer and a reinsurer agree to share losses arising from more than one policy, usually a whole line or book of the insurer's business. The ceding of losses arising from a policy is usually automatic and does not require the reinsurer to specifically accept the policy as long as it falls within the categories of policies covered by the treaty reinsurance agreement.

Facultative and treaty reinsurance, which are often used together in an insurer's reinsurance program, usually serve different purposes. Facultative reinsurance might provide capacity above the limits of a treaty for a single large risk exposure or fill in coverage gaps in a treaty. Treaty reinsurance might stabilize the insurer's net (of reinsurance) underwriting results for an entire line of business or reimburse it for losses arising from a catastrophe, such as a hurricane, which involves losses from many different insurance policies.

After an insurer pays its policyholder for a loss, the amount of reimbursement from a reinsurer for that loss depends on the terms of the reinsurance contract between the insurer and the reinsurer. A reinsurer could agree to pay the insurer a percentage of each loss, such as 60 percent of a $2 million loss, or $1,200,000. Alternatively, a reinsurer could agree to pay the insurer an amount for each loss in excess of a certain loss level, or attachment point, such as $1,250,000 in excess of a $750,000 attachment point for a $2 million loss.

Pro Rata Reinsurance

When a reinsurer agrees to reimburse an insurer for a percentage of each loss, the agreement is called a **pro rata reinsurance agreement** (sometimes called a **proportional reinsurance agreement**). Under this

In a **pro rata reinsurance agreement** (also called a **proportional reinsurance agreement**), an insurer and a reinsurer share premiums in the same proportion as they share losses. For example, if a reinsurer receives 80 percent of the premium, it pays 80 percent of each covered loss.

agreement, the reinsurer receives a percentage of the policy premium charged by the insurer that is equal to the percentage of each loss that the reinsurer will pay. With pro rata reinsurance the loss ratio (ratio of losses to premium) is the same for both the insurer (net of reinsurance) and the reinsurer because they share a set percentage of both premium and losses. The pro rata method of sharing premium and loss can be used with either facultative or treaty reinsurance.

Exhibit 6-4 shows the relationships between premiums and losses for a sample pro rata reinsurance agreement. The figures for the insurer are shown net of reinsurance. Assume that the insurer issues a policy with a limit of $1 million for a premium of $160,000 and experiences losses of $120,000 for a loss ratio (losses divided by premium) of 75 percent. Further, assume the insurer cedes 80 percent of the premium and losses to a reinsurer.

Exhibit 6-4

Pro Rata Reinsurance With 80 Percent Ceded to the Reinsurer

Policy Limit is $1,000,000.		Insurer (20% net)	Reinsurer (80%)
Premium	$160,000	$32,000	$128,000
Loss	$120,000	$24,000	$ 96,000
Loss Ratio	75%	75%	75%

20% Net Retention by the Insurer

80% Ceded to the Reinsurer

The reinsurer receives 80 percent of the premium and pays 80 percent of the losses, while the insurer retains 20 percent of the premium and pays 20 percent of the losses, net of reinsurance. The insurer's loss ratio is the same (75 percent) regardless of whether or not it purchases the pro rata reinsurance. The insurer's and reinsurer's loss ratios are equal.

Excess of Loss Reinsurance

When a reinsurer agrees to reimburse an insurer for the portion of each loss that exceeds a specific attachment point, the agreement is called an **excess of loss reinsurance agreement**. The attachment point can apply

An **excess of loss reinsurance agreement** means that a reinsurer agrees to reimburse an insurer for the portion of each loss that exceeds a specific attachment point.

on a per policy basis or on a per occurrence basis. In the latter case, excess of loss reinsurance attaches excess of the sum of all the insurer's losses from a single occurrence, such as a hurricane, regardless of the number of insurance policies involved.

Exhibit 6-5 shows the relationships between premiums and losses for a hypothetical excess of loss reinsurance agreement. The figures for the insurer are shown net of reinsurance. The excess of loss reinsurance attaches at $250,000 per occurrence and covers up to an insurer's policy limit of $1 million per occurrence. Therefore, the reinsurance provides a limit of $750,000 excess of $250,000 per occurrence. The insurer receives a premium of $200,000 for a $1 million policy and pays a reinsurance premium of $50,000 for the $750,000 excess of $250,000 layer.

Exhibit 6-5
Excess of Loss Reinsurance for a $1 Million Policy With a $250,000 per Occurrence Attachment Point

		Insurer (net)	Reinsurer $750,000 Excess of $250,000
Premium	$200,000	$150,000	$ 50,000
Loss	$125,000	$125,000	$ 0
Loss ratio		83%	0%
Loss	$350,000	$250,000	$100,000
Loss ratio		167%	200%

$750,000 Excess
of $250,000
Transferred to the
Reinsurer

$250,000 Net
Retention by the
Insurer

Two losses, one for $125,000 and the other for $350,000, are examined in Exhibit 6-5. For the $125,000 loss, the insurer receives no reimbursement from the reinsurer because the loss is below the $250,000 attachment point. For the

$350,000 loss, the insurer pays a net amount of $250,000, with the reinsurer indemnifying the insurer for $100,000.

For excess of loss reinsurance, the loss ratios usually differ between the insurer and reinsurer. For example, with the $350,000 loss, the insurer's net loss ratio is 167 percent while the reinsurer's loss ratio is 200 percent.

Unlike with pro rata reinsurance, the premium for an excess of loss layer of reinsurance is not a straight percentage of the insurer's premium because the insurer and reinsurer do not share losses proportionally. Instead, the reinsurance premium is negotiated between the insurer and reinsurer and is usually based on factors such as the number of policies written by, and the past loss experience of, the insurer.

Finite Risk Reinsurance

An additional type of reinsurance is known as **finite risk reinsurance**, which is similar to finite risk insurance (introduced in Chapter 3). A finite risk reinsurance arrangement works in the same manner as the finite risk insurance example illus-

> **Finite risk reinsurance** is a nontraditional type of reinsurance whereby the insurer transfers a limited amount of risk to the reinsurer. Finite risk reinsurance is similar to finite risk insurance.

trated in Chapter 3, except that the contract is written on a reinsurance basis rather than on an insurance basis. Finite risk reinsurance is a nontraditional type of reinsurance that doesn't fit neatly into the general categories of facultative, treaty, pro rata, and excess of loss, but it can be written on any of these bases. Finite risk reinsurance is best described by its characteristics, which include the following:

- The reinsurer accepts a limited amount of risk.
- The reinsurer shares with the insurer any profit on the arrangement.
- The reinsurer provides the insurer with credit for investment income earned.

There is usually an aggregate limit that applies over the term of the reinsurance agreement, which usually extends over multiple years.

The finite risk reinsurance premium is generally a substantial percentage of the policy limit. This relationship between premium and limits reduces the reinsurer's potential underwriting loss to a level that is much lower than the potential underwriting loss typically associated with conventional types of reinsurance. The insurer is usually able to share in favorable loss experience by receiving a profit-sharing distribution from the reinsurer, which helps to compensate for the higher-than-normal reinsurance premium.

The reinsurer's cash flow (receiving premium before paying losses) is also recognized in a finite risk reinsurance agreement. In general, the cash flow accrues to the insurer's benefit through an investment income credit. However, if the reinsurer's losses exceed its premium, the reinsurer usually uses the investment income to pay for the losses, reducing the reinsurer's chance of losing money on the arrangement.

A finite risk reinsurance plan can be an effective way for an insurer to transfer a limited amount of risk associated with large and unusual risks that generally cannot be reinsured efficiently with traditional reinsurance. In addition, it provides the insurer with a predictable reinsurance cost over the term of the cover. Chapter 10 further discusses finite risk arrangements.

Functions of Reinsurance

Reinsurance can perform several functions for an insurer:

- Enhancing capacity,
- Providing stability,
- Providing catastrophe protection,
- Providing surplus relief,
- Providing underwriting expertise, and
- Assisting with withdrawal from a territory or line of business.

Each of these functions is discussed below.

Enhancing Capacity

An insurer needs two types of capacity: large-line capacity and premium capacity. **Large-line capacity** is an insurer's ability to provide a high limit of insurance under a single policy, such as $50 million for a commercial office building or $30 million for a jet plane. **Premium capacity** refers to the aggregate premium volume that an insurer can write.

Large-line capacity is an insurer's ability to provide a high limit of insurance for a single risk exposure.

Premium capacity is the aggregate premium volume that an insurer can write.

Few insurers are able or willing to provide the large-line capacity needed to underwrite a commercial office building or a jumbo jet. Even if an insurer were willing to take such a risk, most U.S. state regulations prohibit an insurer from retaining a single risk of loss net of reinsurance that exceeds 10 percent of its policyholders' surplus.[4]

Reinsurance serves a useful purpose by enabling insurers to accept large risks that they could not otherwise accept. For example, an insurer could underwrite a $100 million jumbo jet and cede $90 million of the policy limit to several reinsurers, therefore retaining a $10 million risk of loss net after reinsurance. By purchasing reinsurance, the insurer is able to provide sufficient large-line capacity to cover the jumbo jet but is able to limit its net retention to an acceptable level.

An insurer's premium capacity is constrained by regulations that limit the ratio of an insurer's net written premium to its policyholders' surplus. Financial analysts and insurance rating organizations look at insurers' ratio of net written premium to policyholders' surplus and are concerned if the ratio is higher than a certain figure, generally 3 to 1. Just as reinsurance enables an insurer to provide large-line capacity, it also enhances an insurer's premium capacity because the reinsurance premium is netted out before calculating an insurer's ratio of net written premium to policyholders' surplus.

Providing Stability

An insurer, like most other organizations, must have a reasonably steady flow of profits both to attract and retain capital so as to support growth. Insurance losses sometimes fluctuate widely because of demographic, economic, social, and natural forces, as well as simple chance. Smoothing the peaks and valleys of an insurer's random variation in loss experience, a function of reinsurance, helps to ensure steady profits for an insurer.

For example, an insurer might purchase reinsurance to limit the net amount it would pay for any one large loss. Limiting the net amount paid for a single large loss through reinsurance provides stability in an insurer's net underwriting results.

Providing Catastrophe Protection

Insurers are subject to major catastrophe losses from earthquakes, hurricanes, tornadoes, industrial explosions, plane crashes, and similar disasters. A catastrophic event might result in a large number of property and liability losses for a single insurer. Total insured losses have exceeded $15 billion in one hurricane, and insured catastrophe losses exceeding $100 million are common.

A specific form of excess of loss reinsurance, called **catastrophe reinsurance**, reimburses an insurer for its losses from a

Catastrophe reinsurance is a specific form of excess of loss reinsurance that reimburses an insurer for losses from a single catastrophic event that, in total, exceed a specific amount. Catastrophic events include hurricanes, tornadoes, and earthquakes.

single catastrophic event that, in total, exceed a predetermined amount. A distinguishing feature of catastrophe reinsurance is that it covers multiple losses under many policies, with all the losses arising from a single catastrophic event.

Providing Surplus Relief

A United States insurer is required to file financial statements prescribed by statute in the various states of the U.S. using a method called statutory accounting. Statutory accounting practices are conservative when compared with Generally Accepted Accounting Principles (GAAP). The conservatism results in a temporary reduction in an insurer's reported policyholders' surplus, which can be offset by purchasing reinsurance. This function of reinsurance, which is called surplus relief, is explained below.

In order to understand surplus relief, it is important to consider **policy-acquisition costs**. These are costs that an insurer incurs upfront to issue an insurance policy. They include items such as U.S. state premium taxes and agents' commissions that,

> **Policy-acquisition costs** are upfront costs, such as U.S. state premium taxes and agents' commissions, incurred by an insurer at the time of policy issuance.

under statutory accounting practices, must be charged immediately as expenses at the beginning of the policy period on the insurer's income statement. The associated premium revenue from a policy is not recognized by the insurer until the premium is earned throughout the policy period. Therefore, under statutory accounting practices, there is a mismatch between the recognition of revenue (over the policy period) and the recognition of policy-acquisition costs (immediate), resulting in a conservative net income figure for the insurer on the date a policy is issued.

For a single policy, this reduction in net income is temporary because it is eliminated by the end of the policy period once all the premium revenue from the policy is recognized by the insurer. However, the aggregate effect is a permanent reduction in net income for an insurer that issues policies on an ongoing basis. (The net income reductions under newly issued policies take the place of net income reductions that are eliminated as policies mature.) In fact, the reduction in net income increases over time for an insurer that is growing in terms of premium revenue, with a resulting drain on policyholders' surplus that possibly can threaten the insurer's solvency. This occurs because the premium and expense amounts for newly issued policies grow at a higher rate than those for expiring policies.

By contrast, under Generally Accepted Accounting Principles (GAAP), policy-acquisition costs are charged as an expense throughout the policy period as the associated premium revenue is recognized by the insurer throughout the policy period. Therefore, GAAP allows for the matching of premium revenue with the associated policy-acquisition costs, which provides a realistic net income figure throughout the life of a policy. Under GAAP, a growing insurer does not experience a drain on its policyholders' surplus because its aggregate premium revenue and policy-acquisition costs are properly matched at any point in time.

Pro rata reinsurance relieves the drain on an insurer's statutory surplus because it pays the insurer a **ceding commission** (a percentage of the reinsurance premium) to reimburse the insurer for the policy-acquisition costs it incurs on the reinsured business.[5] On the insurer's statutory financial statement, the ceding commission revenue offsets the effect of the immediately charged policy-acquisition costs, in effect mitigating the reduction in the insurer's statutory policyholders' surplus.[6] This benefit provided by reinsurance is called **surplus relief**.

A **ceding commission** is a percentage of a reinsurance premium that reimburses an insurer for its policy-acquisition costs. It usually applies only to pro rata reinsurance.

Surplus relief is a function of pro rata reinsurance whereby a reinsurer pays a ceding commission to an insurer. The ceding commission, which offsets the insurer's policy-acquisition costs, relieves the insurer from the temporary reduction of its surplus due to the effect of statutory accounting practices.

Providing Underwriting Expertise

Reinsurers deal with a wide variety of insurers. Consequently, reinsurers accumulate a great deal of information on various insurers, including their loss experience and methods of rating, underwriting, and handling various coverages. A reinsurer can use its knowledge to help an insurer improve its underwriting for a line of business or to help it enter a new line of business.

For example, a medium-sized insurance company reinsured 95 percent of its umbrella liability coverage over several years, relying heavily on the expertise of the reinsurer in rating and underwriting the umbrella policies. In another example, a large insurer issued package policies that included boiler and machinery coverage and reinsured this line with a reinsurer that specializes in that coverage.

Assisting With Withdrawal From a Territory or a Line of Business

An insurer or a reinsurer sometimes decides to withdraw from a territory or a line of business. There are two ways to achieve that end. The insurer could merely cancel the unwanted policies and refund the unearned premiums to its policyholders. That process can be unwieldy and expensive, and it is likely to create ill will among policyholders, agents/brokers, and regulatory authorities. Alternatively, an insurer could reinsure the unwanted business. This method not only avoids the ill will resulting from cancellation, but it also might be less expensive than the cost of processing and paying premium refunds on canceled policies. An arrangement whereby an insurer reinsures an entire class, line, territory, or book of business in order to withdraw from that business is known as **portfolio reinsurance**, which the next section further discusses.

> **Portfolio reinsurance** is an arrangement whereby an insurer stops writing a particular line of insurance and transfers the book of business to a reinsurer.

Risk Managers' Direct Dealings With Reinsurers

Normally, a risk manager is not involved with negotiating reinsurance contracts. Only insurers and reinsurers typically enter into reinsurance contracts. However, there are situations whereby a risk manager would deal directly with a reinsurer:

- A reinsurer takes the place of an insurer as a result of a portfolio reinsurance arrangement.

- A reinsurer takes the place of an insurer through a cut-through endorsement added to an insurance policy.

- An organization's risk manager directs business to a particular insurer and uses another insurer as a "front."

- An organization purchases reinsurance for its captive insurer or for a pool, of which it is a member.

- A reinsurer or several reinsurers team up with an insurer or several insurers to provide coverage.

Risk Management in Practice
Risk Managers' Contact With Reinsurers
Various surveys have shown that an increasing percentage of risk managers' time is spent with reinsurers as opposed to insurers. Subjects that risk managers discuss directly with reinsurers include integrated risk plans, reinsurance of captive insurance companies, and other alternative risk products.[7]

Portfolio Reinsurance Arrangements

With a portfolio reinsurance transaction, the reinsurer often becomes the insurer for the affected business and deals directly with the policyholders. A risk manager whose insurance plan has been reinsured through a portfolio reinsurance arrangement should learn the details of the transaction in order to ascertain that coverage is maintained and that the reinsurer is at least as financially sound as the retiring insurer.

Cut-Through Endorsements

A **cut-through endorsement** (also called an **assumption certificate**) is attached to an insurance contract and states that reinsurance proceeds will be paid directly to a named payee in the event of the insurer's insolvency. Therefore, an insured's or a third party's right of recovery from an insurer "cuts through" directly to the reinsurer.

> A **cut-through endorsement** (also called an **assumption certificate**) is an endorsement to an insurance policy that states that reinsurance proceeds will be paid directly to a named payee in the event of the insurer's insolvency.

In general, cut-through endorsements are difficult to obtain and can result in problems when an insurance company is liquidated. A liquidator of an insurance company wants to maximize the amount of reinsurance proceeds available to all policyholders and does not want to allow one policyholder to enjoy preferential treatment because it has a cut-through endorsement. A reinsurer that issues a cut-through endorsement could find itself in the unenviable position of having to pay twice for the same losses: once to the liquidator for the full amount of the reinsurance payable to the liquidated insurer and again to the named payee in the cut-through endorsement.

In the United States, cut-through endorsements are allowed on a limited basis for policies covering property that is used as collateral for a loan. A lender usually requests a cut-through to the reinsurer when it is not comfortable with the financial security of the insurer of the property. Many cut-through endorsements agree to pay the lender, not the insured, and only pay to the extent of a lender's secured interest subject to the limit of reinsurance.

Reinsuring Fronted Coverage

An organization might decide it wants a particular insurer to provide coverage. If the chosen insurer is not licensed in the organization's jurisdiction to provide the type of insurance sought, the organization can arrange for a licensed insurance company to front the coverage. The licensed insurer would issue an insurance policy and then reinsure all the risk with the chosen insurer. In this type of arrangement, the risk manager should investigate not only the chosen insurer's financial strength but also the fronting company's financial strength.

Similarly, an insurer itself might arrange for another insurer to front for it. This situation might arise because the insurer does not have an established credit rating or the necessary underwriting skills for the type of business it is underwriting.

Reinsuring a Captive or Pool

A risk manager for an organization with a captive insurer is usually an officer of the captive subsidiary or an informal adviser to its management. The same is true of a pool.

Because captives and pools often purchase reinsurance, a risk manager frequently participates in reinsurance decisions. Consequently, a risk manager must be concerned with the reinsurers' financial strength, integrity, and operating efficiency, which all affect the captive's or the pool's reliability as well as the solidity and effectiveness of the organization's risk financing program.

The Functions of Reinsurance for a Captive or a Pool

Captive insurance companies and pools often purchase excess of loss reinsurance in order to provide large-line capacity to their insureds and to stabilize their net underwriting results. Although this excess of loss reinsurance is usually purchased on a treaty basis, it is sometimes purchased on a facultative basis.

Reinsurers can be helpful to the management of a captive insurer or pool by providing underwriting expertise. In many cases, reinsurers assist a captive or a pool in underwriting unrelated third-party business (business not related to its owners).

Reinsurers and Insurers Cooperate To Provide Capacity

Insurers and reinsurers sometimes form an alliance to provide high limits of capacity. In recent years, there have been several instances of insurers and reinsurers cooperating to provide a single high limit of insurance, usually for an excess layer.

Summary

- A transfer of risk between two insurance companies is called reinsurance. By reinsuring its risk of loss, an insurance company can increase its capacity to underwrite risks and can better control its net underwriting results. A reinsurer itself might also purchase reinsurance to spread the cost of its losses. This transaction is referred to as a retrocession. Through a series of reinsurance and retrocession agreements, losses can be shared by many reinsurers located throughout the world.

- Every insured organization depends on the financial soundness of its commercial insurers. Because commercial insurers usually depend on reinsurance, any disruption to the reinsurance network, such as the bankruptcy of a major reinsurer, can threaten an organization's risk financing program.

- A reinsurance transaction involves premiums and losses that are exchanged between an insurer and a reinsurer (or reinsurers), often with an intermediary's involvement.

- Reinsurance transactions fall into one of two major categories: facultative and treaty. With facultative reinsurance, an insurer and a reinsurer agree to share part or all of the losses arising from a single policy, while treaty reinsurance covers a whole line or book of business. Each of these categories is further broken down into pro rata and excess of loss. With pro rata reinsurance, an insurer and a reinsurer share premiums in the same proportion as they share losses. With excess of loss reinsurance, a reinsurer agrees to reimburse an insurer for the portion of each loss that exceeds a specific attachment point. Finite risk reinsurance does not fit neatly into these categories and is a nontraditional type of reinsurance whereby the insurer transfers a limited amount of risk to a reinsurer and receives profit sharing for favorable loss experience.

- The functions of reinsurance for an insurer include the following: (1) enhancing capacity, (2) providing stability, (3) providing catastrophe protection, (4) providing surplus relief, (5) providing underwriting expertise, and (6) assisting with withdrawal from a territory or line of business.

- Pro rata reinsurance provides surplus relief to an insurer because the reinsurer pays the insurer a ceding commission, which offsets the insurer's policy-acquisition costs. Policy-acquisition costs can temporarily reduce policyholders' surplus because they must be immediately charged as expenses when incurred under statutory accounting practices.

- A risk manager might deal directly with a reinsurer in the following situations: (1) a reinsurer takes the place of an insurer through a portfolio reinsurance arrangement; (2) a reinsurer takes the place of an insurer through a cut-through endorsement added to an insurance policy; (3) an organization places coverage with a particular insurer and uses another insurer to front the coverage; and (4) an organization purchases reinsurance for its captive insurer or for a pool, of which it is a member.

Chapter Notes

1. Parts of this chapter are based on material in the text for ARe 141: Michael W. Elliott, Bernard L. Webb, Howard N. Anderson, and Peter R. Kensicki, *Principles of Reinsurance* (Malvern, PA: Insurance Institute of America, 1995).

2. Robert W. Strain, CPCU, CLU, *Reinsurance Contract Wording* (Athens, TX: Strain Publishing and Seminars, 1996), p. 776. Quoted with permission from Robert W. Strain Publishing & Seminars Incorporated, P.O. Box 1520, Athens, TX 75751.

3. Robert W. Strain, CPCU, CLU, *Reinsurance Contract Wording* (Athens, TX: Strain Publishing and Seminars, 1996), p. 776. Quoted with permission from Robert W. Strain Publishing & Seminars Incorporated, P.O. Box 1520, Athens, TX 75751.

4. Policyholders' surplus is an amount on an insurer's balance sheet that is available for policyholders and is determined by this equation: Assets − liabilities = Policyholders' Surplus.

5. The ceding commission is usually greater than the insurer's policy-acquisition costs because it reimburses the insurer for additional expenses and, sometimes, a share of the profit on the reinsured business.

6. Of course, if the reinsurer itself is subject to U.S. statutory accounting, it would experience a reduction in its policyholders' surplus.

7. For more information, see Lisa S. Howard, "RMs Moving to Direct Contact With Reinsurers," *National Underwriter*, June 14, 1999, p. 9.

Chapter 7

Self-Insurance

Introduction

Chapter 3 introduced *self-insurance* as a loss retention plan for which an organization keeps records of its losses and maintains a formal system to pay for them. Self-insurance was contrasted with informal retention under which an organization simply pays for its losses with its cash flow and/or current (liquid) assets but has no formal payment procedures or method of recording losses.

> *Self-insurance* is a loss retention plan for which an organization keeps records of its losses and maintains a formal system to pay for them.

Using the definition of the term "self-insurance" given here, one could argue that it includes the retained portion of losses under deductible plans, retrospective rating plans, captive insurance plans, pools, and finite risk plans. However, this text discusses those plans as being separate from self-insurance plans.

Self-insurance is best practiced by organizations having tolerance for retaining risk of loss and a willingness to devote capital and resources to financing and administering a self-insurance program. It is best applied to losses that are both low-severity and high-frequency. These types of losses are somewhat predictable in total over a defined period of time, such as a year. (Losses that are both low-severity and low-frequency are easily self-insured; however, they are usually informally retained, which avoids the administrative costs involved with self-insurance.) Some organizations also self-insure medium-severity losses, although the resulting financial impact on an organization can be unpredictable, depending on the frequency of these losses.

A self-insurance plan is usually combined with a transfer or a hybrid plan that covers high-severity losses. Exhibit 7-1 shows these relationships.

Exhibit 7-1
Self-Insurance Combined With Other Risk Financing Plans

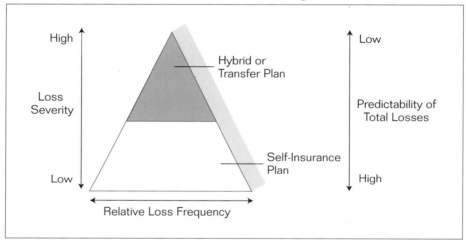

For example, excess insurance (transfer) or a finite/integrated risk plan (hybrid) could sit directly above the self-insured layer.

Because self-insurance involves certain overhead costs and other expenses as well as the assumption of risk of loss, an organization should have a sufficient amount of loss exposure for self-insurance to be economically feasible. Rules of thumb exist as to what an organization's minimum insurance premium (if the loss exposure were insured) should be in order to make self-insurance an economically feasible alternative to guaranteed cost insurance. One source reports the annual minimum premium as $500,000 for any one line of casualty coverage.[1]

Self-insurance is particularly well suited for losses that are paid out over a period of time, therefore providing a cash flow benefit to the organization retaining its losses. For this reason, workers compensation, general liability, and automobile liability loss exposures are often self-insured.

Hospitals often self-insure their professional liability losses. During the 1970s and 1980s, hospital professional liability insurance was either unavailable or extremely expensive. As a result, many hospitals self-insured their low-to-medium-severity professional liability losses and purchased excess insurance for their high-severity losses.[2]

In the United States, certain requirements apply to the self-insurance of workers compensation and automobile liability. Although most states allow these exposures to be self-insured, they require that an organization obtain approval to self-insure. To be approved, an organization must show to the state that it is financially secure and, therefore, able to meet its loss payment obligations to its employees and third-party claimants. For example, some states require a self-insured organization to purchase excess insurance and obtain a bond to secure the payment of retained losses. These requirements are discussed later in this chapter.

Self-insurance is usually applied to losses for which there is a high frequency of occurrence. Because of the large volume of claim transactions, self-insurance demands substantial administration on the part of the self-insured organization. This involves duplicating many of the services normally provided by an insurance company under an insurance plan, such as claim adjusting and regulatory filings. A self-insured organization can provide these services directly or contract with an outside organization that provides them.

For financial accounting purposes, a self-insured organization must recognize its retained losses as they are incurred,[3] just as an insurance company does. Reserves for future payments of losses (loss reserves) that have occurred must be reported as a liability on the organization's balance sheet and charged as an expense on its income statement.

These reserves for self-insured loss payments can be funded or unfunded. If they are unfunded, the self-insured organization pays for losses out of its cash flow or available current (liquid) assets. If they are funded, the reserves are backed by an internal fund that is recorded as an asset on the organization's balance sheet. This fund is used by the organization to pay for its retained losses as they become due. (As discussed in Chapter 2, an organization that maintains an internal fund incurs an opportunity cost because the cash is tied up in relatively liquid assets.)

Exhibit 7-2 summarizes some general characteristics of self-insurance.

Exhibit 7-2
Characteristics of Self-Insurance

Retention/Transfer	Severity of Losses	Funded/Unfunded	Administrative Requirements
Retention	Low to Medium	Either	High

Advantages and Disadvantages of Self-Insurance

As with any other risk financing plan, self-insurance has certain advantages and disadvantages. Some are similar to those of any other retention plan, while others are unique to self-insurance.

Advantages

As a retention technique, self-insurance provides several advantages to an organization when compared with a transfer plan. (The advantages of retention were discussed in Chapter 1.) In addition, self-insurance allows an organization to exercise more control over its claims than it could by using most other risk financing plans.

Control Over Claims

A major advantage of self-insurance is that an organization is able to exercise direct control over the adjustment of its claims. (This advantage also exists with some of the other plans that involve retention.) The self-insured organization can select its own panel of defense attorneys and set specific guidelines for the handling of its claims. For example, this allows the organization to determine the amount of effort it will put into defending rather than settling a claim. The ability to set guidelines for settlement offers could be particularly important to an organization with claims that could affect its reputation, such as those involving allegations that the organization negligently manufactured a product.

Risk Control

Another major advantage of self-insurance is that it encourages risk control. When an organization directly pays the cost of its own losses, it has an incentive to prevent and reduce them because, by doing so, the organization saves the loss payments and the expense of adjusting the losses. Also, the organization avoids having to devote resources in the aftermath of a loss, such as time spent tending to workers' injuries or cleaning up after a loss. Furthermore, the organization avoids possible major disruptions in its operations, such as those caused by a plant's total shutdown following an explosion.

Long-Term Cost Savings

Another major advantage of self-insurance is that its long-run cost tends to be lower than the cost of transfer. For example, an organization usually saves money over the long run using self-insurance rather than guaranteed cost insurance because it does not have to contribute to an insurance company's overhead costs and profits, which are included in the expense component of a guaranteed cost insurance premium. The organization also does not have to pay an insurance company's risk charge, which is an extra charge that an insurer includes as part of its premium to cover the chance that losses will be higher than expected. Just as with a large deductible insurance plan (discussed in Chapter 3), a self-insurance plan avoids premium taxes and residual market loadings. However, as discussed later in this chapter, self-insurance is subject to various other taxes, assessments, and fees.

Cash Flow

An organization that self-insures rather than buys insurance is able to benefit from cash flow generated by retained losses that are paid over a period of time. Chapter 2 explained how present value analysis could be used to measure the cash flow benefit of retained losses. This same analysis can be applied to the retained loss payments under a self-insurance plan.

Present value analysis should be applied to all the costs of a self-insurance plan, not just paid losses. That way, the present value cost of a self-insurance plan can be compared with the present value cost of other plans that involve retaining low-to-medium-severity losses, such as a large deductible plan, a retrospective rating plan, or a captive insurer plan. Present value analysis can also be used to compare the cost of self-insurance and guaranteed cost insurance.

Disadvantages

Self-insurance has disadvantages similar to those of any retention plan. In addition, self-insurance requires a substantial amount of administration and may not be recognized as fulfilling contractual requirements to purchase insurance. These disadvantages are discussed below.

Uncertainty of Retained Loss Outcomes

A major disadvantage of self-insurance is the associated uncertainty of retained loss outcomes, which can negatively affect an organization's earnings, net worth, and cash flow. When an organization decides to finance losses by self-insuring rather than transferring them with guaranteed cost insurance, it faces the possibility that self-insured losses will be much greater in number (frequency) or size (severity) than initially expected. Because of this uncertainty, an organization should limit its self-insured loss retention to a level at which it is comfortable with the potential uncertainty of the retained loss outcomes.

A self-insured loss retention can apply on a per occurrence/accident basis, an aggregate stop-loss basis, or a combination of the two. With a per occurrence/accident basis, there is a limit on the amount that the self-insured organization will pay for each loss occurrence or accident, regardless of the number of claims (losses) arising from a single occurrence or accident. With aggregate stop-loss, there is a limit on the amount that the self-insured organization will pay in total for all loss occurrences or accidents that take place over a period of time, such as a year.

Financial Accounting Requirements for Self-Insurance

For financial accounting purposes, a self-insured organization must recognize its retained losses as they are incurred rather than paid out, just as an insurance company does. When a loss occurs, reserves for future payments (loss reserves) on losses that have occurred but have not been fully paid must be recorded as a liability on the organization's balance sheet and charged as an expense on its income statement. In addition, paid amounts must be recognized as an expense on the organization's income statement. Therefore, when incurred self-insured losses are higher than expected during a period covered by an organization's income statement, the organization must immediately recognize those higher-than-expected incurred loss amounts on its income statement, substantially lowering its net income.

Loss reserves cannot be deferred or set arbitrarily. Under Generally Accepted Accounting Principles (GAAP), a loss reserve must be established if the following two conditions are met:

- The loss occurred before the date of the financial statements, and
- The amount that will be paid on the loss can be "reasonably determined."[4]

Some losses may have occurred, but no claim for payment has been made. These are known as incurred-but-not-reported (IBNR) losses. A self-insured organization should include reserves for its retained IBNR losses if they can be "reasonably determined." A self-insured organization with a large volume of losses per year usually can "reasonably determine" its retained IBNR loss liability.

The financial accounting rules mentioned above help to prevent a self-insured organization from using self-insured loss reserves as a tool to smooth out its reported profits and losses over time. For example, under GAAP, a self-insured organization cannot post loss reserves as a liability and an expense on its financial statements if the losses have not yet occurred. If it were able to do this, the organization could later use these reserves and prematurely charged expenses to cover itself for a year of higher-than-normal self-insured losses.

Administrative Requirements

As previously mentioned, self-insurance imposes certain administrative requirements on an organization. Claims must be recorded, adjusted, and reserved; litigation must be managed; regulatory filings must be made with the states (depending on the type of loss exposure); and taxes and fees must be paid (depending on the type of loss exposure). These services are normally provided by an insurance company under an insured plan. The self-insured organization's own staff can provide these services, or the organization can hire other organizations for a fee to perform some or all of these services on its behalf. Administrative requirements are discussed in detail later in this chapter.

Tax Deductibility

Chapter 2 mentioned income taxes as a consideration in managing an organization's cost of risk. An important tax issue with regard to risk financing is the timing of deductions of expenses from an organization's taxable income.

Although all risk retention and transfer expenses are tax-deductible, an organization maximizes the present value of its cash flows by taking a tax deduction as soon as possible. In other words, the organization enjoys a cash flow benefit when it takes a tax deduction immediately rather than at a future point in time.

Under a self-insurance plan, an organization is allowed a tax deduction only as losses are paid out rather than as they are incurred. Depending on the type of loss exposure involved, losses might not be paid out until several years after the losses are incurred. Therefore, tax deductions are delayed under a self-insurance plan when compared with the timing of the tax deductions under many other types of risk financing plans. An organization is not allowed to deduct its self-insured loss reserves, which are estimates of loss amounts that have occurred but will not be paid until future years.

This deferral of tax deductions is a disadvantage for self-insurance because with some other plans that involve retention, an organization is allowed a tax deduction for both paid and reserved losses during the year in which the losses are incurred. This disadvantage to self-insurance is more significant for liability losses (long-tail) than for property losses, which tend to be paid soon after a loss occurs.

Measuring the Disadvantage of Taking a Tax Deduction on Losses as Paid Rather Than Incurred

Chapter 2 introduced the concept of present value analysis and illustrated how it can be used to measure the cash flow advantage from paying out losses over several years. In a similar way, present value analysis can be used to measure the

---

Continued on next page.

cash flow disadvantage to taking a tax deduction on self-insured losses as they are paid rather than as they are incurred.

Take the case of a large manufacturer that self-insures its workers compensation exposure. Assume that it has thousands of workers compensation claims each year. When workers are injured on the job (losses are incurred), they do not immediately receive payment for the full amount of their losses. Instead, the self-insured manufacturer pays lost wages and other expenses over a period of time— usually many years. In addition, the self-insured manufacturer usually pays lump sum settlements for loss of limb and other specified injuries many years after an injury occurs. Therefore, workers compensation losses usually are paid out over a long period of time, and the organization self-insuring its losses must estimate future payments by placing reserves on each loss soon after it occurs.

The manufacturer, because it is self-insured, is able to take a tax deduction only as the losses are paid rather than as they are incurred. This is a disadvantage that can be measured using present value analysis.

Assume that the manufacturer incurs $1 million in retained workers compensation losses in Year 1 and that the losses are paid out as shown below over Year 1 through Year 5.

	Year 1	Year 2	Year 3	Year 4	Year 5	Total
Incurred Losses	$1,000,000					$1,000,000
Percentage Paid	25	25	20	15	15	
Amount Paid	$250,000	$250,000	$200,000	$150,000	$150,000	$1,000,000
Loss Reserve	$750,000	$500,000	$300,000	$150,000	$0	

Even though $1 million in losses is incurred in Year 1, only $250,000 is paid to claimants in Year 1. Therefore, the manufacturer establishes a reserve for future loss payments (loss reserve) of $750,000 at the end of Year 1.[5] This reserve is reduced as losses are paid out in Year 2 through Year 5.

Assume that the manufacturer has an after-tax cost of capital of 10 percent yearly. Therefore, it values any after-tax deferred cash outflow benefits at 10 percent yearly because it is able to invest the additional cash back into its business and, therefore, is able to avoid raising additional capital. Further, assume that the manufacturer is in a 30 percent marginal tax bracket.

What is the present value of the disadvantage to the manufacturer of taking a tax deduction as the $1 million in losses is paid in Year 1 through Year 5 rather than taking the tax deduction on the $1 million in incurred losses in Year 1? The present value calculation for each option is shown on the next page. The present value factors are taken from the present value table shown in Chapter 2. (To simplify the analysis, assume that the saving in taxes occurs at the end of each year.)

Tax Deduction for Losses as Incurred

	Year 1
Incurred Losses	$1,000,000
Savings in Taxes (30%)	$ 300,000
Present Value Factor (10%)	.9091
Present Value of the Tax Savings	$ 272,730

Tax Deduction for Losses as Paid

	Year 1	Year 2	Year 3	Year 4	Year 5	Total
Paid Losses	$250,000	$250,000	$200,000	$150,000	$150,000	$1,000,000
Savings in Taxes (30%)	$75,000	$75,000	$60,000	$45,000	$45,000	$300,000
Present Value Factor (10%)	.9091	.8264	.7513	.6830	.6209	
Present Value of the Tax Savings	$68,183	$61,980	$45,078	$30,735	$27,941	$233,917

Note that under each option the manufacturer saves $300,000 in income taxes ($1 million losses × 30 percent marginal tax rate). However, the tax savings occur at different points in time depending on whether the manufacturer is able to deduct its losses as they are incurred or as they are paid.

The calculations show that $272,730 is the present value of the tax savings if the manufacturer takes a tax deduction at the end of Year 1 for the incurred losses. By contrast, they show $233,917 as the present value of the tax savings if the manufacturer takes a tax deduction as it pays losses in Year 1 through Year 5. The difference between the two numbers is the present value disadvantage to the manufacturer of taking a deduction as losses are paid rather than incurred.

$272,730	Present value advantage of deducting losses as incurred
$233,917	Present value advantage of deducting losses as paid
$ 38,813	Present value disadvantage of deducting losses as paid rather than as incurred

Contractual Requirements

Contracts often require one party to purchase insurance for the benefit of another party. Sometimes an organization finds it difficult to use its self-insurance plan for this purpose. For example, if an organization leases a building, it might be required to name the landlord as an additional insured under a general liability insurance policy covering liability arising from the occupancy of the building. The landlord might not accept the tenant's self-insurance plan and, instead, might insist that the tenant purchase a general liability insurance policy for this purpose.

Often, a self-insured organization can persuade those requiring proof of insurance to accept its self-insurance plan. This persuasion is particularly effective if the self-insurance plan has adequate financial security arrangements, such as a trust fund or a bond to secure the payment of any losses.

Weighing the Advantages and Disadvantages

When comparing self-insurance to other risk financing alternatives, an organization should weigh all the advantages and disadvantages of each plan. For example, although self-insurance has disadvantages compared with some other plans in terms of the administration and the timing of tax deductions, it has several advantages in terms of control, cost, and cash flow.

Regulatory Requirements

In order to self-insure workers compensation and/or automobile liability in most U.S. states, an organization must qualify as a self-insurer. It must qualify separately in each state in which it seeks to self-insure its workers compensation and/or automobile liability loss exposures. For an organization that has operations in several states, the process for qualifying as a self-insurer can be complex and time-consuming because each state has its own unique set of requirements.

Often, an organization self-insures its automobile liability and/or workers compensation in some states but not others in which it has operations. This is because the organization might only have a few automobiles or employees in some states, so in those states it is not large enough to qualify as a self-insurer. Additionally, self-insurance is probably not economically feasible for the organization in those states.

The qualification requirements differ by state and specify items such as financial security, filing fees, taxes, assessments, excess insurance, and periodic reports. Exhibit 7-3 illustrates some of those requirements by comparing the workers compensation self-insurance qualifications of South Carolina and Pennsylvania.

Exhibit 7-3
Comparison of Workers Compensation Self-Insurance Qualifications[6]

	South Carolina	Pennsylvania
Security	Determined individually subject to a minimum amount of $250,000. A surety bond or letter of credit is acceptable.	Based on actuarially developed outstanding liability. Surety bond, letter of credit, or government securities held in trust are acceptable.
Filing Fee	$250 per self-insurer plus $100 per subsidiary.	$500 initially, $100 upon renewal.
Taxes, Assessments, and Fees	2.5% of total cost. Also a second-injury fund contribution.	Annual assessments for various funds, including second-injury fund.
Excess Insurance Requirements	Specific excess required—minimum self-insured retention of $250,000.	Specific excess required for organizations with quick assets less than $100 million.
Required Reports	Annual financial statements.	Annual financial statements and report of historical loss experience.
Term	Continuous.	One year.

Administration of a Self-Insurance Plan

A self-insurance plan involves keeping records of claims and adjusting and reserving them. It also involves managing litigation, making regulatory filings, paying taxes and fees, and maintaining excess insurance. These activities can be time-consuming, especially for an organization that is self-insured in several states. The self-insured organization can perform these activities itself or hire another organization to perform these activities on its behalf. Each of these activities is discussed below.

Recordkeeping

A self-insured organization needs a recordkeeping system to keep track of its self-insured claims. The information contained in this system should be similar to that contained in a loss report from an insurance company. It should include claims identified by number and type, as well as the amount paid and reserved for each claim. Also, information on the causes of each loss should be included because it is helpful for implementing a risk control program.

Claim Adjustment

A self-insurer must devote considerable resources to claim adjustment. As with an insured plan, claims must be investigated, evaluated, negotiated, and paid. Also, subrogation opportunities must be pursued. Handling claims properly takes specialized knowledge and skills.

Third-Party Administrators

Some self-insured businesses create an in-house department to handle claims. Others hire a **third-party administrator**, which is an outside organization that handles claims on the organization's behalf. Third-party administrators usually settle claims, keep claim records, and perform statistical analysis. When a third party is hired to handle claims, the arrangement is sometimes referred to as an administrative services only (ASO) plan.

Claims must be investigated and evaluated to determine facts about damages and liability. Depending on the type of claim, a claim adjuster must determine which property is damaged, who was liable for the loss, and how much money should be paid.

During his or her investigation and evaluation of a claim, a claim adjuster must obtain information, verify the information, and compare the information with that available from other sources. For example, a claim adjuster might do any of the following:

- Investigate an accident scene to obtain information
- Verify a claimant's statement of his or her salary amount by checking with the claimant's employer
- Compare a claimant's statement of the circumstances surrounding an accident with a police report

When new information contradicts previously known information, a claim adjuster reexamines all of the information and investigates further to resolve the conflict or to determine which information is the most credible.

To determine the value of a loss, a claim adjuster usually consults numerous sources of information, such as valuation guides and facts regarding previous claims with similar characteristics. The claim adjuster must have a thorough grasp of all the facts and be an expert in communication in order to negotiate the settlement of a claim.

Loss Reserving

Self-insured organizations must reserve for estimated future payments on self-insured losses that have occurred. This includes both reported and incurred-but-not-reported (IBNR) losses. Claim adjusters and actuaries usually provide loss reserving services for organizations.

Claim adjusters play a vital role in establishing a self-insurer's loss reserves. After the claim adjuster receives a notice of a claim, obtains initial information, and verifies that the self-insurance plan covers the loss, he or she establishes a reserve for the loss.

Loss reserving is fairly straightforward for most property claims in which the adjuster can readily establish that damage has occurred and can estimate its amount. On the other hand, reserves for future payments on complex claims, especially liability claims, are often very difficult for an adjuster to estimate.

Reserving an Automobile Liability Loss

Assume that one of a self-insured organization's trucks is involved in a serious accident with a pedestrian, who is hospitalized with severe injuries. The cause of the accident is not immediately clear because of conflicting testimony of witnesses, and it is difficult to determine whether the self-insured organization is wholly or partly liable for the accident. How should the self-insured's claim adjuster establish the loss reserve? The amount eventually paid for the loss could range from almost nothing (if the self-insured organization is not found to be legally responsible) to hundreds of thousands of dollars (if the self-insured organization is found to be responsible and if the injured victim dies or is permanently disabled). It is extremely difficult to establish accurate reserves for some types of losses.

Self-insurers often employ actuaries to calculate overall or aggregate loss reserves for a particular period. Using the individual claim reserves set by adjusters, actuaries smooth out the estimates and add amounts for incurred-but-not-reported losses. However, the estimates of overall loss reserves produced by actuaries can only be accurate if the underlying reserves on individual claims set by the claim adjusters are reasonably accurate.

An organization's self-insured loss reserves should be as accurate as possible for each financial period. If an organization discovers that it has under-reserved losses that occurred in the past, it must immediately increase those reserves, which reduces the current period's net income on its income statement. An organization that chronically under-reserves its self-insured losses can suddenly discover that it must charge a huge expense for additional loss reserves on its income statement. The opposite is true for an organization that is over-reserved, with an immediate reduction in self-insured loss reserves increasing its net income. Because it is difficult to reserve for self-insured losses (or any other retained losses) accurately, organizations frequently must adjust their net income to account for changes in reserves for losses that occurred in the past.

> **Risk Management in Practice**
>
> **Effect of Reserve Changes for Retained Losses on Net Income**
> The following report of an organization's financial results shows the effect that over-reserving can have on its net income.
>
> > Roy F. Weston Inc., an infrastructure redevelopment services firm, today reported results for the second quarter ended June 30, 1999. Net revenues for the quarter were $36.1 million compared to $34.9 million for the second quarter of 1998. Net income for the quarter was $91,000, or $.01 per share, compared to $152,000, or $.02 per share, for the second quarter of 1998. These results include an after-tax gain of $300,000 from reduction of the company's reserve for insurance claims.[7]

Loss reserving takes a great deal of careful thought. Reserving for an individual claim is not a one-time activity; the loss reserve must be constantly evaluated and reevaluated as new information becomes available.

Litigation Management

A self-insurer should practice **litigation management**, which involves controlling the cost of legal expenses for claims that are litigated. Litigation management involves evaluating and selecting defense lawyers, supervising them during litigation, and keeping records of their costs. It also involves specific techniques such as auditing legal bills and experimenting with alternative fee-billing strategies.

> **Litigation management** involves controlling the cost of legal expenses for claims that are litigated. It includes tasks such as evaluating and selecting defense lawyers, auditing legal bills, and experimenting with alternative fee-billing strategies.

Another important aspect of litigation management involves the cost-effective resolution of disputes. A self-insured organization should set guidelines for the conditions under which it settles rather than fights a claim so as to avoid continuing litigation. It should also set guidelines for the use of alternative dispute resolution (ADR) techniques, such as mediation and arbitration.

Insurance companies, third-party administrators, and large self-insured organizations often employ litigation managers. These professionals are technical specialists who oversee the litigation management process.

Regulatory Filings

A self-insured organization must make periodic filings with each U.S. state. Because requirements vary by state, these filings can be time-consuming, particularly for an organization that is self-insured in several states.

For example, an organization that self-insures its automobile liability in Hawaii must annually file an application and related documents. The related documents include a tax clearance certificate and a schedule of vehicles, among others.[8] As another example, an organization that self-insures its workers compensation in Tennessee must file the following reports:

- Annual payroll
- Statement of loss reserves
- Renewal application
- Annual report
- Tennessee experience modifier
- Names and address of third-party administrators[9]

In addition to these filings, organizations must pay taxes and fees to each state in which they self-insure. These taxes and fees vary in amount by state.

Excess Insurance

Many states require a self-insurer to purchase excess insurance. Some states specify the conditions under which a self-insurer must purchase excess insurance. In other states, the state agency responsible for self-insurance reviews each applicant and decides whether or not to require excess insurance.

Excess Insurance and Self-Insurance Plans

Specific excess insurance and aggregate excess insurance are commonly used in connection with self-insurance plans. (These two types of policies were previously discussed in Chapter 5.)

A specific excess policy requires the insured organization to self-insure (retain) a stipulated amount of loss from the first dollar *for all losses resulting from a single accident/occurrence.* The excess insurer pays losses above the self-insured retention, subject to the policy limit. For example, if the policy required a self-insured retention of $100,000 per occurrence, the self-insurer would pay the first $100,000 of each loss occurrence, and the excess insurer would pay amounts in excess of $100,000 per occurrence up to the policy limit.

An aggregate excess policy (also called a stop-loss excess policy) requires the insured organization to self-insure a total amount of loss (regardless of the number of accidents or occurrences) *during a specified period of time,* usually one year. The excess insurer then pays, up to the policy limit, all loss for that period that exceeds the self-insured retention, which is an aggregate amount for the period.

Note the similarities between specific/aggregate excess insurance and the transferred losses under a retrospective rating plan as shown in Exhibit 3-4.

If excess insurance is required, specifications must be put together and bids obtained from various insurance companies. Also, the excess insurance program must be reviewed periodically.

Group Self-Insurance

Many states allow organizations to band together to self-insure their workers compensation exposures as a group. A **group self-insurance plan** operates in a manner similar to that of a pool (pools were introduced in Chapter 3). However, a group self-insurance plan differs in that it applies only to workers compensation in a single state.

> A **group self-insurance plan** is one in which organizations band together to self-insure their workers compensation exposures as a group. It applies to a single state, and it is similar in operation to a pool.

A group self-insurance plan operates like an insurance company by pooling the loss exposures of its members. The administrator of the group self-insurance plan issues member agreements, collects premiums, and manages claims. It also purchases excess insurance (or excess of loss reinsurance) and makes various regulatory filings with the state.

Group self-insurance can benefit an organization that is too small to self-insure its loss exposures on its own. Savings are achieved through economies of scale in administration, claim handling, and the purchase of excess insurance (or reinsurance).

Relationship of Self-Insurance to an Organization's Risk Financing Objectives

When designing a risk financing program, an organization should consider self-insurance along with other alternatives for retaining low-to-medium-severity losses. These other alternatives include hybrid plans, such as large deductible plans; retrospective rating plans; and captive insurer plans. An organization that decides to self-insure should design the self-insurance plan so that it helps the organization meet its risk financing objectives.

Exhibit 7-4 discusses self-insurance in relation to each of the risk financing objectives introduced in Chapter 2. A properly designed and managed self-insurance plan can help an organization to meet its risk financing objectives.

Exhibit 7-4
Self-Insurance and Risk Financing Objectives

Risk Financing Objective	Relationship to Self-Insurance
Paying for Losses	Self-insurance can help meet this objective if an organization carefully chooses the loss retention level, purchases appropriate excess insurance, and has sufficient cash flow or liquid assets.
Maintaining Liquidity	Self-insurance can help meet this objective if an organization carefully chooses the loss retention level, purchases appropriate excess insurance, and accurately forecasts paid amounts for retained losses.
Managing Uncertainty of Loss Outcomes	With self-insurance, retained loss outcomes are uncertain. The higher the retention, the higher the degree of uncertainty of retained loss outcomes. Therefore, self-insurance can help meet this objective if an organization carefully chooses the loss retention level and purchases appropriate excess insurance.
Managing the Cost of Risk	Self-insurance can reduce an organization's cost of risk over the long run. A self-insured organization must administer its own claims (either with its own staff or a contractor) but can save insurance company operating expenses, profits, and risk charges.
Complying With Legal Requirements	A self-insurer must meet certain legal requirements because, in most U.S. states, an organization must qualify as a self-insurer for workers compensation and automobile liability.

Summary

- Self-insurance is a loss retention plan for which an organization keeps records of its losses and maintains a formal system to pay for them.
- Self-insurance is best practiced by organizations that have tolerance for retaining risk and a willingness to devote capital and resources to financ-

ing and administering a self-insurance program. It is best applied to low-severity losses, although some organizations also self-insure medium-severity losses.

- Because self-insurance involves certain overhead costs and other expenses as well as the assumption of risk of loss, an organization should be financially strong and have a sufficient amount of loss exposure for self-insurance to be economically feasible.

- A self-insurance plan is usually combined with a transfer or a hybrid plan that covers high-severity losses.

- For financial accounting purposes, a self-insured organization must recognize its retained losses as they are incurred, just as an insurance company does. However, for tax purposes, a self-insured organization can only deduct its retained losses as they are paid rather than as they are incurred.

- A self-insurance plan has many advantages and disadvantages that are similar to those that apply to all retention plans. However, some are unique to self-insurance, such as the substantial amount of control that the self-insured has over its claims and the complex administration required.

- In order to self-insure workers compensation and/or automobile liability in most U.S. states, an organization must qualify as a self-insurer. This can be complex and time-consuming because each state has its own unique set of requirements.

- The administration of a self-insurance plan involves activities such as recordkeeping, claim adjustment, loss reserving, litigation management, regulatory filings, and the purchase of excess insurance.

- Under a group self-insurance plan, organizations band together to self-insure their workers compensation exposures as a group. A group self-insurance plan is similar to a pool; however, group self-insurance differs in that it applies only to workers compensation in a single state.

- A properly designed and managed self-insurance plan can help an organization to meet its risk financing objectives.

Chapter Notes

1. International Risk Management Institute, *Risk Financing: A Guide to Insurance Cash Flow* (Dallas: International Risk Management Institute, Inc., 2000), p. IV.E.3, 3d Reprint, September 1997.
2. In order to receive Medicare reimbursement for their professional liability loss costs, self-insured hospitals must establish a trust fund for paying losses and abide by other requirements, such as maintaining a viable claim administration program.

3. Incurred losses = Paid losses + Loss reserves

4. *Financial Accounting Standards Board Statement #5.*

5. This example assumes that the manufacturer is able to accurately determine its reserves for incurred losses at the end of Year 1.

6. For a complete listing of self-insurance qualifications, see the following: International Risk Management Institute, *Risk Financing: A Guide to Insurance Cash Flow,* vol. II (Dallas: International Risk Management Institute, Inc., 2000), p. C.39, C.41, 5th Reprint, January 2000.

7. "Weston Inc. Reports Gains for Quarter," *Daily Local News,* July 30, 1999, p. C1.

8. International Risk Management Institute, *Risk Financing: A Guide to Insurance Cash Flow,* vol. II (Dallas: International Risk Management Institute, Inc., 2000), p. D.12, 6th Reprint, January 2000.

9. International Risk Management Institute, *Risk Financing: A Guide to Insurance Cash Flow,* vol. II (Dallas: International Risk Management Institute, Inc., 2000), p. C.43, 4th Reprint, January 2000.

References

Harrington, Scott E., and Gregory R. Niehaus. *Risk Management and Insurance.* Burr Ridge, IL: Irwin/McGraw-Hill, 1999.

International Risk Management Institute, *Risk Financing: A Guide to Insurance Cash Flow.* Dallas: International Risk Management Institute, Inc., 2000.

Williams, Arthur C., Jr., Michael L. Smith, and Peter C. Young. *Risk Management and Insurance,* 8th ed. Burr Ridge, IL: Irwin/McGraw-Hill, 1998.

Chapter 8

Retrospectively Rated Insurance Plans

Introduction

Chapter 3 introduced retrospectively rated insurance plans (also called retro-spective rating plans), which are hybrid plans containing elements of both retention and transfer. Retrospective rating plans are used by insureds to finance low-to-medium-severity losses and are usually combined with another risk financing plan, such as a transfer plan, which covers high-severity losses. An organization needs a substantial premium, usually amounting to several hundred thousand dollars per year, to benefit from a retrospective rating plan.

On the surface, a retrospective rating plan appears to be the same as a guaranteed cost insurance plan. With a retrospective rating plan, an insurance company issues an insurance policy and agrees to pay covered losses up to a policy limit. However, a retrospective rating plan differs significantly from a guaranteed cost insurance plan because a retrospective rating plan takes a cost-plus approach to calculating a major portion of the premium, which is why it is categorized as a hybrid rather than as a pure transfer plan. A later section of this chapter covers premium calculations for retrospective rating plans in detail.

Characteristics of Retrospective Rating Plans

Retrospective rating plans operate differently than do other risk financing plans that cover low-to-medium-severity losses, such as self-insurance plans, large deductible plans, and captive insurer plans. Most significantly, retrospective rating plans differ in the way that losses are funded and paid.

Losses and Coverages

In general, organizations use retrospective rating plans to finance their low-to-medium-severity losses.[1] These types of losses usually have a high frequency and therefore are somewhat predictable in total. Exhibit 8-1 shows the characteristics of losses usually covered by retrospective rating plans.

Exhibit 8-1
Characteristics of Losses Usually Covered by a Retrospective Rating Plan

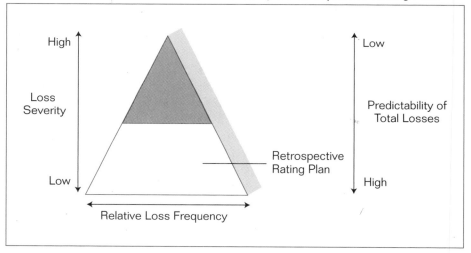

Organizations commonly use retrospective rating plans for losses arising from their liability loss exposures that are covered by workers compensation (including employers liability), automobile liability, and general liability policies. Organizations also use them to finance losses arising from automobile physical damage, crime, and glass exposures. A single retrospective rating plan can be used for more than one type of exposure. For example, workers compensation, automobile liability, and general liability are commonly combined under a single plan.

Premium

As with any insurance plan, the insured organization under a retrospective rating plan pays a premium to the insurance company, which reimburses claimants for losses and pays other expenses such as premium taxes, residual market loadings, loss adjustment costs, and legal defense fees. The premium also includes an amount to cover the insurer's overhead and profit.

With a guaranteed cost insurance plan, the premium rate is fixed for the policy period and does not vary with the insured's losses that occur during the policy period. Therefore, a guaranteed cost plan is a transfer plan.

With a retrospective rating plan, a deposit premium is paid at the beginning of the policy period, and the premium rate is adjusted after the end of the policy period to include a portion of the insured's covered losses that occur during the policy period. Because the premium is adjusted upward or downward based directly on a portion of covered losses, the insured is, in effect, retaining a portion of its own losses. Therefore, a retrospective rating plan is categorized as a hybrid plan.

loss limit

The portion of each covered loss that is included in the premium is subject to a limit, or maximum amount, called a *loss limit*. The loss limit can vary and is negotiated between the insurer and the insured. For example, the loss limit under a retrospective rating plan might be $100,000 per occurrence. In that case, the first $100,000 of each covered loss occurrence is included in the premium and used to adjust the deposit premium upward or downward, and the amount of each loss occurrence that exceeds $100,000 up to the policy limit is transferred to the insurer.

> A *loss limit* is a maximum amount of each loss (from ground-up) that is used to adjust the retrospective premium.

For a specific retrospective rating plan, the higher the loss limit in relation to the policy limit, the greater the degree of retention as opposed to transfer under the plan. For example, a retrospective rating plan with a loss limit of $250,000 per occurrence and a policy limit of $1 million per occurrence has a higher degree of retention than if the loss limit were $50,000 per occurrence.

The adjusted premium under a retrospective rating plan is subject to a maximum amount, called the **maximum premium**. By agreeing to limit the amount by which the premium can be adjusted upward based on covered losses, the insurer takes the risk that the total losses under the loss limit (retained losses) will exceed a maximum amount. The adjusted premium

> A **maximum premium** is a maximum amount that the retrospective rating plan premium will not exceed.

Maximum amt

also is often subject to a minimum amount, called a **minimum premium.**

> A **minimum premium** is a minimum amount that the retrospective rating plan premium will not fall below.

Exhibit 8-2 shows the relationship between retained and transferred losses under a retrospective rating plan.

Exhibit 8-2
Retained and Transferred Losses Under a Retrospective Rating Plan

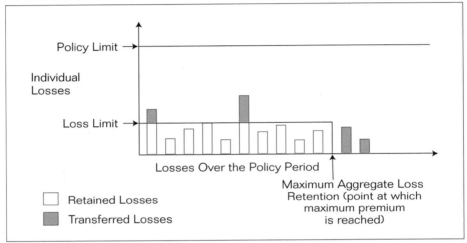

The premium under a retrospective rating plan includes costs other than retained losses, such as insurance company overhead and profits, residual market loadings, service bureau charges, and premium taxes. The retrospective rating plan premium also includes a guaranteed cost (risk transfer) premium that compensates the insurer for accepting the risk that the following might occur:

- An individual loss will fall between the loss limit and the policy limit (this component is called an excess loss premium), and

- Total losses under the loss limit for the policy period will exceed the aggregate amount that causes the retrospective premium to reach the maximum premium (this component is called an insurance charge).

To summarize, the purpose of the risk transfer (guaranteed cost) portion of a retrospective rating plan premium is to compensate the insurer for limiting the amount of an insured's covered losses that is included in the retrospective premium adjustments. The risk transfer premium is split into the two components mentioned above, an *excess loss premium* for limiting individual losses and an *insurance charge* for limiting total losses. These premium components are further discussed later in this chapter.

Exhibit 8-3 shows the relationship between losses and premium for a typical retrospective rating plan. Note that the premium is limited by both the maximum and minimum premiums.

Exhibit 8-3
Relationship Between Losses and Premium for a Retrospective Rating Plan

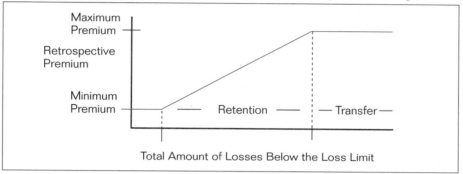

To summarize, a retrospective rating premium includes a portion of the insured's covered losses during the policy period and is subject to maximum and minimum amounts. Therefore, an insured is, in effect, retaining a portion of its losses. If an insured incurs higher-than-average losses during a policy period, the final adjusted premium under a retrospective rating plan is higher than the premium that the insured would pay under a guaranteed cost insurance plan to cover the same losses. The opposite is true if losses are lower than average. The portion of losses not retained is transferred to the insurer, which is compensated through risk transfer premium charges (the excess loss premium and the insurance charge) that are built into the retrospective plan premium. The retrospective plan premium also includes charges for other expenses such as residual market loadings, service bureau charges, premium taxes, and insurance company overhead and profits. A later section of this chapter discusses the premium formula for a retrospective rating plan in more detail.

Major Types of Retrospective Rating Plans

The two major types of retrospective rating plans are paid loss retrospective rating plans and incurred loss retrospective rating plans. They differ in terms of whether or not the insured must pay premium to the insurer to account for retained loss reserves, and, therefore, they differ in terms of the degree of cash flow benefit provided to the insured.

With a *paid loss retrospective rating plan*, the insured pays a relatively small deposit premium during the policy period to cover the insurer's estimated expenses, such as the risk transfer premium charges, premium taxes, residual market loadings, and insurer overhead and profits. In addition, the insured reimburses the insurer for retained losses as the insurer pays for them. For most liability losses, payment usually takes place over a period of several years after the losses occur. Therefore, the insured organization benefits from the cash flow available on the reserves for retained losses. The insured organization must provide the insurer with security, such as a letter of credit, to guarantee future payments on retained losses that have occurred.

> A *paid loss retrospective rating plan* is a retrospective rating plan whereby the insured pays a small deposit premium at the beginning of the policy period and reimburses the insurer for its losses as the insurer pays for them. The total amount paid is subject to minimum and maximum amounts.

Exhibit 8-4 shows the relationship between losses and premium payments for a paid loss retrospective rating plan. Note that the cumulative paid premium tracks the cumulative paid losses rather than the cumulative incurred losses, providing a sizeable cash flow benefit to the insured because premium is not fully paid until several years after the policy period. Just as with any retrospective rating plan, the paid loss amounts are subject to a loss limit and a maximum premium, so a paid loss retrospective rating plan has an element of risk transfer.

Exhibit 8-4
Relationship Between Losses and Premium Payments
for a Paid Loss Retrospective Rating Plan

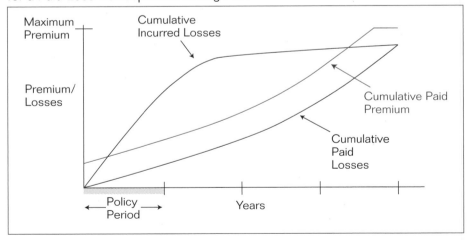

With an *incurred loss retrospective rating plan*, the insured pays a larger deposit premium than that under a paid loss retrospective rating plan. The deposit is based on projected average *incurred* losses (paid plus reserved amounts) for the

> With an *incurred loss retrospective rating plan*, the insured pays a deposit premium during the policy period. After the end of the policy period, the insurer adjusts the premium based on the insured's actual incurred losses.

policy period plus the insurer's estimated expenses. Shortly after the end of the policy period, the insurer adjusts the deposit premium using a formula that is based on the retained portion of the insured's actual incurred losses during the policy period. At that time, depending on the level of the retained incurred losses, the insured pays an additional premium or receives a return premium. Subsequent adjustments, usually on an annual basis, continue based on subsequent valuations of incurred losses from the original policy period until all losses are paid. Because it pays premium as losses are incurred rather than as they are paid, the insured does not receive the cash flow available on its loss reserves.

Exhibit 8-5, which is comparable in format to Exhibit 8-4, shows the relationship between losses and premium payments for an incurred loss retrospective rating plan. Note that the premium payments track the incurred losses rather than the paid losses, providing less cash flow benefit to the insured than with a paid loss retrospective rating plan.

Exhibit 8-5
Relationship Between Losses and Premium Payments
for an Incurred Loss Retrospective Rating Plan

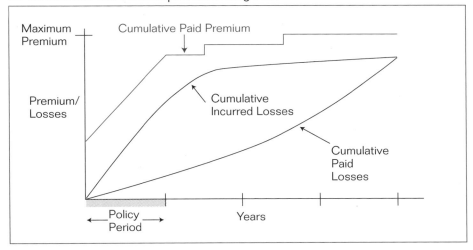

Funded Versus Unfunded Plans

Depending on the type of retrospective rating plan, the retained portion of losses is either funded or unfunded. A paid loss retrospective rating plan is an unfunded plan because the insured must periodically raise cash to reimburse the insurer for retained losses as the insurer pays for them. An incurred loss retrospective rating plan is a funded plan because the premium is paid based on incurred rather than paid losses. The insurer receives premium not only for the paid amount of retained losses but also for the reserved amount as well and is able to use this amount to pay losses as they come due.

With all retention plans and some hybrid plans, cash and other liquid assets made available to pay for retained losses are shown as an asset, and reserves for retained losses are shown as a liability on the balance sheet of the organization retaining the losses. This is not the case with an incurred loss retrospective rating plan. The insurer rather than the insured organization holds the assets that fund the loss reserves. The insurer must show the assets and the loss reserves (a liability) on its balance sheet, whereas the insured does not do so because it has paid a premium (and previously taken it as an expense) to fund the loss reserves. Therefore, from the insured organization's point of view, an incurred loss retrospective rating plan is an "off-balance sheet" funding plan for the portion of losses that it retains.

With a paid loss retrospective rating plan, the insured must calculate what the premium would be at any point in time if incurred rather than paid losses were used to calculate it. The difference between that premium and the amount paid by the insured organization should be recognized as a liability on its balance sheet. This and other financial accounting issues for retrospective rating plans are further discussed later in this chapter.

Administration

Retrospective rating plans require a moderate amount of administration by the insured organization. The insurer rather than the insured is responsible for many of the administrative tasks, such as adjusting claims, making necessary filings with the states, and paying applicable premium taxes and residual market loadings. The insured's responsibility is limited to making premium payments and arranging for any required security, such as a letter of credit to guarantee future loss payments under a paid loss retrospective rating plan.

Because a portion of the premium includes the insured's covered losses, the insured organization periodically should audit the insurance company's claim handling, loss payment, and loss reserving practices. Often, a broker or a risk management consultant performs this audit function on the insured's behalf.

Comparison to Other Risk Financing Plans

An organization should compare the cost of a retrospective rating plan with other risk financing plans that are suited to low-to-medium-severity losses, such as self-insurance plans, large deductible plans, and captive insurer plans. The retained portion of losses under a retrospective rating plan is directly comparable to the losses under a self-insurance plan or the retained portion of losses under a large deductible plan or a captive insurer plan. Expenses and cash flow benefits under the different risk financing plans vary and should be carefully analyzed.

Summary of Characteristics

Exhibit 8-6 summarizes the general characteristics of retrospective rating plans.

Exhibit 8-6
General Characteristics of Retrospective Rating Plans

Retention/ Transfer	Severity of Losses	Administrative Funded/Unfunded	Requirements
Hybrid	Low to Medium	Either, depending on the type of plan	Moderate

Combining Retrospective Rating Plans With Other Risk Financing Plans

To put together a risk financing program, an organization usually combines a retrospective rating plan with a hybrid or a transfer plan. The retrospective rating plan is generally used for the first layer of loss where there is a relatively high frequency of loss and low-to-moderate severity of loss, with a hybrid or a transfer plan sitting directly above the retrospective rating plan covering the higher-severity losses.

For example, assume that an organization purchases a retrospective rating plan to cover its general liability and automobile liability loss exposures, with a policy limit of $1 million per accident/occurrence and a loss limit of $250,000 per accident/occurrence. Excess insurance (transfer) or a finite/integrated risk plan (hybrid) might sit directly above the $1 million per accident/occurrence layer of loss covered by the retrospective rating plan.

Exhibit 8-7 shows how the organization might combine excess insurance (Case 1) or combine excess insurance and finite/integrated risk insurance (Case 2) with the retrospective rating plan described in the above paragraph.

Under Case 1, the organization purchases excess insurance on a guaranteed cost basis with a limit of $25 million per accident/occurrence to sit directly above the retrospective rating plan. Therefore, the total limit of insurance available is $26 million per accident/occurrence.

Under Case 2, the organization purchases a finite/integrated risk plan with a limit of $20 million per accident/occurrence to sit directly above the retrospective rating plan and excess insurance with a limit of $5 million per accident/ occurrence to sit directly above the finite/integrated risk plan. Therefore, the organization still has a total limit available of $26 million per accident/occurrence.

Exhibit 8-7

Retrospective Rating Plan Combined With Excess Insurance
and a Finite/Integrated Risk Plan

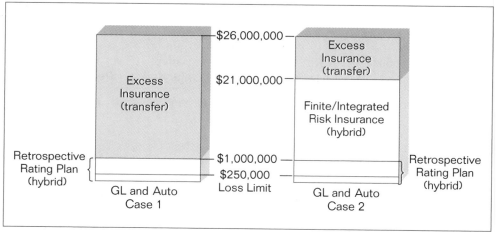

Under both Case 1 and Case 2, the organization retains the first $250,000 per accident/occurrence because the retrospective rating plan premium is calculated based on a loss limit of $250,000 per accident/occurrence. The portion of each covered loss that exceeds $250,000 up to the retrospective plan policy limits of $1 million per accident/occurrence is transferred to the insurer, with a risk transfer insurance premium built into the retrospective rating plan premium to cover the risk that losses will fall into this layer. The risk transfer insurance premium also is meant to compensate the insurer for the risk that the retrospectively rated premium might exceed the maximum premium.

Losses in the $25 million per accident/occurrence layer in excess of $1 million per accident/occurrence are also transferred to an insurer. However, in Case 2, the organization funds a portion of its own losses through a finite/integrated risk plan.

Advantages and Disadvantages of Retrospective Rating Plans

Because they are hybrid risk financing plans, retrospective rating plans have many of the advantages and disadvantages of both retention and transfer. The degree to which these advantages and disadvantages apply to a specific retrospective rating plan depends on the design of that plan—that is, the degree of retention versus the degree of transfer built into the plan.

Advantages

A major advantage of retention is that its long-run cost tends to be lower than the cost of transfer. By retaining a portion of losses under a retrospective rating plan rather than transferring all losses under a guaranteed cost plan, an organization is able to save certain expenses. One significant expense saved is insurance company risk charges, which are extra charges that an insurer includes as part of its guaranteed cost premium to cover the chance that losses will be higher than expected. In addition, savings result from the cash flow gained by retaining losses under a paid loss retrospective rating plan.

A second major advantage of retrospective rating plans is that they encourage risk control. With a retrospective rating plan, an organization that is able to reduce its losses will quickly realize a premium savings compared with what it would pay under a guaranteed cost plan. This direct link between losses and premium is a major incentive for an insured to control its losses.

If designed properly, a retrospective rating plan also provides many of the advantages of transfer. If the loss limit and the maximum premium are set so as to reduce the uncertainty of the insured's retrospective premium adjustments to a level that it can tolerate, then the insured benefits from the relative stability that the retrospective rating plan provides for its earnings, net worth, and cash flow. For a retrospective rating plan covering more than one type of loss exposure, the insured also benefits from the stability provided through diversification by retaining losses from different types of loss exposures under a single plan.

Disadvantages

If a retrospective rating plan is not properly designed, it can make financial planning difficult for the insured. For example, if the loss limit and maximum premium are set at a high level, the insured might not be able to tolerate the uncertainty created by the possibility of upward premium adjustments that reduce its earnings, net worth, and cash flow.

Another disadvantage to retrospective rating plans is that the insurance company might set unrealistically high reserves for the retained portion of losses. Therefore, under an incurred loss retrospective rating plan, the insured would pay a premium based on inflated loss reserve figures, resulting in a loss of cash flow. Under this scenario, the premium would eventually be adjusted downward as losses are paid because the inflated loss reserves would be eliminated. In the meantime, however, the insurer would have use of the insured's money.

Some people contend that an insurance company might not diligently adjust claims when it knows the insured is retaining them, resulting in loss payments that are higher than necessary. These people state that this might be the case for the retained portion of losses under a retrospective rating plan. However, insurance companies contend that they adjust claims in the same manner regardless of the type of plan involved and that the loss adjuster for a specific claim typically has no knowledge of the type of plan involved.

Another disadvantage of retrospective rating plans is that the losses that are ultimately retained are nevertheless paid for as "premium," which attracts premium taxes and residual market loadings. As explained in Chapter 3, these costs can be avoided for the retained portion of losses under a large deductible insurance plan.

Calculating the Retrospective Rating Plan Premium

As previously discussed, a retrospective rating plan premium is adjusted based on a portion of the insured's covered losses. The retrospective rating plan premium can be expressed as a mathematical formula, called the retrospective premium formula.

Retrospective Premium Formula

The formula for calculating premium, or the **retrospective premium formula**, is as follows:

$$\text{Retrospective rating plan premium} = \left(\begin{array}{c} \text{Basic premium} + \\ \text{Converted losses} + \\ \text{Excess loss premium} \end{array} \right) \times \text{Tax multiplier}$$

Subject to maximum and minimum amounts

In order to understand the retrospective premium formula, one should analyze each of the components separately.

Standard Premium

Before analyzing the elements of a retrospectively rated premium, one should understand what a standard premium is and how it is calculated. A **standard premium** is calculated by using state rating classifica-

A **standard premium** is calculated by using state rating classifications and rates and applying them to an insured's exposures, allowing for various adjustments.

tions and rates and applying them to an insured's estimated exposures for the policy period, allowing for various adjustments. For a guaranteed cost plan, a discount to the standard premium is available based on the insured's size. Therefore, in general, the standard premium minus the discount is the amount that an insured would pay to transfer all of its losses under a guaranteed cost insurance plan. Some of the components of the retrospective premium formula are based on an insured's standard premium, without an allowance for the discount.

At the beginning of the policy period, the standard premium is estimated based on an insured's estimated exposures for the period. The standard premium is adjusted after the end of the policy period based on the insured's actual exposures for the period. Therefore, if an insured's exposures, such as sales, turn out to be higher than initially estimated at the beginning of the policy period, its standard premium is adjusted upward.

Basic Premium

The **basic premium** is the first component of the retrospective premium formula. It covers the insurer's acquisition expenses, administrative costs, profit, overhead, and other costs for the retrospective rating program.

An important element of the basic premium is the **insurance charge** (mentioned previously), which provides the insurer with a risk transfer premium to compensate it for taking the risk that the insured's retained losses might be high enough for the maximum premium to be exceeded. There is also a chance that losses will be so low that the calculated retrospective premium falls below the minimum premium, in which case the insurer benefits because the insured must still pay the minimum premium. The insurer provides a credit to the insurance charge to account for this possibility and, therefore, the overall insurance charge is actually a net charge.

A **basic premium** is a component of the retrospective premium formula that covers insurer acquisition expenses, administrative costs, overhead, and profit. It also includes the insurance charge. The basic premium is expressed as a percentage of the standard premium.

An **insurance charge** is included in the basic premium to provide the insurer with premium to compensate it for the risk that the calculated retrospective premium might be higher than the maximum premium or lower than the minimum premium. The insurance charge is a net charge because it accounts for the possibility that the insurer will benefit if the calculated retrospective premium is lower than the minimum premium.

The basic premium is expressed as a percentage of the insured's standard premium. Therefore, when the standard premium is adjusted after the end of the policy period based on actual exposures, the dollar amount of the basic premium automatically adjusts as well.

Converted Losses

Converted losses, which are the second component of the retrospective premium formula, are incurred losses with a factor applied to them to account for the unallocated portion of loss adjustment expenses. The "losses" included in converted losses are the retained losses under the retrospective rating plan, that is, the losses limited at the loss limit and a maximum amount. The losses include allocated loss adjustment expenses but not unallocated loss adjustment expenses. These expenses are explained below.

> **Converted losses** are a component of the retrospective premium formula that consists of retained incurred losses times the applicable loss conversion factor.

Allocated and Unallocated Loss Adjustment Expenses

Loss adjustment expenses are divided into allocated and unallocated amounts. **Allocated loss adjustment expenses** relate directly to the individual loss being adjusted and include items such as legal defense costs, litigation management expenses, court fees, and premiums for bonds. **Unallocated loss adjustment expenses** are expenses that cannot be attributed to individual losses, such as insurer claim staff salaries and office rent.

In order to understand the meaning of converted losses, one must also understand the meaning of a loss conversion factor. A **loss conversion factor** is a factor that is applied to incurred losses to account for the unallocated portion of loss adjustment expenses.

> A **loss conversion factor** is applied to incurred losses to account for the unallocated portion of loss adjustment expenses.

Converted losses are calculated by applying a loss conversion factor to retained losses. Converted losses are represented by the following formula:

Converted Losses = Loss conversion factor × Retained losses

For example, a loss conversion factor for general liability losses might be 1.12, and the incurred amount of general liability losses (including allocated loss adjustment expenses) that is retained might be $300,000. In this case, the converted losses are $336,000 ($300,000 × 1.12).

Excess Loss Premium

The **excess loss premium** (mentioned previously), which is the third component of the retrospective premium formula, is a risk transfer premium that compensates the insurer for taking the risk that a covered loss

> **Excess loss premium** is a component of the retrospective premium formula that compensates the insurer for the risk that an individual loss will exceed the loss limit.

will exceed the loss limit. For example, assume that the loss limit is $250,000 per accident/occurrence and that the policy limit is $1 million per accident/occurrence. The excess loss premium compensates the insurer for the risk that losses will fall in the layer between $250,000 and $1 million per accident/occurrence.

The excess loss premium is expressed as a percentage of the standard premium. For example, if the standard premium is $600,000, and the excess loss premium is 15 percent, the excess loss premium is $90,000 ($600,000 × 15 percent). When the standard premium is adjusted after the end of the policy period based on actual exposures, the dollar amount of the excess loss premium automatically adjusts as well.

The excess loss premium amount varies with the loss limit. In the example above, the excess loss premium percentage would be higher if the loss limit were $100,000 per accident/occurrence rather than $250,000 per accident/occurrence because the insurer's risk of loss would be greater.

Tax Multiplier

The **tax multiplier** is a component of the retrospective premium formula that adds an amount for state premium taxes, license fees, service bureau charges, and residual market loadings that the insurer must pay. The tax multiplier is expressed as a factor that, when multiplied by the other premium components, adds a specified percentage to them. For example, if the amount to be added is 4 percent, the tax multiplier is 1.04.

> The **tax multiplier** is a component of the retrospective premium formula that adds an amount for state premium taxes, license fees, service bureau charges, and residual market loadings. It is expressed as a factor applied to the other components of the retrospective premium formula.

Maximum and Minimum Premiums

Maximum and minimum premiums are expressed as a percentage of the standard premium. For example, if the maximum premium is 150 percent and the standard premium is $900,000, the maximum premium is $1,350,000 ($900,000 × 150 percent). In this case, a minimum premium of 50 percent would equal $450,000. When the standard premium is adjusted after the end of the policy period based on actual exposures, the dollar amounts of the maximum and minimum premiums automatically adjust as well.

Premium Adjustments

With an incurred loss retrospective rating plan, the insured initially pays a deposit premium that is usually equal to the standard premium. This deposit

premium is usually paid in equal installments throughout the policy period. In
some cases the insurer negotiates a **depressed pay-in** feature by allowing the insured to pay the standard premium over a
period longer than the policy period. An

Depressed pay-in is a feature of
an incurred loss retrospective rating plan whereby the insured is allowed to pay the standard premium
over a period that extends beyond
the actual policy period.

example of a depressed pay-in is a situation in which a policy period is for
twelve months and the insurer allows the insured to pay the standard premium
in equal installments over a period of eighteen months, six months beyond the
end of the policy period.

The initial standard premium is based on estimated exposures. Sometime after
the end of the policy period, the insurer adjusts the standard premium based on
actual exposures for the policy period. About the same time, the insurer
applies the retrospective premium formula to the adjusted standard premium,
taking into account the paid and reserved amount of retained losses for the
policy period. The result is the retrospective rating plan premium.

In subsequent periods, usually annually, further adjustments are made to the
retrospective rating plan premium for the policy by applying the retrospective
premium formula to subsequent evaluations of losses that occurred during the
policy period. Under an incurred loss retrospective rating plan, if the evaluation of incurred losses for the policy period shows an increase in cumulative
incurred losses from one adjustment to the next, an additional premium is due.
If the evaluation shows that cumulative incurred losses for the policy period
have decreased, premium is returned to the insured. This series of premium
adjustments, which can go on for several years after the policy period, contin-
ues until all retained losses are paid or until the insurer and the insured agree
that there will be no further retrospective premium adjustments. Therefore, a
retrospective rating plan premium for a single policy period usually is not
finalized until many years after the policy period.

Exhibit 8-8 illustrates the relationship between incurred losses and premium
adjustments for an incurred loss retrospective rating plan. The standard
premium is paid during the policy period and is adjusted at two evaluation
points, Evaluation Point #1 and Evaluation Point #2. Because this example
assumes that the cumulative incurred losses at Evaluation Point #1 were less
than those anticipated by the standard premium, a return premium is due to
the insured at Evaluation Point #1. At Evaluation Point #2, this example
assumes that cumulative incurred losses further increased, so the insured pays
an additional premium. Although the exhibit shows only two evaluation
points, usually there are many subsequent evaluation points with corresponding adjustments to the cumulative premium.

Exhibit 8-8

Relationship Between Incurred Losses and Premium Adjustments
for an Incurred Loss Retrospective Rating Plan

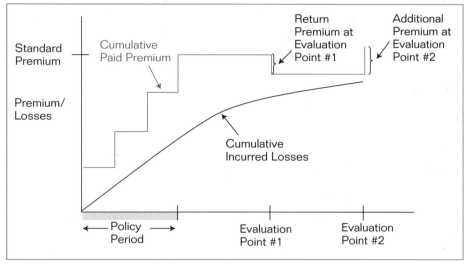

Example of a Retrospective Rating Plan Premium

Assume that ABC Corporation (ABC) has the following cost factors for its incurred loss retrospective rating plan:

Policy Limit	$1,000,000 per occurrence
Standard Premium	$700,000
Discount	$50,000
Basic Premium	20%
Loss Conversion Factor	1.10
Loss Limit	$500,000 per occurrence
Excess Loss Premium	5%
Tax Multiplier	1.04
Maximum Premium	150%
Minimum Premium	40%

Analysis

• The standard premium of $700,000 less the premium discount of $50,000 ($650,000) is the amount that ABC would pay for a guaranteed cost plan.

Continued on next page.

- The basic premium is 20 percent of standard premium, or $140,000. (The basic premium includes an "insurance charge.")
- The excess loss premium is 5 percent of the standard premium, or $35,000.
- The maximum premium is 150 percent of standard premium, or $1,050,000, and the minimum premium is 40 percent of standard premium, or $280,000.
- Using the retrospective premium formula, the retrospective rating plan premium is calculated as follows:

(Basic premium + Converted losses + Excess loss premium) × Tax multiplier

($140,000 + Losses × 1.10 + $35,000) × 1.04

With the use of the above formula, the retrospective plan premium is calculated to equal each of the following amounts at various incurred loss levels:

Incurred Losses	Premium	
$ 50,000	$280,000	Minimum Premium Applies
$100,000	$296,400	
$200,000	$410,800	
$300,000	$525,200	
$400,000	$639,600	
$500,000	$754,000	
$600,000	$868,400	
$700,000	$982,800	
$800,000	$1,050,000	Maximum Premium Applies

Losses of $50,000 cause the minimum premium to apply, whereas losses of $800,000 cause the maximum premium to apply.

ABC pays the standard premium of $700,000 as a deposit during the policy period. The premium is adjusted upward or downward as incurred losses for the policy period are evaluated at subsequent annual intervals. For example, if at the first evaluation date ABC's incurred losses are $600,000, then an additional premium of $168,400 is due ($868,400 − $700,000).

Financial Accounting Issues

For financial accounting purposes, an organization must recognize its retained losses as they are incurred. Therefore, it follows that an organization using a retrospective rating plan should recognize any future premium payments that will be due based on current retained losses that have been incurred. These amounts must be posted as a liability on the organization's balance sheet and charged as an expense on its income statement.

For example, assume that an organization pays a deposit premium for an incurred loss retrospective rating plan and discovers at the end of the policy period that its incurred losses are much higher than expected. When it prepares its next set of financial statements, the organization should recognize the additional premium that will be due at the next adjustment by using the retrospective premium formula and applying it to the incurred losses. The higher-than- expected incurred losses have created an obligation (liability) on the insured's part. The additional premium that will be due should be posted as a liability on the organization's balance sheet and charged as an expense on its income statement.

With a paid loss retrospective rating plan, premium payments are based on paid rather than incurred losses. However, for financial accounting purposes, the insured must calculate what the premium would be at any point in time if incurred losses rather than paid losses were used. The difference between the amount of premium using incurred losses and the amount currently paid should be recognized as a liability on the organization's balance sheet and an expense on its income statement.

With either type of retrospective rating plan, an organization might need to recognize an amount for the incurred-but-not-reported (IBNR) amount of retained losses. If an IBNR amount can be estimated with reasonable accuracy, then the organization should use it when applying the retrospective premium formula to its losses. The organization should include any resulting additional premium estimate due to IBNR losses as a liability on its balance sheet and as an expense on its income statement.

Tax Issues

Chapter 2 mentioned income tax as a consideration in managing an organization's cost of risk. An important tax issue with regard to risk financing is the timing of expense deductions from an organization's taxable income.

In general, under a retrospective rating plan, an organization is able to take a tax deduction on premiums as they are paid. Therefore, an incurred loss retrospective rating plan, in effect, allows an organization to deduct its reserves for the retained portion of its losses because premiums are paid based on incurred losses. This favorable timing of the tax deduction helps offset some of the cash flow disadvantage of paying premium based on incurred rather than paid losses. A paid loss retrospective rating plan does not allow an organization to deduct its reserves for retained losses because, in general, premiums are paid, and thus deductible for tax purposes, only as losses are paid.

Comparison of Paid Loss With Incurred Loss Retrospective Rating Plans

Given the previous discussion of paid loss and incurred loss retrospective rating plans, it would seem that an insured would always favor a paid loss over an incurred loss retrospective rating plan. With both plans, the insured pays for the insurer's estimated expenses, but with the paid loss plan the insured pays premium only as its retained losses are paid rather than incurred, benefiting from the cash flow on the loss reserves. Even being able to take a tax deduction on the premium based on incurred rather than paid losses under an incurred loss plan does not make up for the cash flow disadvantage of not benefiting from the cash flow on loss reserves.

However, it should be noted that under a paid loss retrospective plan an insurer usually adds an amount to the basic premium to compensate itself for the fact that it does not have the use of the cash flow on the loss reserves. Therefore, an insured should not automatically choose a paid loss plan over an incurred loss plan because the decision depends on the relationship between the amount that the insurer adds to the basic premium and the value of the cash flow benefit to the insured.

For example, assume ABC Corporation (ABC) is trying to decide between an incurred loss retrospective rating plan and a paid loss retrospective rating plan with the following cost factors:

	Incurred Loss Plan	Paid Loss Plan
Policy Limit	$1,000,000 per occurrence	Same
Standard Premium	$700,000	Same
Basic Premium	20%	28%
Loss Conversion Factor	1.10	Same
Loss Limit	$500,000 per occurrence	Same
Excess Loss Premium	5%	Same
Tax Multiplier	1.04	Same
Maximum Premium	150%	158%
Minimum Premium	40%	Same

Note that the difference between the two plans is the charge for the basic premium, which is higher under the paid loss plan. The maximum premium is also adjusted upward to account for the influence of the higher basic premium as part of the retrospective premium formula. This higher charge for the basic premium is meant to compensate the insurer for its loss of use of cash flow on the loss reserves under the paid loss retrospective rating plan.

Present value analysis should be used to compare the paid loss and incurred loss plans. The cash flow benefit from paying premium as the losses are paid under the paid loss plan might or might not offset the additional amount loaded into the basic premium.

Relationship of Retrospective Rating Plans to an Organization's Risk Financing Objectives

As with any risk financing plan, an organization should evaluate a retrospective rating plan in terms of its ability to meet the organization's risk financing objectives. Exhibit 8-9 discusses retrospective rating plans in relation to each of the risk financing objectives introduced in Chapter 2.

Exhibit 8-9
Retrospective Rating Plans and Risk Financing Objectives

Risk Financing Objective	Relationship to Retrospective Rating Plans
Paying for Losses	A retrospective rating plan meets this objective because, as with any insurance plan, the insurer pays for losses as they become due.
Maintaining Liquidity	A retrospective rating plan, particularly a paid loss plan, can help meet this objective if the loss limit and maximum premium are carefully chosen.
Managing Uncertainty of Loss Outcomes	A retrospective rating plan can help meet this objective if the loss limit and maximum premium are carefully chosen.
Managing the Cost of Risk	Because it includes a significant amount of retention, a retrospective

Continued on next page.

	rating plan can reduce an organization's cost of risk over the long run. The cash flow available under a paid loss retrospective rating plan further reduces costs.
Complying With Legal Requirements	Retrospective rating plans meet legal requirements for purchasing insurance because a policy is issued by an insurance company, which guarantees that all claims will be paid.

Summary

- Retrospective rating plans differ from other risk financing plans that cover low-to-medium-severity losses, particularly in the way that losses are funded and paid.

- A retrospective rating plan also differs from other types of insurance plans in the way that the premium is calculated. The premium is adjusted to include a portion of the insured's covered losses during the policy period. The portion of losses included in the premium calculation is subject to a loss limit, and the adjusted premium is limited to a maximum and a minimum amount. Because the premium includes a portion of the insured's covered losses, a retrospective rating plan is categorized as a hybrid plan.

- The two major types of retrospective rating plans are paid loss retrospective rating plans and incurred loss retrospective rating plans. With a paid loss plan, the insured pays a deposit premium to cover the insurer's estimated expenses and risk transfer charges and pays the rest of the premium as the insurer pays the retained losses. Therefore, the insured is able to benefit from the cash flow on the loss reserves for its retained losses. With an incurred loss plan, the insured pays a deposit premium based on the insurer's estimated expenses and projected incurred losses that are retained under the plan. Therefore, the insured is not able to benefit from the cash flow on the loss reserves for its retained losses. For the portion of losses that is retained, a paid loss plan is an unfunded plan, while an incurred loss plan is a funded plan.

- Retrospective rating plans require a moderate amount of administration. The insurer rather than the insured is responsible for many of the administrative tasks, such as adjusting claims, making necessary filings with the states, and paying applicable premium taxes and residual market loadings.

- In designing a risk management program, an organization generally uses a retrospective rating plan for the first layer of an insured's losses, with a transfer plan, a hybrid plan, or both sitting above it. The cost of a retrospective rating plan should be compared with the cost of other risk financing plans for low-to-medium-severity losses, such as self-insurance plans, large deductible plans, and captive insurer plans.

- Retrospective rating plans have several advantages over guaranteed cost plans, including a lower long-term cost and direct savings as a result of successful loss control efforts. However, if the loss limit and maximum premium are set at too high a level, financial planning can be difficult for the insured because of the uncertainty of the size of upward premium adjustments. Another disadvantage is that the insurance company might set unrealistically high reserves for the retained portion of losses, with the premium payments for an incurred loss retrospective rating plan based on these reserve amounts, resulting in a loss of cash flow for the insured. A further disadvantage is that the losses that are retained under a retrospective rating plan are paid for as premium, upon which premium taxes and residual market loadings are levied. These costs can be avoided with a large deductible plan.

- A retrospective rating premium is calculated using a formula that includes a basic premium, converted losses, an excess loss premium, and a provision for taxes. The formula is as follows:

$$\text{Retrospective rating plan premium} = \left(\begin{array}{l} \text{Basic premium +} \\ \text{Converted losses +} \\ \text{Excess loss premium} \end{array} \right) \times \text{Tax multiplier}$$

- The retrospective rating plan premium is subject to maximum amounts and minimum amounts.

- For financial accounting purposes, an organization that uses a retrospective rating plan should recognize on its financial statements any future premium payments that will be due based on current incurred retained losses. For tax purposes, premium is deductible when paid, which, in effect, allows for the deduction of loss reserves under an incurred loss retrospective rating plan.

- A properly designed retrospective rating plan can help an organization meet its risk financing objectives by providing an appropriate balance between retention and transfer of its losses.

Chapter Note

1. For workers compensation, a retrospective rating plan also covers high-severity losses because a workers compensation policy covers statutory benefits, which are theoretically unlimited in amount.

References

Harrington, Scott E., and Gregory R. Niehaus. *Risk Management and Insurance*. Burr Ridge, IL: Irwin/McGraw-Hill, 1999.

International Risk Management Institute. *Risk Financing: A Guide to Insurance Cash Flow*. Dallas: International Risk Management Institute, Inc., 2000.

Malecki, Donald S., Ronald C. Horn, Eric A. Wiening, and Arthur L. Flitner. *Commercial Liability Insurance and Risk Management*. Vol. 2. Malvern, PA: American Institute, 1996.

Williams, Arthur C., Jr., Michael L. Smith, and Peter C. Young. *Risk Management and Insurance*. 8th ed. Burr Ridge, IL: Irwin/McGraw-Hill, 1998.

Chapter 9

Captive Insurance Companies

Introduction

Chapter 3 introduced captive insurance companies. A *captive insurance company* is a subsidiary formed to insure the risks of its parent and affiliates, although a captive is sometimes owned by and insures more than one parent. Because it is an insurance company, a captive performs many of the same functions as those of a typical insurance company.

> A *captive insurance company* is a subsidiary formed to insure the risks of its parent and affiliates, although a captive is sometimes owned by and insures more than one parent.

Since the 1960s, thousands of captive insurance companies have been formed worldwide. The vast majority of large multinational organizations use one or more captive insurers to finance their loss exposures.

Exhibit 9-1 shows the relationships between a captive insurer and its parent(s). Just as any other insurance company does, a captive collects premium, issues policies, and pays covered losses (both first-party and third-party losses).

Most captive insurers purchase reinsurance, usually on an excess of loss basis, to transfer some of their risk of loss to another insurance company. Reinsurance provides a captive insurer with many of the benefits discussed in Chapter 6, including large-risk capacity and stability of underwriting results.

Exhibit 9-1
The Relationship of a Captive to its Parent(s) (Insured)

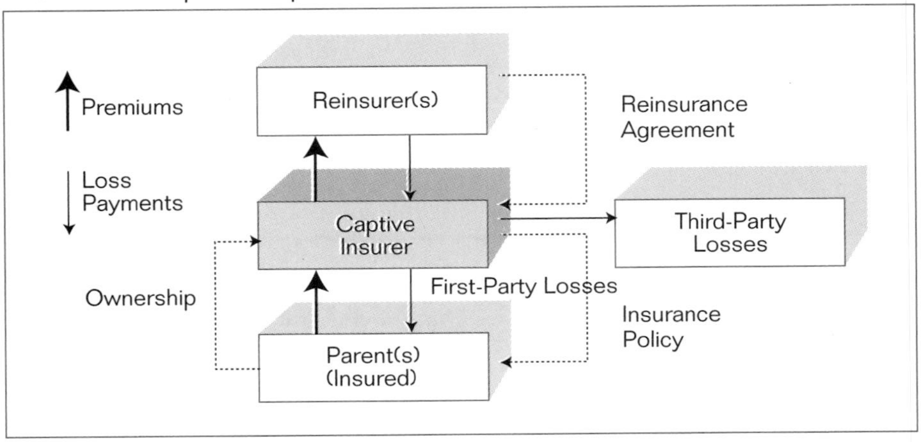

Types of Captive Insurers

A captive insurer owned by one parent is called a *single-parent captive*, or a *pure captive*.[1] When a captive insurer is owned by multiple parents, usually from the same industry, it is called a *group captive*. A group captive is similar to a mutual insurance company except that the insureds (owners) under a group captive exercise a great deal more control over the management of the company than do the insureds under a typical mutual insurance company. A group captive sponsored by an association is referred to as an *association captive*. For example, an association of paint manufacturers might sponsor a captive insurer for the benefit of its members.

A *single-parent (pure) captive* is a captive insurer that is owned by one parent.

A *group captive* is a captive insurer owned by multiple parents, usually from the same industry.

An *association captive* is a group captive sponsored by an association.

Because a captive is an insurance company, it requires an investment of capital by its parent(s), as well as expenditures to manage the company, including accounting, auditing, legal, and underwriting expenses. Therefore, in order for a captive insurer to be economically feasible, an organization should have loss exposures that generate a substantial premium revenue for the captive. One source places the minimum annual premium at $2,500,000 for a single-parent captive.[2]

This text classifies a single-parent captive as a hybrid risk financing plan because, from its parent's point of view, a single-parent captive usually combines elements of retention and transfer. Because a single-parent captive covers its parent's losses and is part of the same economic family as its parent, losses retained by the captive are, in effect, retained by its parent. For the same reasons, losses transferred by the captive (for example, through reinsurance or some other means) are, in effect, transferred by its parent. Some single-parent captive insurers do not purchase reinsurance, so they are classified as retention plans instead of hybrid plans.

A group captive (or an association captive) is classified as a hybrid or a transfer plan, depending on its design. If each member (insured) of a group captive retains a portion of its own losses within the captive and pools the balance of its losses with other members, then the group captive is classified as a hybrid plan. If each member pools all of its losses with the other members, then the group captive is classified as a transfer plan.

Retaining and Transferring Losses

Exhibit 9-2 illustrates the retained and transferred losses under a hypothetical captive insurance plan whereby the captive issues policies and purchases both per occurrence and annual aggregate excess of loss reinsurance. (Bear in mind that aggregate excess of loss reinsurance is usually difficult to obtain, so most captive insurers don't purchase it.) The net retention of the captive for each occurrence is the amount below the per occurrence attachment point of the reinsurance. This is similar in concept to a loss limit under a retrospective rating plan. If the captive is able to purchase annual aggregate excess reinsurance, then its annual retained losses are capped at an annual maximum amount, similar in concept to a maximum premium under a retrospective rating plan.

Exhibit 9-2
Retained and Transferred Losses Under a Hypothetical Captive Insurer Plan

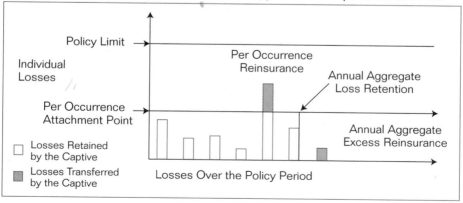

Combining a Captive Insurer Plan With Transfer and Hybrid Risk Financing Plans

To put together a risk financing program, a captive insurer plan is usually combined with a hybrid or a transfer plan. As with a retrospective rating plan, the captive insurer plan generally is used for the first layer of loss where there is a relatively high frequency and low-to-medium severity, with a transfer or a hybrid plan sitting directly above it covering the higher-severity losses.

For example, assume that an organization establishes a single-parent captive to cover its general liability loss exposures. The captive issues a policy with a limit of $1 million per occurrence to the organization (the owner of the captive). Further, assume that the captive purchases excess of loss reinsurance of $750,000 excess of $250,000 per occurrence.

Excess insurance or a finite risk plan might sit directly above the $1 million layer of loss covered by the captive insurer. Exhibit 9-3 shows how the organization might combine excess insurance (Case 1) or combine excess insurance and finite risk insurance (Case 2) with the single-parent captive insurer plan described above.

Exhibit 9-3
Single-Parent Captive Insurer Plan Combined With Excess Insurance and a Finite Risk Plan

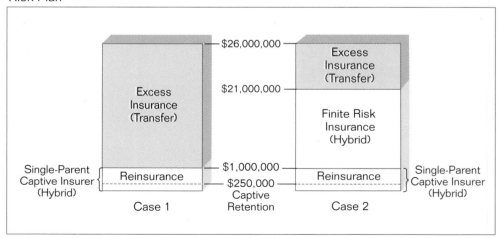

Under Case 1, the organization purchases excess insurance on a guaranteed cost basis with a limit of $25 million per occurrence to sit directly above the

$1 million per occurrence layer of loss covered by the captive insurer. Therefore, the total limit of insurance available per occurrence is $26 million.

Under Case 2, the organization purchases finite risk insurance with a limit of $20 million per occurrence to sit directly above the $1 million per occurrence layer of loss covered by the captive insurer. It also purchases excess insurance with a limit of $5 million per occurrence to sit directly above the finite risk insurance plan. Again, the organization has a total limit available of $26 million per occurrence.

Under both Case 1 and Case 2, the organization, in effect, retains the first $250,000 per occurrence because its captive insurer retains $250,000 per occurrence, net of reinsurance. The portion of each covered loss that exceeds $250,000 per occurrence up to the policy limits of $1 million per occurrence is transferred to reinsurers through the organization's captive.

To transfer risk, an organization might purchase excess insurance rather than purchase reinsurance through its captive. For example, with the captive insurer plan described above, the organization might decide to purchase insurance for $750,000 per occurrence excess of $250,000 per occurrence rather than have the captive purchase reinsurance for the same layer of loss. In this case, the captive would issue a policy with a limit of $250,000 per occurrence rather than $1 million per occurrence. Exhibit 9-4 shows this alternative.

Exhibit 9-4
Purchasing Excess Insurance Instead of Reinsuring a Captive

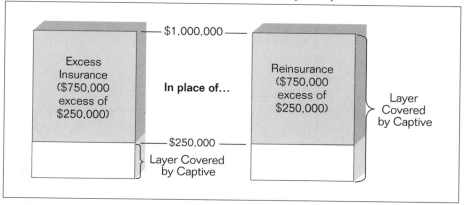

Operating a Captive Insurer

There are many considerations in operating a captive insurer, including coverages, domicile, management, and the method of writing business (for example, fronted or direct basis). The following sections discuss these various considerations in detail.

Coverages

Captive insurers are commonly used to cover losses that offer substantial cash flow, such as those covered by workers compensation, general liability, and automobile liability policies. An advantage to covering these types of losses through a captive is that it is able to earn investment income on the substantial cash flow generated by the loss reserves. Captives are also used to cover property losses as well as losses that fall under specialized lines of business, such as products and environmental liability.

Operating as a Reinsurer

Most countries have regulatory requirements that state an insurance company must be licensed. For example, in the United States, the states require an insurance company to be licensed to provide insurance for workers compensation and automobile liability loss exposures. The majority of captive insurers are not licensed to write these lines of business in the various U.S. states, and it would be time-consuming and expensive for them to obtain licenses. Because of these regulatory requirements, captive insurers usually operate as reinsurers behind U.S.-licensed insurance companies, which act as fronting companies.

Fronting Company

A **fronting company** is a licensed insurance company that issues an insurance policy and reinsures the risk of loss back to a captive insurer owned by the insured. By having its captive reinsure a fronting company, the insured is able to benefit from using a captive insurer and at the same time comply with regulations that require the insurance company issuing the insurance policy to be licensed. In addition, a licensed fronting company usually satisfies outside parties that require the insured organization to purchase insurance from an established insurance company with an acceptable claim-paying-ability rating from one of the rating agencies, such as A.M. Best or Standard & Poor's.

Exhibit 9-5 shows the relationships among the various parties for a captive that uses a fronting company. Premiums are paid by the captive's parent (and affiliates) to the fronting company, which issues an insurance policy. The fronting company takes out its fees and expenses and passes on the balance of the premium and the risk of loss to the captive insurer, which is acting as a reinsurer of the fronting company. (In some cases, the fronting company retains a small quota share percentage of the risk of loss.) The captive insurer, in turn, transfers some of its risk of loss by passing a portion of the premium to a reinsurer or to several reinsurers.

Exhibit 9-5
Operating a Captive as a Reinsurer

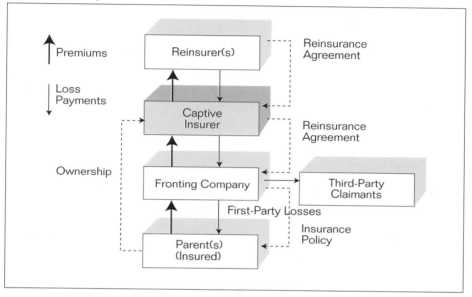

Because the fronting company issues an insurance policy, it is responsible for paying covered losses, both first-party losses to the parent and third-party losses to other claimants. The fronting company is reimbursed for losses by the captive insurer. In effect, a licensed insurer (the fronting company) is guaranteeing the payment of losses covered by the captive insurer in order to satisfy jurisdictional regulations.

The relationship between the insured (the owner of the captive) and the fronting company is the same as a typical relationship between an insured and its insurance company. The fronting company issues a policy to the insured, collects premium from the insured, and pays all losses, just as any other insurance company would.

However, a fronting company usually does not retain any underwriting risk (on a net basis) because it has a reinsurance agreement to transfer all premiums (less fees and expenses) and losses to the captive insurer. However, the fronting company does retain the risk that the captive might not have sufficient funds to reimburse it for payment of covered losses. To offset this risk, the fronting company usually requires a letter of credit or some other type of financial guarantee from the captive insurer.

The insured, through its ownership interest in the captive, is, in effect, retaining its own losses to the extent that they are retained by the captive. If the captive's premium (net of reinsurance premium) plus the investment income it earns on its cash flow exceeds its retained losses plus its expenses, the captive owner benefits because its ownership interest increases in value. The opposite applies if the captive's premium (net of reinsurance premium) plus investment income is less than retained losses plus captive expenses.

The fronting company often provides claim handling services for a fee, although sometimes the insured contracts with a third-party administrator to handle claims. The fronting company must pay expenses such as state premium taxes, license fees, service bureau charges, and residual market loadings. The fronting company deducts these expenses from the premium before it passes the balance on to the captive.

Operating as a Direct Writer

For some lines of business, a captive is able to operate as a **direct writer**, meaning that it issues policies directly to its parent(s) and affiliates and does not use a fronting company. A direct-writing captive operates in a manner similar to that shown near the beginning of this chapter in Exhibit 9-1.

> A **direct writer** is a captive that issues policies directly to its parent(s) and affiliates and does not use a fronting company.

For example, in the United States an insurer does not need to be licensed for many lines of property, marine, and liability coverage. Therefore, a captive insurer can issue policies directly to its parent(s) and affiliates for these lines of coverage. However, the captive must comply with nonadmitted insurer regulations in each state and pay premium taxes. As another example, a captive insurer domiciled in Dublin, Ireland, does not need to be licensed to write insurance directly for its parent's (and affiliates') operations located throughout the European Union.

A major advantage of operating as a direct writer is that a captive is able to save the fees charged by the fronting company, which range between 5 percent and 30 percent of premium.[3] This cost savings can make a direct-writer captive insurance plan less expensive than commercial insurance and many other risk financing plans.

Premium

The premium arrangement between the parent (and affiliates) and the captive insurer (with or without a fronting company) can be on a guaranteed cost basis or a retrospectively rated basis. Under a guaranteed cost arrangement, the insured pays a fixed premium rate, transferring the entire risk of loss to its captive. However, as previously mentioned, because the captive is part of the insured's economic family, any risk retained by the captive is, in effect, retained by the insured. If the premium arrangement is on a retrospectively rated basis, the premium rate adjusts based on a portion of the insured's covered losses during the policy period. In this case the insured and its captive share the risk of loss (again, with any residual loss retained by the captive, in effect, retained by the parent).

The retrospectively rated premium can be paid to the captive on a paid loss or an incurred loss basis. If the premium is on a paid loss basis, the cash flow benefit of the loss reserves for the insured's retained losses resides with the insured rather than with its captive insurer. The opposite is true if the premium is on an incurred loss basis.

Using a Retrospective Rating Plan With a Captive Insurer

Assume that DKF Manufacturing (DKF) establishes a single-parent captive insurer and uses it to cover losses arising from its automobile liability and general liability loss exposures up to a limit of $1 million per occurrence/accident. In order to comply with regulatory requirements, DKF's captive reinsures a fronting company, which issues the policies to DKF.

Also assume that the insurance arrangement between DKF and the fronting company is an incurred loss retrospective rating plan with a loss limit of $100,000 per occurrence/accident. Therefore DKF retains the first $100,000 of its own losses. DKF's captive reinsures the fronting company on the same retrospectively rated basis. Therefore, the deposit premium and retrospective adjustments are passed among DKF, the fronting company, and DKF's captive as follows:

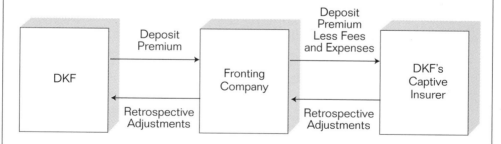

Assume that DKF's captive insurer purchases excess of loss reinsurance of $500,000 excess of $500,000 per occurrence/accident. (It does not purchase aggregate excess of loss reinsurance.) Therefore, the net risk assumed by DKF's captive insurer is $400,000 per occurrence/accident excess of $100,000 per occurrence/accident, which is shown in the following diagram:

Continued on next page.

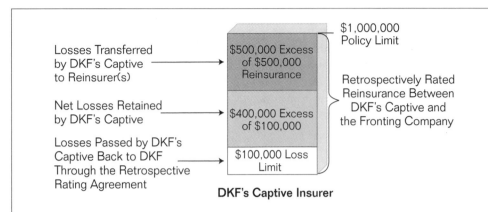

DKF's Captive Insurer

Because all retrospective rating agreements have a maximum premium, DKF's captive assumes the risk that the losses subject to the loss limit of $100,000 will exceed the maximum premium under the retrospective rating plan between the fronting company and DKF.

To cover its reinsurance cost and its net retained risk, DKF's captive builds an insurance charge (to account for the risk that the maximum premium might be exceeded) and an excess loss premium charge (to limit losses subject to retrospective rating to $100,000 per occurrence/accident) into the retrospective premium formula. In addition, DKF's captive includes its administrative costs and overhead in the basic premium, which is part of the retrospective premium formula.

A captive insurer plan is a funded plan if a guaranteed cost or an incurred loss retrospective rating plan is used to determine the premium paid by the insured. With these types of premium plans, funds are available within the captive to pay for losses as they become due. When a paid loss retrospective rating plan is used with a captive, the captive is unfunded for the portion of losses that the insured retains.

Domicile

Many jurisdictions encourage captive insurers to locate within their territories through favorable regulations and little (or no) taxes. These jurisdictions see captive insurance as an industry that boosts their economies by providing employment and other income such as annual registration fees. Examples of these jurisdictions are Barbados, Bermuda, Dublin, Isle of Man, Guernsey, Singapore, British Columbia, Cayman Islands, Hawaii, Vermont, Colorado, and Tennessee.

Although, theoretically, a captive insurer can be domiciled anywhere in the world, an organization usually chooses a jurisdiction that is favorable for the formation and operation of captives. For example, some states of the U.S. require a single-parent captive to maintain a minimum capital and surplus of several million dollars, which is the same requirement as that for a large, commercial insurer. Tying up this much capital would make most single-parent captives uneconomical. By contrast, the state of Vermont has a minimum capital and surplus requirement of $250,000 for a single-parent captive.

When evaluating a domicile for a captive insurer, one should consider the following:

- Capital requirements
- Incorporation fees and annual registration fees
- Types of business permitted to be written by the captive
- Taxes
- Premium restrictions
- Investment restrictions
- Ease of travel to and from the domicile
- Support infrastructure in terms of accountants, bankers, lawyers, captive managers, and other services

---

Requirements for Forming a Captive Insurer in Barbados[4]

Barbados is a domicile for many captive insurers. The following requirements illustrate Barbados' favorable regulatory and tax climate for establishing and operating a captive insurer:[5]

Requirement	Details
Minimum Premium Requirements	None.
Minimum Capitalization Requirements	$125,000 single-owner and group captives; letter of credit is permitted in place of cash.
Solvency Requirements	Assets must exceed liabilities by $125,000 if prior year's premiums do not exceed $750,000. If premiums are between $750,000 and $5 million, assets must exceed liabilities by 20 percent of the premium and 10 percent for the portion of premium that exceeds $5 million.

Continued on next page.

Incorporation and Registration Expenses	$250 application fee; $390 incorporation fee; $2,500 initial license fee; $2,500 annual renewal fee.
Local Taxes	None.
Kinds of Insurance That Can Be Written	All, subject to approval of Superintendent of Insurance.
General Regulatory Environment	Fairly lenient.
Investment Restrictions	None.

Management

A captive insurer requires most, if not all, of the same management functions as any commercial insurer requires. For example, underwriting decisions must be made, policies must be issued, premium must be billed and collected, and losses must be adjusted and paid. Other major functions include purchasing reinsurance, investing assets, and producing financial statements.

A single-parent captive, particularly one operating as a reinsurer, requires substantially less management than that needed for a group captive. A single-parent captive, by definition, is underwriting only its parent's (and affiliates') loss exposures, so it usually does not need to devote as many resources as a group captive would to underwriting and rating. For single-parent captives that operate as reinsurers, the fronting company performs many of the required functions, such as issuing policies, making filings, and adjusting claims.

Because of the limited amount of administration required, a single-parent captive usually hires a management company to oversee and coordinate tasks such as accounting, annual filings, purchase of reinsurance, and investment of assets. Dozens of companies, located in the popular captive domiciles, specialize in managing captives. Many of these management companies are owned by a broker or an insurer, while others are independently owned.

Most group captives require the same amount of management as a large insurance company requires, so a group captive can justify employing full-time staff. The volume of daily transactions can be equal to or greater than that of a large insurer. For example, some group captives insure (or reinsure) thousands of members, such as individual doctors or lawyers. On a daily basis, the group captive must issue insurance policies and certificates and adjust and settle claims.

Administration by the Insured

A single-parent captive plan can require more administration on the part of the insured (the parent) than do other risk financing plans that usually are applied to low-to-medium-severity losses, such as retrospective rating or self-insurance plans. This is especially true in the formative stage when the captive company must be incorporated and a domicile chosen. At this stage, relationships must be developed with bankers, accountants, lawyers, regulators, and others. In addition, the parent must appoint a board of directors for the captive.

On an ongoing basis, the parent must oversee the management of its captive. Board meetings must be held on an annual basis, usually in the captive's domicile. The parent needs to oversee the adjustment of claims and make sure the fronting company (if used) is making the proper filings and passing on the premium to the captive on a timely basis.

Group captives might or might not require substantial administration on the part of one of its members, depending on the degree of involvement of that member with the management of the group captive. In many cases, an individual member of a group captive has no more administration responsibilities than if it were purchasing insurance from a commercial insurer.

Third-Party Business

Some domiciles allow a captive insurer to write **third-party business**, which is business that is not directly related to the parent(s) and affiliates of the captive. Often, a captive accepts third-party business on a reinsurance basis because it is not licensed in the jurisdiction in which the third-party risk exposure is located.

> **Third-party business** is business written by a captive that is not directly related to the business of its parent(s) and affiliates.

Although third-party business potentially can generate profit for a captive, in the past many captives have lost large sums of money writing third-party business. In many cases the captives did not have a good understanding of the risk involved.

In recent years, many organizations have found that there is a benefit to writing third-party business over which they have some control, such as warranties on the products they sell. In general, organizations have an understanding of this type of third-party business and, therefore, a reasonable chance of making a profit by insuring it.

Summary of General Characteristics

Exhibit 9-6 summarizes the general characteristics of a single-parent captive insurer plan.

Exhibit 9-6
General Characteristics of a Single-Parent Captive Insurer Plan

Retention/ Transfer	Severity of Losses	Funded/ Unfunded	Administrative Requirements
Hybrid (usually)	Low to medium	Usually funded	High

Advantages and Disadvantages of Captive Insurer Plans

Because it is usually a hybrid risk financing plan, a single-parent captive insurer plan has many of the advantages and disadvantages of both retention and transfer. The degree to which these advantages and disadvantages apply to a specific single-parent captive insurer plan depends on the design of the plan—that is, the amount of retention versus transfer built into the plan. The same is true of a group captive.

Advantages

A captive insurer plan has many advantages when compared with other risk financing plans. Included are the usual advantages associated with retention, as well as the ability to obtain insurance when it is not available, direct access to reinsurers, centralized loss retention, and potential tax savings.

Benefiting From Cash Flow

As with most other plans that involve loss retention, a captive insurance company allows the insured(s) to benefit from the cash flow available on losses that are paid out over time because, under a funded plan, the captive earns investment income on premium funds that have not yet been paid out for claims. The insured benefits because it is part of the same economic family as the captive insurer.

However, the insured has an opportunity cost by having funds tied up in its captive because the investment income earned by the captive is likely to be less than the insured's cost of capital. In other words, the insured would realize a net savings if it could use some or all of the cash tied up in the captive as capital. As previously explained, it is possible for the insured to retain some of the cash by using a paid loss retrospective rating arrangement for paying premium to its captive. Also, some jurisdictions allow a captive to loan back funds to its parent (the insured), which also overcomes the opportunity cost problem.

Obtaining Insurance Not Otherwise Available

A second advantage is that a captive insurer can be used by its parent to obtain insurance coverage that is not available from commercial insurers. Examples of coverages in this category are some types of environmental liability insurance, depending on the related loss exposure. The parent pays a premium to its captive, which issues an insurance policy for the needed coverage.

One could argue that using a single-parent captive to insure hard-to-place coverages does not constitute insurance because the parent owns the captive and, therefore, retains the premium and losses arising from its own loss exposures. However, for hard-to-place insurance coverages, the captive might be able to negotiate a favorable reinsurance arrangement, which, in effect, transfers the parent's risk just as an insurance arrangement would. Also, using a fronting company and a captive for these coverages would satisfy outside parties that require insurance with a policy issued by a licensed insurance company.

Negotiating With Insurers

The existence of a captive insurer can improve an insured's negotiating power with commercial insurers. Take the case of an airline that forms a single-parent captive insurer to retain a quota share percentage of its aircraft hull insurance. If premiums increase in the aircraft hull insurance market, the airline might increase the share it places in its captive to take advantage of the increased premiums. However, the fact that the airline has this option might increase its bargaining power with its commercial insurers, who might lower the airline's premium so as not to lose business to the captive.

Having Direct Access to Reinsurers

Another advantage of a captive insurer is that it gives the insured direct access to reinsurers, which are sometimes more flexible than insurers in terms of underwriting and rating. Also, the captive is able to capture any ceding commission on the reinsurance that would otherwise be paid to a commercial insurer.

This advantage of going direct to reinsurers is not as great as it used to be in years past. As previously discussed in Chapter 6, risk managers now deal directly with reinsurers, even in the absence of a captive insurance arrangement.

Retaining Losses on a Centralized Basis

A further advantage of a captive insurer plan is that the insured can use it to retain a large amount of its losses on a centralized basis. This action can result in savings to the insured organization due to the lower long-term cost of retention.

For example, the management of a large multinational corporation might want to retain a significantly higher level of loss than does each of its subsidiaries. Therefore, the corporation can use a single-parent captive to pool its losses on a worldwide basis and take a higher loss retention than that taken by each of its subsidiaries, which purchase insurance from the captive. Exhibit 9-7 illustrates the operation of this type of plan:

Exhibit 9-7
Retaining Worldwide Risk of Loss in a Captive

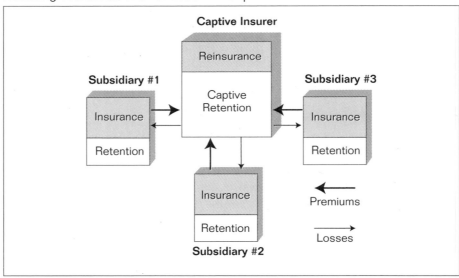

Subsidiary #1, #2, and #3 each pay premium to the captive, which takes a higher per occurrence retention than any of the subsidiaries.

Potential Cash Flow Advantages on Income Taxes

A key issue with regard to captive insurers is whether premium paid by an insured to its captive is tax-deductible. If premium is not tax-deductible, then the insured can deduct the associated losses and other expenses as they are paid by the captive. However, there is a cash flow disadvantage to deducting losses and expenses as they are paid by the captive rather than deducting the premium as it is paid to the captive.

Since the 1970s a series of U.S. tax cases have denied a tax deduction for premium paid by a parent (and its affiliates) to its captive insurer because the Tax Court determined there was no risk shifting and distribution outside the economic family of the parent's organization. However, in 1989 there was a landmark Tax Court case involving Humana Corporation and its subsidiary hospitals. Humana owned a captive insurer to which it and each of its subsidiaries paid premium. The Tax Court denied a deduction of premium paid by Humana because it was the parent of the captive, but it allowed a deduction for premium paid by each of Humana's subsidiaries. The Court cited a **brother-sister relationship** between Humana's subsidiaries and the captive as the basis for allowing the tax deductions. It determined that this relationship was sufficient to establish risk shifting and distribution to the captive insurer. The Humana case was reaffirmed in a similar case in 1993.

> A **brother-sister relationship** exists between one subsidiary and another subsidiary of the same parent. In the Humana case, this concept was used as the basis for allowing a tax deduction of premium to a captive.

The writing of third-party business has always been considered a way to increase the likelihood that premium to a captive insurer would be tax-deductible when paid. Some early tax rulings commented that if a large percentage of the captive's premium is for third-party business, then the captive is considered to be operating as an arm's-length insurance company from its parent and the premium paid by the parent to the captive is deductible. However, these early rulings never cited what a sufficient percentage is. In 1991, in three separate cases involving AMERCO, Harper, and Sears, the Tax Court allowed a deduction for premium paid by each of the parents to their insurance subsidiaries. In each case, the insurance subsidiary wrote substantial third-party business, ranging from 99 percent of the premium in the Sears case (Allstate was the insurance subsidiary in question) to under 30 percent in the Harper case. These cases helped solidify the argument that substantial third-party business should enable a company to take tax deductions for premium paid to its captive.

The issue as to whether the premium paid to a captive insurer is tax-deductible is quite complex. There will continue to be cases applied to specific fact situations that help define the conditions under which premium paid to a captive insurer is and is not tax-deductible.

Most captive insurers are domiciled in a jurisdiction with little or no income tax. Therefore, a parent located in a high-income tax country is able to save taxes if it deducts the premium it pays to its captive and generates profits in the captive that are subject to little or no income tax. In recent years, many countries, including the United States and the United Kingdom, have closed this loophole by requiring the parent to pay tax in its home country on some or all of the profit generated by its offshore captive, even if the profit has not been paid as a dividend back to the parent.

Controlling Losses

Because a captive insurer is, in part, a retention plan, an insured that controls its losses is able to save payments for losses and loss expenses. For a premium arrangement with a captive on a guaranteed cost basis, the savings are immediately captured within the captive. For a premium arrangement with a captive on a retrospectively rated basis, much of the savings accrues directly to the insured.

Managing Uncertainty of Loss Outcomes

A captive insurer can help an insured reduce the uncertainty of its retained losses to a tolerable level. A single-parent captive is a wholly owned subsidiary and, therefore, its financial statements are consolidated with those of its parent (the insured). Any volatility in the underwriting results of the captive insurer creates volatility in the parent's financial results. However, if the captive purchases reinsurance that is sufficient to stabilize its underwriting results, the parent's financial uncertainty is reduced.

Disadvantages

When compared with other risk financing plans, a captive insurer plan's disadvantages include capital and start-up costs, availability of fronting and reinsurance, and payment of premium taxes and residual market loadings.

Capital and Start-Up Costs

A captive involves a commitment of capital and start-up costs not incurred with other risk financing plans, such as retrospective rating plans. One source states that the range of start-up and annual operating costs for a captive is $35,000 to above $150,000.[6]

Availability of Fronting and Reinsurance

Another possible disadvantage of a captive insurer plan is that fronting companies may charge an unreasonably high amount for their services. Also, reinsurance might not be available at a level that sufficiently reduces the uncertainty of the retained losses in the captive.

Premium Taxes and Residual Market Loadings

Another disadvantage of a captive is that the losses retained by a captive insurer are paid for by the insured as a premium, upon which premium taxes and residual market loadings are levied. As explained in Chapter 3, these costs can be avoided by using a large deductible plan.

Financial Accounting Issues

As previously mentioned, as a wholly owned subsidiary, a single-parent captive insurer's financial statements should be consolidated with those of its parent. Therefore, any profit or loss generated in the captive is reflected on the financial statements of its parent, just as with self-insurance.

Just as with any insurance company, a captive insurer must recognize on its financial statements all losses as they are incurred. This includes an estimate for incurred-but-not-reported losses if they can be determined with reasonable accuracy.

With a group captive, if there is risk shifting and distribution between the insured and the captive, the financial accounting treatment of the premium is the same as with a guaranteed cost insurance plan. The premium is treated by the insured as an expense, and any dividends paid by the captive are treated as a return of premium to the insured.

Relationship of a Captive Insurer Plan to an Organization's Risk Financing Objectives

As with any risk financing plan, a captive insurer plan should be evaluated in terms of its ability to meet an organization's risk financing objectives. Exhibit 9-8 discusses a captive insurer plan in relation to each of the risk financing objectives introduced in Chapter 2.

Exhibit 9-8

Captive Insurer Plan and Risk Financing Objectives

Risk Financing Objective	Relationship to Captive Insurer Plan
Paying for Losses	If properly funded, a captive insurance plan meets this objective.
Maintaining Liquidity	A captive insurance plan can help meet this objective if the retention of the captive is carefully chosen and the captive is properly capitalized.
Managing Uncertainty of Loss Outcomes	A captive insurance plan can help meet this objective if the retention of the captive is carefully chosen and an appropriate amount of reinsurance is purchased.
Managing the Cost of Risk	Because it involves retention, a captive insurance plan can reduce an organization's cost of risk over the long run. In addition, a group captive, if operated efficiently, can reduce a member organization's cost of risk.
Complying With Legal Requirements	In the U.S., a captive insurance plan meets legal requirements for workers compensation and automobile liability when a licensed fronting company issues an insurance policy and reinsures the risk with a captive insurer. When it is a direct writer of U.S. business, a captive must operate as a nonadmitted insurer.

Special Types of Captive Insurers

There are variations of the single-parent and group captives previously discussed. These include risk retention groups, rent-a-captives, and protected cell companies.

Risk Retention Groups

A **risk retention group** is a group captive formed under the Liability Risk Retention Act of 1986. This is a United States federal law that allows the formation of risk retention groups (group captives) to insure any type of liability coverage, except personal lines, employers liability, and workers compensation. In order to form a risk retention group, all owners must be from the same industry and must be insured by the risk retention group. Conversely, all insureds must be

> A **risk retention group** is a group captive formed under the requirements of the Liability Risk Retention Act of 1986. A major benefit to a risk retention group is that it needs to be licensed in only one state in the United States in order to write liability coverages in all fifty states.

owners. A major benefit to a risk retention group is that it needs to be licensed in only one state in the U.S. in order to write liability coverage in all fifty states. This benefit saves the risk retention group the expense of complying with regulations in each of the fifty states.

Rent-a-Captives

A **rent-a-captive** is an arrangement whereby an organization benefits from using a captive insurer but does not put up its own capital. Instead, the organization rents the capital of a rent-a-captive organization, which provides a captive facility to which the organization pays premium and receives reimbursement for its losses. Each

> A **rent-a-captive** is an arrangement whereby an organization rents capital from a rent-a-captive facility, to which it pays premium and receives reimbursement for its losses. The organization also receives credit for underwriting profits and investment income.

insured keeps its own premium and loss account, so no risk shifting or distribution occurs among the members of a rent-a-captive. With some types of rent-a-captives, the insured organization must purchase nonvoting preferred stock and receives dividends on the stock equal to its underwriting profit and the investment income earned on its unearned premium and loss reserves. If a plan does not involve the purchase of nonvoting preferred stock, then the rent-a-captive organization returns underwriting profit and investment income through some other means, such as policyholder dividends. The rent-a-captive organization charges a fee for its services. Rent-a-captives provide a means for an organization to quickly form a captive insurer without tying up capital.

Protected Cell Companies

A **protected cell company (PCC)** is a fairly new concept that is similar in structure to a rent-a-captive. An organization pays premium to a PCC and receives reimbursement for its losses, while receiving credit for underwriting profits and investment in-

> **Protected cell companies (PCCs)** are similar to rent-a-captives in which an organization pays premium and receives reimbursement for its losses and credit for underwriting profits and investment income. Each member is assured that the other members cannot access its capital and surplus and that third parties cannot access its assets.

come. As with a rent-a-captive, each organization keeps a premium and loss account separate from those of other members.

However, with a PCC, each member is assured that other members will not be able to access its capital and surplus in the event the cells of those other members are insolvent. This is not necessarily the case with a rent-a-captive in which members purchase preferred stock. In addition, with a PCC, the assets of each member's cell are protected from the claims of any third parties.

Summary

- A captive insurance company is a subsidiary formed to insure the risks of its parent and affiliates, although a captive is sometimes owned by and insures more than one parent. Just as any other insurance company does, a captive collects premium, issues policies, and pays covered losses (both first-party and third-party).

- A captive insurer owned by one parent is called a single-parent captive, or pure captive. When a captive insurer is owned by multiple parents, usually from the same industry, it is called a group captive. A group captive sponsored by an association is referred to as an association captive.

- This text classifies a single-parent captive as a hybrid risk financing plan because, from its parent's point of view, a single-parent captive usually combines elements of retention and transfer. A group (or an association) captive is also classified as a hybrid or a transfer plan, depending on its design.

- To put together a risk financing program, a captive insurer plan is usually combined with a hybrid or a transfer plan. As with a retrospective rating plan, the captive insurer plan generally is used for the first layer of loss where there is a relatively high frequency and low-to-medium severity, with a transfer or a hybrid plan sitting directly above it covering the higher-severity losses.

- There are many considerations in operating a captive insurer, including coverages, domicile, management, and method of writing business (for example, fronted or direct basis). Captive insurers are commonly used to cover losses that are paid over a substantial period of time, such as those arising under workers compensation, general liability, and automobile liability policies.

- Many captives operate as a reinsurer by reinsuring a fronting company, which collects premiums, issues policies, and pays losses. The captive receives the premium (less the fronting company's fees and expenses) from the fronting company and reimburses the fronting company for losses. Operating in this way enables the captive to comply with the licensing requirements of various countries. Other captives operate as direct writers.

- The premium paid to a captive insurer can be on a guaranteed cost or on a retrospectively rated basis, which enables the insured to retain some of its own losses directly.

- Many jurisdictions allow a captive to write third-party business, which is business that is not directly related to the parent(s) or affiliates of the captive.

- A captive insurer plan has many advantages when compared with other risk financing plans. Included are the usual advantages associated with retention, as well as the ability to obtain insurance when it is not available, direct access to reinsurers, centralized loss retention, and potential tax savings.

- When compared with other risk financing plans, a captive insurer plan's disadvantages are capital requirements and start-up costs, and possible nonavailability of fronting and reinsurance.

- As a wholly owned subsidiary, a single-parent captive insurer's financial statements should be consolidated with those of its parent. Therefore, any profit or loss generated in the captive is reflected on the financial statements of its parent, just as with self-insurance. Just as with any insurance company, a captive insurer must recognize on its financial statements all losses as they are incurred. With a group captive, if risk shifting and distribution occur between the insured and the captive, the insured's financial accounting treatment of the premium is the same as with any insurance plan.

- There are variations of single-parent and group captives. These include risk retention groups, rent-a-captives, and protected cell companies.

Chapter Notes

1. Some individuals define "pure captive" as any type of captive that has no third-party business. (Third-party business is discussed later in this chapter.)

2. International Risk Management Institute, *Risk Financing: A Guide to Insurance Cash Flow* (Dallas: International Risk Management Institute, Inc., 2000), 1st reprint, p. IV.K.5, March 1997.

3. Felix H. Kloman, "Captive Insurance Companies," in Skipper, Harold D., Jr.; *International Risk and Insurance* (Burr Ridge, IL: Irwin/McGraw-Hill, 1998), p. 671.

4. These are the requirements for an "exempt insurance company," which is defined as a business (1) whose risks and premiums originate outside of Barbados and (2) which is owned by persons resident outside the Caribbean Community.

5. International Risk Management Institute, *Risk Financing: A Guide to Insurance Cash Flow* (Dallas: International Risk Management Institute, Inc., 2000), p. B6, 2d reprint, September 1998, and PricewaterhouseCoopers, "Barbados Insurance Companies" (PricewaterhouseCoopers, Inc., 2000), pp. 11-12.

6. Felix H. Kloman, "Captive Insurance Companies," in Skipper, Harold D., Jr.; *International Risk and Insurance* (Burr Ridge, IL: Irwin/McGraw-Hill, 1998), p. 668.

References

Harrington, Scott E., and Gregory R. Niehaus. *Risk Management and Insurance*. Burr Ridge, IL: Irwin/McGraw-Hill, 1999.

Malecki, Donald S., Ronald C. Horn, Eric A. Wiening, and Arthur L. Flitner. *Commercial Liability Insurance and Risk Management*. Vol. 2. Malvern, PA: American Institute for CPCU, 1996.

International Risk Management Institute. *Risk Financing: A Guide to Insurance Cash Flow*. Dallas: International Risk Management Institute, Inc., 2000.

Skipper, Harold D., Jr. *International Risk and Insurance*. Burr Ridge, IL: Irwin/McGraw-Hill, 1998.

Williams, Arthur C., Jr., Michael L. Smith, and Peter C. Young, *Risk Management and Insurance*, 8th ed. Burr Ridge, IL: Irwin/McGraw-Hill, 1998.

Chapter 10

Finite and Integrated Risk Insurance Plans

Introduction

This chapter provides an overview of both finite risk and integrated risk insurance plans, which were introduced in Chapter 1 and Chapter 3. As explained throughout this chapter, these plans enable an organization to efficiently manage many of its enterprisewide risks. As explained in Chapter 3, a *finite risk plan* is an insurance plan whereby an insured transfers a limited (finite) amount of risk to an insurer because a large component of the insured's premium is used to fund its own losses. An **integrated risk plan** is an insurance plan that provides an insured with a single block of risk-transfer capacity over several types of risk exposures, which can include financial/market risk (such as that involving interest rate, foreign exchange, and commodity price risks) as well as hazard risk exposures.

> An **integrated risk plan** is an insurance plan that provides an insured with a single block of risk-transfer capacity over several types of risk exposures, which can include financial/market risk (for example, risk related to interest rate and foreign exchange) along with hazard risk exposures.

An integrated risk plan is sometimes written on a finite risk basis. Under such a plan, the insurer provides a large block of risk-transfer capacity over several types of risk exposures, with the premium structured so that the insurer takes only a limited amount of risk. This type of plan is sometimes referred to as a **finite/ integrated risk plan**.

> A **finite/integrated risk plan** is an integrated risk plan written on a finite risk basis.

In general, an organization uses a finite and/or an integrated risk plan for high-severity losses above a plan that involves retention, such as a self-insurance plan, a retrospective rating plan, or a captive insurer plan. (As explained later, in certain circumstances an organization uses finite risk insurance for its working-level losses.) An insured needs a substantial annual risk cost in order to justify the expenses involved with a finite and/or an integrated risk plan. One source places this annual risk cost in excess of $1 million.[1]

Finite Risk Plans

Finite risk plans, which are often categorized as hybrid plans, can be thought of as a blend of self-insurance and guaranteed cost insurance. With a finite risk plan, the insurer returns a portion of the premium if it makes a profit, as specified by the plan. This structure benefits an insured that is able to control its losses. Conversely, an insured that is not able to control its losses is protected because losses that exceed an aggregate retained amount are transferred to the insurer.

Most finite risk plans are somewhat similar in concept to a retrospective rating plan. A major difference between them is that a finite risk plan usually covers an insured's high-severity losses over several years under a single contract, while a retrospective rating plan is usually applied to an insured's low-to-medium-severity losses over a single year. Because a finite risk plan deals with high-severity losses, the losses that will fall under it are usually more difficult to predict than the losses that will fall under a retrospective rating plan.

Finite risk insurance plans are flexible and are custom-tailored to insureds' needs. Although no two finite risk plans are exactly alike, they do share common characteristics:

- The limits of coverage apply on an aggregate basis.
- The term of coverage is usually for multiple years (up to fifteen years in some cases, although five to ten years is more common) and is noncancelable.
- The premium is generally a substantial percentage of the policy limits (often 50 percent or more).
- The insurer shares profit with the insured, including investment income arising from the cash flow.

- The insured is allowed to commute the plan within a specified time frame. Commutation extinguishes all liabilities between the parties and is the means by which a share of the profit is returned to the insured.

Commutation

A **commutation** occurs when the parties to an insurance (or a reinsurance) contract agree to extinguish all liabilities between them. The previously insured organization, rather than the insurer, is then responsible for all future payments on losses, including losses that have been reported but not paid. The previously insured organization usually receives money from the insurer for agreeing to commute the agreement.

With a finite risk plan, the insurer uses commutation as a means to share its profit with the insured. In order to receive a share of the insurer's profit, the insured must exercise its option to commute.

A finite risk plan can be written as insurance or reinsurance. When written as reinsurance, a finite risk plan can reinsure a captive insurance company or a commercial insurance company.

Example of a Finite Risk Plan

Finite risk is best illustrated with an example. Much of the rest of this section refers to the facts presented below for ABC Corporation.

ABC Corporation (ABC) is a publicly traded corporation that manufactures sports helmets, which are considered by insurance underwriters to be high-risk products from a liability standpoint. However, because of its high-quality manufacturing process and its consumer education campaign, ABC has an excellent historical liability loss record with its helmets, which it has been manufacturing for fifteen years.

Under its risk management program, ABC is willing to retain a great deal of the products liability risk arising from its helmets. It retains the first $5 million per occurrence through its captive insurer, which purchases no reinsurance. In the past, ABC purchased guaranteed cost products liability insurance with a limit of $45 million per occurrence and aggregate to sit above the $5 million per occurrence layer covered by its captive.

Currently, ABC's broker is renewing the insurance program and is able to obtain the same limit of guaranteed cost products liability coverage, but above an attachment point of $30 million rather than $5 million per occurrence. This leaves an uncovered layer in ABC's liability program of $25 million per occurrence excess of $5 million per occurrence as Exhibit 10-1 illustrates:

Exhibit 10-1
ABC's Liability Program Without Finite Risk Insurance

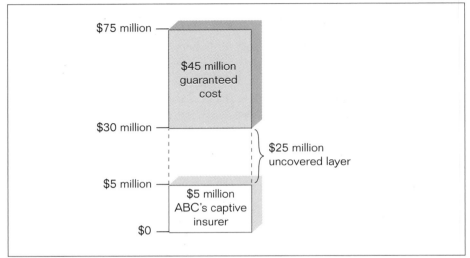

ABC has the financial resources to retain losses in the uncovered layer and, based on its historical record, believes it will suffer no losses in that layer. However, in the unlikely event that a loss occurs in the uncovered layer, ABC's reported net income for the year would drop significantly and, as a result, the financial markets would probably bid down its share price.

ABC asks its insurance broker to devise a finance/insurance product that would enable it to spread over time the cost of any large losses that fall into the uncovered layer. ABC's insurance broker suggests a finite risk insurance plan and obtains the following quotation, as shown in Exhibit 10-2.

Note that the plan shown in Exhibit 10-2 has all the common characteristics of a finite risk plan. ABC pays a premium of $3 million per year for five years in order to obtain a single aggregate limit over the five years of $25 million. By combining premium and limits over five years, ABC is able to obtain a higher limit in this layer than it would be able to obtain with a single year's premium. By giving ABC the option to commute the agreement, the insurer is offering to return profit to ABC. Upon commutation, ABC would obtain a refund based on the formula shown.

In the ABC case, the insurer is taking a limited (finite) amount of risk. A single large products liability loss or a series of moderately sized products liability losses probably would not be fully paid for until many years after they occur. Therefore, the insurer has a long period of time over which to earn investment income on the net premium of $13.8 million ($15 million premium minus the $1.2 million margin). The most that the insurer would ever have to pay over the five-year period is $25 million (including defense costs). The insurer's risk is limited to $25 million minus the sum of the $13.8 million net premium and the earned investment income. For taking this limited amount of risk and to cover its expenses, the insurer receives the margin of $1.2 million plus the opportunity to earn investment income that exceeds the six-month T-bill rate, which is the rate of interest that it credits to the experience fund.

Exhibit 10-2
ABC's Finite Risk Quotation

Coverage:	ABC's Products Liability
Limit:	$25 million per occurrence/five-year aggregate (including defense costs)
Attachment Point:	$5 million per occurrence
Deposit Premium:	$3 million per year for five years (total of $15 million)
Margin:	8 percent of the deposit premium (.08 × $15 million) or $1.2 million
Term:	Five years, noncancelable
Investment Income Credited:	Six-month Treasury bill (T-bill) rate
Commutation:	At the end of the five-year policy term and at each anniversary thereafter, ABC has the option to commute the agreement. Upon commutation, any funds returned to ABC (profit sharing) are based on the following formula:
	$15 million deposit premium plus accrued investment income minus the sum of the $1.2 million margin and the paid losses

Experience Fund

With a finite risk plan, profit sharing is accomplished through the maintenance of an **experience fund**, which is credited with the paid premium less the margin as well as investment income at a specified rate. In the example given in Exhibit 10-2, this is the six-month T-bill rate. Losses are subtracted from the experience fund as they are paid. Upon commutation, any balance in the experience fund is returned to the insured.[2] The insured would elect to commute the agreement only if the experience fund has a positive balance that is more than adequate to make projected future payments for losses that the insurer would no longer cover upon commutation.

Exhibit 10-3 shows the relationship between retained and transferred losses under a finite risk insurance plan.

Exhibit 10-3
Retained and Transferred Losses Under a Finite Risk Insurance Plan

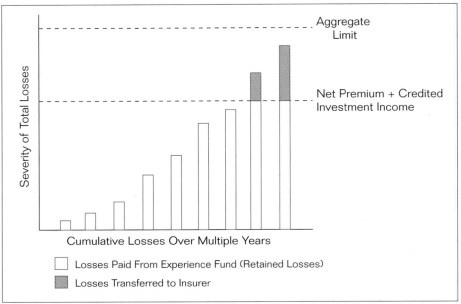

The value of a finite risk plan to an insured depends largely on favorable financial accounting and income tax treatments. In the example previously given, ABC hopes to be able to treat the deposit premium for the finite risk insurance plan in the same way that it would treat the premium for a guaranteed cost insurance plan. This treatment involves charging the $3 million deposit premium as an annual expense over five years for both financial accounting and tax purposes. This would allow ABC to smooth over time the impact of a large loss on its financial statements and would give ABC the benefit of a tax deduction of premium as it is paid. It would also create an off-balance sheet fund[3] (the experience fund) that ABC could use to pay large losses. However, as discussed later in this chapter, favorable financial and tax accounting treatments of a finite risk plan are uncertain and depend largely on the design of a particular plan.

Analysis of Finite Risk Plans

All insurance transactions involve varying degrees of three different types of risk: underwriting risk, investment risk, and credit risk. Finite risk insurance can be better understood if it is analyzed in terms of these various types of risk.

Types of Risk Under an Insurance Plan

Underwriting risk can be defined as the risk that an insurer's losses and expenses will be greater or less than its premiums plus the investment income it expects to earn,[4] therefore exposing its capital to a loss or a gain. For example, an insurer that receives $5 million in premium and expects $3 million in investment income to cover losses and expenses that could be as high as $15 million takes a $7 million underwriting risk.

Investment risk is the risk that an insurer's investment income will be higher or lower than it expects. Investment risk can be broken down into **timing risk** and **interest rate risk**. Timing risk is the risk that the insured's losses will be paid faster or slower than expected, and interest rate risk is the risk that interest rates will be above or below the expected rate over the term of the contract. Timing risk and interest rate risk together constitute investment risk. For example, an insurer's investment income will be lower than it expects if losses are paid sooner than expected and/or interest rates are lower than expected.

Credit risk is the risk that an insured will not pay a premium that it owes an insurer. For example, under a paid loss retrospectively rated plan, an insured pays premium as the insurer pays losses. The insurer is responsible for paying all covered losses under the policy, even those losses not reimbursed by the insured. Therefore, the insurer has a credit risk with this transaction because it might have to pay losses for which it is not reimbursed.[5]

A guaranteed cost plan contains all three types of risk previously mentioned. When pricing a guaranteed cost plan, an insurer calculates an expected amount of losses, expenses, and investment income. If actual losses and expenses on an individual policy are higher than expected, the insurer suffers an underwriting loss on the policy. Alternatively, if actual losses and expenses on the policy are lower than expected, the insurer experiences an underwriting gain. If actual investment income is lower than expected, the insurer suffers a loss due to investment risk. An insurer suffers a credit risk loss if the insured does not pay the premium.

When insurers underwrite on a guaranteed cost basis, they usually issue a large number of policies, each covering similar loss exposures. Using the law of large numbers to its advantage, the insurer charges each insured a guaranteed cost premium that reflects the expected, or average, annual amount of loss that will arise from each insured's exposures. If the insurer suffers an underwriting loss on one policy, it hopes to make it up with an underwriting gain on other policies. If an insured has lower-than-expected losses, it does not receive profit sharing. For the book of business as a whole, the insurer hopes to minimize its underwriting risk by spreading it out among the many policies it writes.

Finite risk does not have this same relationship between premium and losses. An insurer uses the premium and investment income from an individual finite risk policy largely to fund losses that fall under that policy. The insurer charges a deposit premium that is a substantial percentage of the policy limits and sets aside a percentage of the deposit premium for the margin. The **margin** is an amount that is meant to cover the limited degree of underwriting risk as well as the investment risk and credit risk that the insurer takes under the policy. The premium and limit are spread over several years, allowing for a large expected amount of investment income. Therefore, compared with a guaranteed cost insurance policy, a finite risk policy involves a much higher degree of self-funding on the insured's part, and the insurer takes a much lower degree of underwriting risk.

> A **margin** is an amount charged under a finite risk plan to cover the insurer's underwriting risk, investment risk, and credit risk, as well as its administrative expenses.

Exhibit 10-4 illustrates underwriting and investment risks for the finite risk plan mentioned in the ABC case.

Exhibit 10-4
Underwriting and Investment Risk Under ABC's Finite Risk Plan

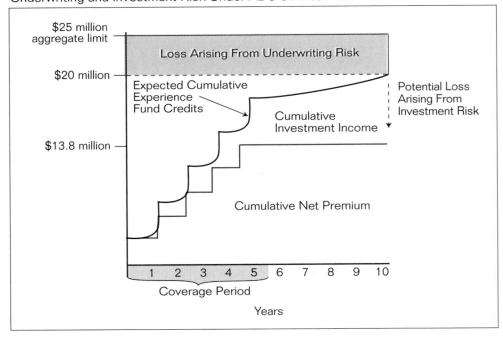

The net premium paid into the experience fund over five years is $13.8 million, and the most that the insurer would ever have to pay in losses is $25 million (including defense costs). Losses are expected to be paid out over ten years and, if the timing of loss payments and investment earnings is as expected, the investment income will equal $6.2 million over the ten-year period. Therefore, the net premium plus the investment income is expected to equal $20 million over the ten-year period. Under this scenario, the following would apply:

- The insurer is subject to a possible loss arising from underwriting risk because the total losses could fall between $20 and $25 million.

- The insurer is subject to a possible loss arising from investment risk because the investment income may be lower than $6.2 million. (Note that at lower loss levels the insurer will probably not realize a loss arising from investment risk because premium plus investment income probably would be sufficient to fund losses.)

- The insurer is subject to a possible loss arising from credit risk because it might have to pay cumulative losses that exceed the experience fund balance before the insured has paid the entire premium. The insurer suffers a credit loss only if the insured does not pay the balance of the premium due.

- To cover its administrative expenses, as well as to obtain compensation for taking the chance of a loss arising from underwriting, investment, and/ or credit risk, the insurer receives a $1.2 million premium (the margin) plus the chance to make an investment gain. The insurer makes an investment gain if it invests the funds at a rate that is higher than the six-month T-bill rate, which is the interest rate it credits to the experience fund.

Calculating the Experience Fund Balance

ABC's experience fund balance at the beginning and end of each year can be calculated as shown in Exhibit 10-5, which is based on the following assumptions:

- The insured pays the premium at the beginning of each year, and the insurer pays losses at the end of each year.

- Losses total $20 million, paid by the insurer based on the amounts shown for each year in the column labeled "Loss Payment."

- The six-month T-bill rate is equal to 6 percent yearly, which is the investment income rate that the insurer credits to the fund.

Exhibit 10-5

Calculation of ABC's Experience Fund Balance

Year	Beginning Experience Fund	Net Premium	Investment Income (6%)	Loss Payment	Ending Experience Fund
1	$0	$2,760,000	$165,600		$2,925,600
2	$2,925,600	$2,760,000	$341,136		$6,026,736
3	$6,026,736	$2,760,000	$527,204		$9,313,940
4	$9,313,940	$2,760,000	$724,436		$12,798,377
5	$12,798,377	$2,760,000	$933,503	$3,000,000	$13,491,879
6	$13,491,879		$809,513		$14,301,392
7	$14,301,392		$858,084		$15,159,475
8	$15,159,475		$909,569	$8,000,000	$8,069,044
9	$8,069,044		$484,143	$1,000,000	$7,553,187
10	$7,553,187		$453,191	$8,000,000	$6,378
Total		$13,800,000	$6,206,378	$20,000,000	

The experience fund balance at the end of year 10 is $6,378. At ABC's option, this amount can be returned to ABC through a commutation or rolled into an experience fund for another coverage period.

Note the similarities between the numbers in Exhibit 10-5 and the graph in Exhibit 10-4. The cumulative net premium paid by ABC is $13.8 million, and the cumulative investment income earned and credited to the experience fund is approximately $6.2 million. The net premium plus the investment income is sufficient to fund $20 million in losses, based on the loss payment schedule shown in Exhibit 10-5.

The experience fund balance can be measured under various loss scenarios to determine whether the fund is sufficient to pay for losses at different levels and with different payment patterns. The insurer can use this information to measure its underwriting and investment risk. ABC can use this information to calculate the net cost of the finite risk plan under various loss scenarios.

Variations in the Terms of a Finite Risk Agreement

ABC has a common type of finite risk plan. There are variations that can be made to this plan depending on the objectives of ABC and the insurer. Some of these variations are discussed below.

Per Occurrence and/or Aggregate Limits per Year

In addition to an aggregate limit over the term of the agreement, a per occurrence limit can be placed on a finite risk plan, reducing the insurer's risk. For example, ABC's finite risk plan could have a per occurrence limit of $10 million as well as the aggregate limit of $25 million over five years. Therefore, if a single $25 million loss occurs, only $10 million of it would be covered under the plan.

In addition to a per occurrence limit and an aggregate limit over the term of the agreement, an aggregate limit can be placed over each year, further reducing the insurer's risk. For example, ABC's finite risk plan could have an aggregate limit of $15 million per year as well as the per occurrence limit of $10 million and the aggregate limit of $25 million over five years. Therefore, if two $10 million losses occur in the first year, only $15 million would be covered under the plan.

Limits on Annual Loss Payout

To lower the insurer's investment risk, a finite risk plan can place limits on the annual payout of losses. For example, ABC's finite risk plan could place a loss payout limit of $2 million per year for the first five years so that during that period the insurer is not placed in a position whereby the cumulative loss payout exceeds cumulative premium received. Placing an annual limit on the loss payout guarantees that a minimum amount of investment income will be credited to the experience account. The annual limit on loss payout does not limit the amount of loss that the insurer will pay over the term of the agreement; it just limits the amount that the insurer will pay in any one year.

Contingent Sharing of Investment Income

A finite risk plan can contain a provision to share investment income if the earned investment income exceeds the rate initially agreed to as an interest credit to the experience fund. For example, ABC's finite risk insurer could agree to credit the experience fund with one-half of the insurer's investment income to the extent that it exceeds the six-month T-bill rate.

Margin Based on a Sliding Scale

With ABC's finite risk plan, the insurer receives a fixed margin of 8 percent of the deposit premium. Instead of being a fixed percentage, the margin could vary based on the loss ratio that falls under the plan, with the margin decreasing for favorable loss experience and increasing for unfavorable loss experience. This arrangement provides the insured with an additional incentive to control losses. The margin could be structured as follows:

Loss Ratio (%)	Margin (%)
70-100	12
30-70	8
0-30	4

Therefore, the margin falls to 4 percent if losses divided by the deposit premium are 30 percent or less and rises to 12 percent if losses divided by the deposit premium are 70 percent or more. Because the margin is subtracted in order to calculate the net premium, which is credited to the experience fund, decreasing the margin increases the amount available in the experience fund. Alternatively, increasing the margin decreases the amount available in the experience fund.

Additional Premium Requirement

A finite risk plan might require that the insured pay an additional premium if total losses exceed a certain level. In effect, the insured is retaining some of the risk that losses will exceed that level. This additional risk retention should be reflected through a lowering of the margin built into the plan.

Prospective vs. Retroactive Plans

The type of finite risk plan discussed up to this point is a **prospective plan**, meaning that it is arranged to cover losses from events that have not yet occurred. Another type of finite risk plan is a **retroactive plan** (sometimes called a "retrospective" plan), meaning that it is arranged to cover losses from events that have already occurred.

> A **prospective plan** is an insurance plan that is arranged to cover losses from events that have not yet occurred.
>
> A **retroactive plan** is an insurance plan that is arranged to cover losses from events that have already occurred.

For example, a pharmaceutical company may have an uninsured multimillion dollar lawsuit against it for an injury alleged to have been caused by one of its products. The pharmaceutical company does not know what the outcome of the suit will be and, therefore, is uncertain as to the magnitude and payout of the loss. A finite risk insurance plan can be designed that covers this loss on a retroactive basis.

Loss Portfolio Transfers

A **loss portfolio transfer** is a type of retroactive plan that applies to a defined portfolio of losses. The losses usually have established reserves, but uncertainty exists as to the timing of the loss payments and the potential for further loss development.

> A **loss portfolio transfer** is a retroactive plan that applies to an entire portfolio of losses.

A loss portfolio transfer can be accomplished with a finite risk agreement. For example, a captive insurer could transfer all of its outstanding workers compensation losses from 1996, 1997, and 1998 with a finite risk plan that provides an aggregate limit and returns funds to the captive if total losses are settled for amounts that are less their outstanding reserves or if investment income is higher than expected.

An insured is usually able to negotiate a loss portfolio transfer for its working-level losses. These are losses characterized by low-to-medium severity and high frequency.

Use of a Finite Risk Plan

Because it is taking a carefully controlled, limited amount of risk, an underwriter of a finite risk plan usually will agree to cover a broader range of exposures than it would cover under a traditional insurance plan. In addition to covering commonly insured property and liability exposures, finite risk can be used for many difficult-to-insure exposures, such as products recall, warranties, environmental liability (including cleanup), and commodity price fluctuations. The terms of coverage are often flexible, with the insured often able to use manuscript policies that are tailored to its exposures.

Finite risk plans can be particularly beneficial in an acquisition or a merger. When the parties to an acquisition or a merger negotiate terms, they often must address an outstanding liability, such as a potential environmental cleanup exposure. Using a retroactive finite risk plan to fund the exposure can help the parties complete their merger or acquisition agreement.

Advantages of Finite Risk Plans

Assuming they receive favorable financial accounting treatment (from the insured's viewpoint), finite risk plans can smooth out over time the impact of large losses on the insured's net income (profit) in its financial statements. Even with guaranteed cost insurance, an insured that suffers a large loss in one year is likely to face an increase in premium the following year, which would lower its net income. Finite risk insurance can help an organization avoid large swings in cost.

As a hybrid plan, finite risk insurance combines many of the advantages of both retention and transfer. An insured that is able to control its losses receives profit sharing, including investment income on the cash flow of the experience fund. However, the insured is also protected by a limited amount of risk transfer in the event that losses are much higher than expected.

A finite risk plan often enables an insured to obtain higher limits than it could get under a traditional guaranteed cost insurance plan. An underwriter is willing to provide the higher limits because premium and limits are combined over several years under a single plan. In addition, by using a finite risk plan an insured is able to certify to third parties that it has insurance that might not otherwise be available.

A major advantage of finite risk plans is that they save the time and expense of annual renewals. Under traditional insurance, the insured, the insurer, and the broker spend a great deal of time each year renewing the insurance program. Underwriting information must be gathered and analyzed, and the premium must be negotiated. Finite risk plans involve these same tasks at renewal, but renewal takes place only once every several years.

Disadvantages of Finite Risk Plans

A disadvantage of finite risk plans that an insured should carefully consider is the opportunity cost on its capital that is tied up in the experience fund. The cash balance in the experience fund usually is credited with a short-term investment rate based on the three- or six-month T-bill rate. The insured's cost of capital is almost certainly above the rate credited to the fund, resulting in an opportunity cost to the insured because the insured could otherwise use the funds as capital. Most finite risk plans build up a large cash balance in the experience fund over time.

Another disadvantage of finite risk plans is that an aggregate limit applies over multiple years. Therefore, if a full-limit loss occurs early in the term, no further limits are available, even though the insured is obligated to pay premium for the remainder of the term.

Premium taxes on finite risk plans can be a large expense. Depending on the structure of a particular plan, state premium taxes or surplus lines taxes and a federal excise tax may be due. For example, if a finite risk plan is placed with an admitted insurer, then state premium taxes are due, which can be 2 to 3 percent of premium. If a finite risk plan is placed with a nonadmitted, offshore insurer, then a surplus lines or a self-procurement tax and a federal excise tax (for premiums paid to offshore insurers) may be due based on the premium amount.

Financial Accounting and Tax Implications of Finite Risk Plans

A great deal of uncertainty exists as to the financial accounting and income tax treatments of finite risk plans. As previously mentioned, the value of a finite risk plan to an insured depends largely on favorable financial accounting and income tax treatments. However, in recent years the Financial Accounting Standards Board (FASB) in the United States has issued accounting standards and opinions that severely limit an insured's ability to treat the premium under a finite risk plan in the same way that it would treat a premium for traditional guaranteed cost insurance.

From the insured's viewpoint, favorable accounting and tax treatments for a finite risk plan mean that it is allowed to treat the annual premium as an expense on its financial statements and its income tax returns. The insured thus is able to smooth out over time its reported expenses for its large losses and take a tax deduction on payments to fund those losses.

Because the premium for a finite risk plan is used both to fund the insured's losses and to transfer a limited amount of risk, determining the appropriate accounting and tax treatments for the annual premium payments is difficult. Many complex financial accounting and income tax issues are involved, and each specific plan is different from others because it is customized for an insured's requirements. Therefore, the terms of each specific plan must be analyzed to determine whether it meets current accounting and tax guidelines. The following section discusses the financial accounting and tax issues related to finite risk plans.

Financial Accounting Issues

Recent statements and pronouncements by the FASB in the United States have tightened the rules for obtaining favorable financial accounting treatment for a finite risk plan. These statements and pronouncements include *Statement of Financial Accounting Standards Number 113 (FAS 113)*, *Emerging Issues Task Force (EITF) 93-6*, and *EITF 93-14*, which are discussed below.

FAS 113

In December 1992, the FASB issued FAS 113, which is titled *Accounting and Reporting for Reinsurance of Short-Duration and Long-Duration Contracts*. FAS 113 applies specifically to reinsurance, including finite risk reinsurance. However there is a widespread belief that auditors will apply its principles to finite risk *insurance* as well.

Treating Contracts as Reinsurance Under *FAS 113*

Two conditions must be met in order to account for a transaction as reinsurance under **FAS 113**:

1. The reinsurer assumes *significant insurance risk* under the reinsured portions of the underlying insurance contracts.

2. It is *reasonably possible* that the reinsurer may realize a *significant loss* from the transaction.[6]

Continued on the next page.

> In order to apply those two guidelines, the italicized words must be interpreted. "Insurance risk" is defined to include both timing and underwriting risk. "Reasonably possible" means "more than a remote" chance exists. "Significant loss" is not defined in the statement. Therefore, the guidelines under *FAS 113* provide some limited guidance as to whether a particular transaction can be accounted for as reinsurance.

If it is determined that a reinsurance transaction meets the guidelines for treating it as reinsurance under *FAS 113*, then the reinsurance premium is allowed as an expense on the insurer's financial statements each year. If a reinsurance transaction does not meet the guidelines for treating it as reinsurance under *FAS 113*, then the insurer must account for the premium as a deposit to fund its losses. The consequence of treating the premium as a deposit is that the insurer is not able to recognize the annual premium payments as an expense but instead must recognize its losses as an expense as they are incurred. This accounting treatment means that the insurer's reported net income can vary significantly from year to year because of the timing and the size of the losses that fall under its finite risk reinsurance plan.

The provisions of *FAS 113* can be applied to finite risk insurance. *FAS 113* makes it clear that in order for a finite risk plan to be treated as insurance, it should transfer underwriting risk as well as timing risk (some of the early finite risk insurance plans transferred timing risk only). In addition, the plan should be designed so that it is "reasonably possible" that the insurer could realize a "significant loss" from the transaction. Although *FAS 113* provides no guidelines as to what is a "reasonably possible significant loss," insurance practitioners hope that certain rules of thumb for implementing these provisions will develop among the auditors of insurers' financial statements. For example, a "10/10 rule" would require that there is a 10 percent chance that the insurer could suffer a loss equal to 10 percent of its premium[7] on the transaction.

With a finite risk insurance arrangement, one could argue that the amount paid for the margin passes the guidelines under *FAS 113*. The margin functions like a guaranteed cost insurance premium, with the insurer using it to fund the underwriting and timing risk on the transaction. Therefore, one could argue that it is reasonably possible for the insurer to realize a significant loss on the margin. In this case, it is only the net premium for which uncertainty exists in terms of financial accounting and tax treatments. The following discussion centers on the financial accounting treatment of the net premium under a finite risk insurance plan.

Finite Risk Payments: Insurance Premiums or Deposits To Fund Losses?

If a finite risk insurance plan does not meet the guidelines under *FAS 113*, the insured organization will probably have to treat the net premium payments as deposits for financial accounting purposes. When an insured treats its net premium payments as deposits to fund its losses rather than as traditional insurance premiums, the insured's reported net income will vary based on the timing and size of its actual incurred losses, just as if it were self-insuring those losses. When treated as a deposit, the cash paid for net premium is booked as an asset on the insured's balance sheet rather than as a premium expense on its income statement. Losses are shown as an expense on the insured's income statement when they are incurred, with the paid amounts taken from the premium deposit assets and the unpaid amounts shown as a liability on the insured's balance sheet.

As an example, assume ABC's finite risk plan has the following amounts of incurred losses in years 1 through 5. (ABC's net premium is the same as mentioned in a previous section.)

Year	Net Premium	Incurred Losses
1	$ 2,760,000	$ 4,000,000
2	2,760,000	500,000
3	2,760,000	10,000,000
4	2,760,000	500,000
5	2,760,000	5,000,000
Total	$13,800,000	$20,000,000

As Exhibit 10-5 illustrated, ABC's net premium of $13.8 million is expected to earn investment income and be sufficient to pay for $20 million in losses, which are assumed to be paid in years 5 through 10.

The following graph shows the expenses that ABC would report on its income statement each year that the finite risk plan is in effect if the net premium payments were (1) treated as insurance premiums or (2) treated as deposits to fund losses. If treated as insurance, the net premium is charged as an expense each year. If the net premium is treated as a deposit, expenses are recognized only as losses are incurred.

Continued on next page.

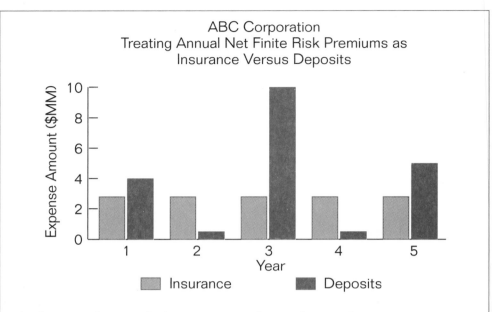

ABC Corporation
Treating Annual Net Finite Risk Premiums as
Insurance Versus Deposits

As the preceding graph shows, treating the net finite risk premiums as insurance premiums spreads out the reported expenses over time and helps stabilize ABC's reported net income. Also, insurance premiums, in effect, are a present-value cost of funding losses, so recognizing the premiums rather than the incurred losses as expenses lowers the total amount of expense that ABC recognizes over the five-year period.

EITF 93-6 *and* EITF 93-14

In 1993, the FASB further investigated the financial accounting issues involved with finite risk reinsurance by issuing EITF 93-6. (An *EITF* is an opinion issued by FASB's Emerging Issues Task Force and does not have the same authority as a financial accounting standard.) Soon thereafter, the provisions of EITF 93-6 were extended to insurance with the issuance of EITF 93-14.

Two important provisions of **EITF 93-6** (and **EITF 93-14** by extension) are

1. A ceding insurer should recognize a liability and the assuming reinsurer should recognize an asset with respect to the cedent's experience-related obligations to pay cash or other consideration to the assuming reinsurer.

2. A ceding insurer should recognize an asset and the assuming reinsurer should recognize a liability with respect to the cedent's experience-related right to a payment from the assuming reinsurer. Failure to do so would, in effect, result in an improper premature recognition of a contingency reserve before losses have actually occurred.

Because EITF 93-14 extends the two provisions to insurance, one could substitute "insured" for "ceding insurer" and "insurer" for "reinsurer" when thinking of the two provisions in terms of *EITF 93-14*.

Under ABC's finite risk plan, *EITF 93-14* suggests that ABC should make the following accruals at the end of each accounting period if it treated the plan as "insurance" under *FAS 113*:

- ABC should accrue any balance in the experience fund as an asset on its balance sheet. ABC should increase its revenue by the same amount. Because the balance in the experience fund is meant to cover outstanding losses, ABC should also accrue any reserves for outstanding losses as an expense on its income statement and as a liability on its balance sheet. (These series of accounting transactions have the same financial accounting effect on ABC as deposit accounting, which was previously discussed.)

- If ABC's incurred losses are large enough to cause ABC to have future premium obligations to cover the losses, then the future premium obligations should be accrued as an expense on ABC's income statement and as a liability on its balance sheet. For example, if a $25 million dollar loss occurred in Year 1, then ABC still would be required to pay $12 million in premium in Year 2 through Year 5, even though it would obtain no future economic benefit from these premium payments because the five-year aggregate coverage limit ($25 million) is exhausted. Therefore, under this circumstance, ABC should accrue the $12 million as an expense on its income statement and as a liability on its balance sheet.

The net effect of *EITF 93-14* is that ABC must recognize the retained portion of its losses as they are incurred, similar to the effect of deposit accounting previously discussed. Therefore, *EITF 93-6* and *EITF 93-14* supported and further tightened the financial accounting provisions of *FAS 113*.

If *FAS 113* or *EITF 93-6* (and *93-14* by extension) forces an organization to, in effect, use deposit accounting treatment for its finite risk plan, then the organization does not have the benefit of smoothing its losses over time on its financial statements. This negates one of the key advantages of these types of plans.

If a finite risk plan is designed so that these accounting pronouncements do not force the insured organization to, in effect, use deposit accounting, then the plan can provide tremendous benefits to an organization for financing its losses. The key is to design a plan whereby it is "reasonably possible" for the insurer to realize a "significant loss" and whereby the insured does not have experience-related obligations to pay cash or experience-related obligations to receive cash. Insurance brokers, consultants, and underwriters continually devise creative strategies for accomplishing this result.

Tax Issues

In the United States, the concepts that apply to financial accounting also apply to the tax treatment of finite risk plans. Many tax accountants believe that *FAS 113*, while applying to financial accounting standards, is also a useful source of guidance in determining the tax deductibility of premiums.

Based on previous Tax Court cases and Revenue Rulings by the Internal Revenue Service (IRS), an insurance premium is tax-deductible if there is both risk shifting and risk distribution. **Risk shifting** means that risk of loss is transferred to the insurer, and **risk distribution** means that the insurer distributes the risks among its insureds. Therefore, the insurer must take underwriting risk and use the profits it makes from some insureds to pay the losses it experiences with other insureds. A transaction that transfers only investment risk is not sufficient to enable an insured to take a tax deduction on the premium.

> **Risk shifting** is the transfer of the risk of loss to an insurer.
>
> **Risk distribution** is the sharing of risk by an insurer among its insureds. Risk shifting and risk distribution are required for an insured to take a tax deduction for an insurance premium.

In the ABC example, the margin is clearly tax-deductible when incurred because the insurer uses it largely to shift and distribute underwriting risk. However, there is a question as to whether the entire premium is tax-deductible when incurred. Does ABC's plan, taken as a whole, contain sufficient risk shifting and distribution? ABC's tax counsel must make that determination.

Integrated Risk Plans

The second major type of plan discussed in this chapter is an integrated risk plan. An integrated risk plan is an insurance plan that provides an insured with a single block of risk-transfer capacity over several types of risk exposures, usually over multiple years. Integrated risk plans usually provide coverage for various types of hazard risk exposures and can include coverage of various types of financial/market risk exposures as well, such as movements in commodity prices, interest rates, and foreign exchange rates. An integrated risk plan is usually written on a guaranteed cost basis; however, it is sometimes written on a finite risk basis, in which case it is referred to as a finite/integrated risk plan.

Traditionally, organizations have analyzed each of their risk exposures separately and decided on a combination of retention and transfer for each exposure. To transfer risk, most large organizations purchase separate annual insurance policies for property, general liability, products liability, automobile liability, marine liability, and directors and officers liability as well as their other loss exposures. In addition, organizations routinely hedge their commodity price, interest rate, and foreign exchange rate risks by purchasing options and engaging in swaps in the financial markets. By contrast, an integrated risk plan can provide a single block of risk-transfer capacity across these multiple types of hazard and financial risk exposures over multiple years (hence the word "integrated").

Chapter 2 mentioned that an organization can manage its risk effectively by retaining a portfolio of various types of risk exposures. A major advantage of this approach is that an organization can retain a large share of each of its risk exposures but at the same time reduce its overall retained risk level through diversification. The benefits of risk diversification also accrue to an insured that transfers risk in a large, single block across all its risk exposures rather than separately for each. This consolidated approach is more efficient than an exposure-by-exposure approach because the risk taker (the insurer) is able to diversify its risk across different types of risk exposures and across time (if the contract is for multiple years). This approach results in a lower risk charge by the insurer.

An example helps illustrate the benefit of risk diversification. Assume that in Year 1 an organization suffers a $500,000 loss from its general liability exposure but that, in that same year, the organization realizes a $1,000,000 gain from its foreign exchange (currency) exposure. In addition, assume that in Year 2 the organization has no general liability losses but realizes a $500,000 loss from its foreign exchange exposure. The organization's total net gain or loss over both Year 1 and Year 2 for both exposures is $0. Therefore, its combined risk over two years is much lower than its net gain or loss on any one risk exposure for any one year.

The Theory Behind Integrated Risk

The following example illustrates the efficiency of transferring risk on an integrated basis. Assume that an insured with two types of risk exposure purchases separate annual insurance policies for each exposure. Each policy has a limit of $50 million per occurrence and a self-insured retention of $5 million per occurrence. The following diagram shows the retention and limits for each policy.

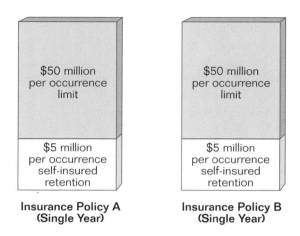

Insurance Policy A
(Single Year)

Insurance Policy B
(Single Year)

Note that the insured is willing to retain a large amount of total losses for a single year because it retains all loss occurrences up to $5 million under both Policy A and Policy B.

The loss exposures covered under Policy A and Policy B could be combined under an integrated risk plan that covers a five-year period with a $10 million per occurrence self-insured retention and a $100 million per occurrence limit. (Other options, including aggregates, are available for the self-insured retention and policy limit.)

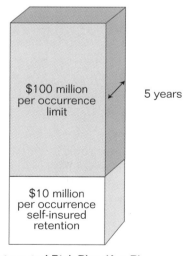

Integrated Risk Plan (A + B)
(Five Years)

The five-year premium for the integrated risk plan is likely to be less than the sum of the annual premiums for Policy A and Policy B over the same five-year period. This is mainly due to the fact that the insurer's risk attaches at a higher per occurrence attachment point ($10 million as opposed to $5 million). Also, the insurer is able to leverage the use of its risk capital by applying it over multiple lines and multiple years. Some industry practitioners estimate the annual savings by using an integrated risk plan to be in excess of 25 percent.[8] This estimated savings includes both premium and administrative costs.

Exhibit 10-6 illustrates the effect of combining, or integrating, coverages under a single contract. Under the integrated risk plan previously described, the $100 million per occurrence limit is available for exposures previously covered under both Policy A and B. Previously, Policy A and Policy B separately provided $50 million of per occurrence coverage with a $5 million per occurrence self-insured retention. For all losses covered under the integrated program, the $10 million per occurrence self-insured retention applies.

Clearly, an insured that switches from a traditional insurance plan to an integrated risk plan engages in a tradeoff. In the example given in Exhibit 10-6, the insured commits to a higher per occurrence retention: $10 million over a five-year period on a combined lines basis as opposed to $5 million for a single annual period for each line separately. In exchange, the insured receives a higher per occurrence limit that applies to the combined exposures for the entire five-year period. Because of this rearrangement of retentions and limits, the insured is likely to save premium over the five-year period.

One could argue that the purported savings from integrated risk is illusory because the insured's premium varies depending on the expected frequency and severity of the transferred losses. If combining loss exposures and limits over time results in a lower annual expected frequency and severity of transferred losses, the insured's annual premium should be correspondingly lower.

Integrated risk does allow for some hard-dollar savings for the following reasons:

- The insurer and the broker negotiate renewals once every several years, rather than annually as under a traditional insurance plan. Also, the insured and the broker usually deal with just one or two insurers rather than several insurers as under a traditional plan. This streamlined approach results in a savings of time and expense and fosters a long-term partnership between the parties.

- With an integrated risk plan, the insured can increase its purchasing power and realize savings by making a single bulk purchase to transfer its risk. This results in a lower risk charge by the insurer than if risk were transferred to it separately by type of risk and by year. Also, policy limits usually go unused in each year (in the sense that each policy does not have a

Exhibit 10-6

Integrating Coverages Under a Single Contract

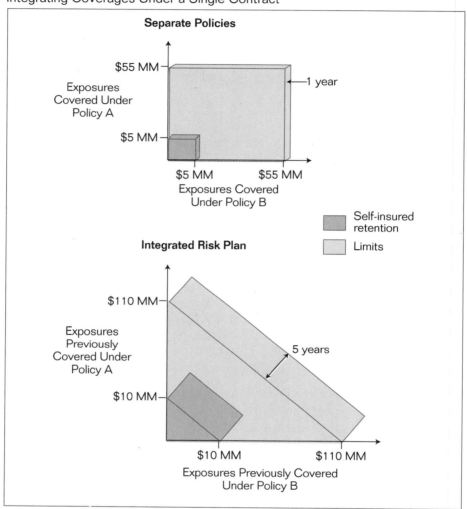

full-limit claim), so purchasing a single limit over different types of risk and multiple years is more efficient than purchasing separate limits for each type of risk and each year.

- Integrated risk results in a more efficient retention by the insured. By combining its retention across different types of risk and multiple years, the insured can reduce its aggregate retained risk through diversification and receive appropriate premium credits.

As long as an integrated risk plan provides an organization with a tolerable retention level and an adequate limit, it can be an efficient way to transfer risk.

Designing an Integrated Risk Plan

As previously mentioned, an integrated risk plan can be designed to cover various types of risk, including hazard risk and financial/market risk, which includes movements in commodity prices, interest rates, and foreign exchange rates (currency risk). To date, insureds have combined property and liability risks (hazard risks) in integrated risk plans. These risks include property, business income, crime, ocean marine, general liability, automobile liability, workers compensation, professional liability, and directors and officers liability, as well as many others. A few insureds have combined financial/market risks with hazard risks in an integrated risk plan, and many are moving in the direction of combining other enterprisewide risks as well. Integrated risk plans are flexible because they are customized for each insured.

Exhibit 10-7 shows one possible design of an integrated risk plan for a large organization that takes a $25 million per occurrence retention for each type of risk. The plan applies over a five-year period. The integrated risk coverage applies to several hazard risks and to currency risk. There is a stop loss protection with a separate limit that applies above an annual aggregate retention for all the risks.[9] The integrated risk layer provides a limit of $50 million per occurrence that sits directly above the $25 million per occurrence retention for each type of risk. The integrated risk layer also has a $150 million aggregate limit that applies over the five-year coverage period. A monoline property coverage, purchased on an annual basis, sits above the integrated risk layer so as to ensure that an adequate limit is available to cover the property risk.

Exhibit 10-7
Integrated Risk Plan Example

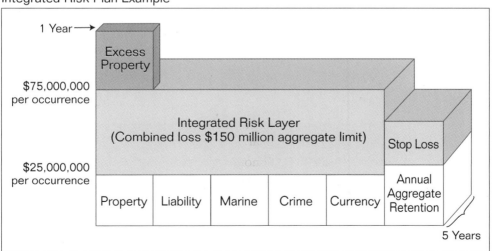

A Numerical Example

A numerical example helps illustrate the integrated risk plan shown in Exhibit 10-7. Assume that, over the five-year period of the plan, an organization incurs the following losses, which total $145 million. (To simplify the analysis, currency losses are not included.) Also, assume that the annual aggregate retention below the stop loss is $35 million.

(Figures in Millions of Dollars)

Coverage	Year 1	Year 2	Year 3	Year 4	Year 5	Total
Property	$1.0		$ 95.0			$ 96.0
Liability			2.0	$32.0		34.0
Marine	2.5	$2.0	6.0		$0.5	11.0
Crime			3.0	1.0		4.0
Total	$3.5	$2.0	$106.0	$33.0	$0.5	$145.0

The following chart shows how the losses are paid under the various layers of the program:

Year	Coverage	Loss	Retained Amount	Stop Loss	Integrated Risk Layer	Property Excess Layer
1	Property	$ 1.0	$ 1.0			
	Marine	2.5	2.5			
2	Marine	2.0	2.0			
3	Property	95.0	25.0		$50.0	$20.0
	Liability	2.0	2.0			
	Marine	6.0	6.0			
	Crime	3.0	2.0	$1.0		
4	Liability	32.0	25.0		7.0	
	Crime	1.0	1.0			
5	Marine	0.5	0.5			
Total		$145.0	$67.0	$1.0	$57.0	$20.0

Of the total losses over five years of $145 million,

- The organization retains $67 million;
- The annual stop loss coverage pays $1 million;
- The integrated risk insurer pays $57 million; and
- The insurer of the excess property losses pays $20 million (assuming the limit of the excess property policy is adequate).

The measurement of the currency risk exposure is unique because it is based on a weighted average of a basket of specific currencies translated into the currency in which the organization reports its profit and loss. The composition of the basket of currencies reflects the size and denominations of the organization's foreign revenues.

Variations in the Terms of an Integrated Risk Plan

Integrated risk plans are customized to meet insureds' needs. Virtually unlimited variations of an integrated risk plan exist, with the common feature being that an integrated risk plan is a single contract that covers more than one type of risk exposure. Two of the common variations are explained below.

Basket Aggregate Retention

Many integrated risk plans are designed to provide coverage that sits above a large aggregate retention spanning multiple types of risk exposures. This type of integrated risk plan is said to apply above a **basket aggregate retention**.

> **Basket aggregate retention** is a large aggregate retention spanning multiple types of risk exposure.

The integrated risk plan attaches at the point at which the basket aggregate retention is exhausted, and the basket aggregate retention itself usually sits above separate per occurrence retentions for each type of risk. This arrangement is illustrated in Exhibit 10-8.

Exhibit 10-8
Integrated Risk Plan With a Basket Aggregate Retention

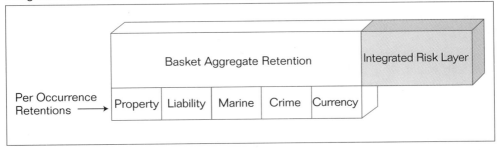

The basket aggregate retention can apply separately to each annual period.

Dual-Trigger Covers

Chapter 1 introduced the concept of dual-trigger covers, which are sometimes called multi-trigger covers. A **dual-trigger cover**, which is a type of integrated risk plan, ties an insured's retention and policy limit to two different types of risk. The distinguishing characteristic of a dual-trigger cover is that a loss above a certain retention threshold must occur under each of the two types of risk during the same time period in order to "trigger" coverage under the policy.

> A **dual-trigger cover** is an integrated risk plan in which the retention and limit are tied to two different types of risk. The distinguishing characteristic of a dual-trigger cover is that a loss above a certain retention threshold must occur under each of two types of risk during the same time period in order to "trigger" coverage under the policy.

A dual-trigger cover provides a means for an organization to tie its retention and policy limit under its hazard risks to its other types of risks, such as its financial/market risks. It is best suited for an organization that is willing to take a high retention on each type of risk but wants to transfer loss in the unlikely event that two large losses arising from different sources of risk occur during the same time period.

Consider the case of a large electricity supplier that distributes but does not generate electricity. Not only does it have property and liability risks (hazard risks) from owning and operating electrical distribution facilities, but it also stands to lose a great deal of profit if the wholesale price of electricity suddenly increases (a financial/market risk). A dual-trigger cover could protect the electricity distributor if it suffers a large property or liability loss related to its distribution facilities (the first trigger), and, during the same time period, if it incurs a significant increase in the price of its purchased electricity (the second trigger). The insurer would reimburse the electricity distributor for the combined loss to the extent it exceeds a specified retention level.

Advantages and Disadvantages of Integrated Risk Plans

Perhaps the greatest advantage to an integrated risk plan is that it can be customized to fit an organization's risk appetite and risk-bearing capacity. Traditional insurance plans are one-size-fits-all. Integrated risk plans can be crafted to address specific needs, improving the efficiency of risk transfer.

Another advantage is that an integrated risk plan provides some hard-dollar savings because of the insured's bulk purchasing power and the avoidance of annual renewal negotiations. Also, an integrated risk plan can be an efficient way for an organization to manage its retentions and limits by spreading them over several lines and several years. It also allows an insured to manage many of its enterprisewide risks under one contract. Depending on the design of the plan, some hard-to-insure risks might be included.

Integrated risk plans have some disadvantages. A single multi-year aggregate limit might not be sufficient for an insured that experiences extremely high losses. A large loss in the first year of the plan could exhaust the aggregate limit, leaving no limit available for the remaining years of the contract. Another disadvantage is that allocating an integrated risk premium among the divisions of a large organization might be difficult. Each division probably has its own unique risk exposures, which makes it difficult to allocate a composite premium that transfers risk for several lines together over multiple years under a single contract. Finally, the pricing for an integrated risk plan can be complex, particularly when it includes both financial/market and hazard risks. As illustrated by the integrated risk plan discussed earlier in this chapter, measuring foreign exchange risk is different from measuring hazard risk.

Summary

- A finite risk plan is an insurance plan whereby a limited (finite) amount of risk is transferred from an insured to an insurer because a large component of the insured's premium is used to fund its own losses. An integrated risk plan is an insurance plan that provides an insured with a single block of risk-transfer capacity over several types of risk exposures, which can include financial/market risk (such as that involving interest rates and foreign exchange) as well as hazard risk. A finite/integrated risk plan is an integrated risk plan written on a finite risk basis.

- A finite risk plan, which is categorized as a hybrid plan, can be thought of as a blend of self-insurance and guaranteed cost insurance. Finite risk plans have the following common characteristics:

  1. The limits of coverage apply on an aggregate basis.
  2. The term of coverage is usually for multiple years (up to fifteen years in some cases, although five to ten years is more common) and is noncancelable.
  3. The premium is a substantial percentage of the policy limits (usually 50 percent or more).
  4. The insurer shares profit with the insured, including investment income arising from the cash flow.
  5. The insured is allowed to commute the plan within a specified time frame. Commutation extinguishes all liabilities between the parties and is the means by which the insurer shares profit on the transaction with the insured.

- From an insurer's point of view, all insurance transactions involve varying degrees of three different types of risk: underwriting risk, investment risk, and credit risk. Underwriting risk, for the purpose of analyzing a finite risk plan, can be defined as the risk that an insurer's losses and expenses will be greater or less than its premiums plus the investment income it expects to earn, therefore exposing its capital to loss or gain. Investment risk is the risk that an insurer's investment income will be higher or lower than it expects. Investment risk can be broken down into timing risk, which is the risk that the insured's losses will be paid faster or slower than expected and interest rate risk, which is the risk that interest rates will be above or below expected interest rates over the term of the contract. Credit risk is the risk that an insured will default on its premium payment to an insurer. Compared with a guaranteed cost insurance policy, a finite risk policy involves a much higher degree of self-funding on the insured's part, and the insurer takes a much lower degree of underwriting risk.

- A cumulative experience fund balance for a finite risk plan is calculated by adding each period's net premium and investment income and subtracting loss payments.

- Some common variations for a finite risk plan are the addition of per occurrence and/or annual aggregate limits to the multi-year aggregate limit. Limits on the amount paid by the insurer for each year can be added. The insurer can agree to share with the insured a percentage of any investment income that is higher than that credited to the experience fund under the plan. Also, the margin can be based on a sliding scale and, therefore, vary with the total losses that fall under the plan. Finally, a finite risk plan might require the insured to pay an additional premium if total losses exceed a certain level.

- A prospective finite risk plan is arranged to cover losses from events that have not yet occurred. A retroactive finite risk plan is a plan that is arranged to cover losses from events that have already occurred. A loss portfolio transfer is a type of retroactive plan that applies to a defined portfolio of losses.

- Because it is taking a carefully controlled, limited amount of risk, an underwriter of a finite risk plan usually will agree to cover a broader range of exposures than it would cover under a traditional insurance plan. Finite risk can be used for many difficult-to-insure exposures, such as products recall, warranties, environmental liability (including cleanup), and commodity price fluctuations.

- Assuming it receives favorable financial accounting treatment, a finite risk plan can smooth over time the impact of large losses on the insured's net income (profit) in its financial statements. As a hybrid plan, finite risk insurance combines many of the advantages of both retention and transfer. An insured that is able to control its losses receives profit sharing, including investment income on the cash flow of the experience fund. However, the insured is also protected by a limited amount of risk transfer in the event that losses are much higher than expected. A finite risk plan often enables an insured to obtain higher limits than it could obtain under a traditional guaranteed cost insurance plan. In addition, a major advantage of a finite risk plan is that it saves the cost of annual renewals.

- A disadvantage of a finite risk plan that must be carefully considered is the opportunity cost of the insured's capital that is tied up in the experience fund. Another disadvantage of a finite risk plan is that an aggregate limit applies over multiple years. Therefore, if a full-limit loss occurs early in the term, no further limits are available, even though the insured is obligated to pay premium for the remainder of the term. Also, premium taxes on a finite risk plan can be a large expense.

- A great deal of uncertainty exists as to the financial accounting and income tax treatments of finite risk plans. In recent years in the United States, accounting standards and opinions have been issued to severely limit an insured's ability to treat the premium under a finite risk plan the same way it would treat a premium for a guaranteed cost insurance plan.

- An integrated risk plan is a single contract that covers more than one type of risk exposure, usually over multiple years. In general, integrated risk plans combine various types of hazard risk and can include various types of financial/market risk as well, such as movements in commodity prices, interest rates, and foreign exchange rates.

- With an integrated risk plan, an insured combines retentions and limits over multiple years, which is likely to result in premium savings. As long as an integrated risk plan provides an organization with a tolerable retention level and an adequate limit, it can be an efficient way to transfer risk.

- Integrated risk plans usually cover a layer of losses that sits above various per occurrence retentions. The limit usually applies on a per occurrence basis, and there is often an aggregate limit.

- An integrated risk plan can be written above a basket aggregate retention, which is a retention that spans multiple types of risk exposure.

- An integrated risk plan can be written as a dual-trigger cover, meaning that the retention and limit are tied to two different types of risk. The distinguishing characteristic of a dual-trigger cover is that a loss above a certain retention threshold must occur under each of the two types of risk during the same time period in order to trigger coverage under the policy.

- The most important advantage of an integrated risk plan is that it can be customized to fit individual organizations' risk appetite and risk-bearing capacity. Another advantage is that an integrated risk plan provides some hard-dollar savings due to an insured's use of bulk purchasing power and avoidance of annual renewal negotiations. Also, an integrated risk plan can be an efficient way for an organization to manage its retentions and limits by spreading them over several types of risk and several years. It allows an insured to manage many of its enterprisewide risks under a single contract. Depending on the design of the plan, the insurer might agree to cover some risks that are normally hard to insure.

- Under an integrated risk plan, the multi-year aggregate limit might not be sufficient for an insured that experiences high-severity losses. A large loss in the first year of the plan could exhaust the aggregate limit, leaving no limit available for the remaining years of the contract. Another disadvantage of an integrated risk plan is that allocating the premium among the divisions of a large organization might be difficult. Finally, the pricing of an integrated risk plan can be complex.

Chapter Notes

1. Elizabeth Eiss, "Enterprising Solutions," Risk Management, August 1999.

2. Most finite risk agreements give the insured an option to use any balance in the experience fund to increase limits for a past period (retroactive coverage) or to purchase limits for a future period.

3. Given favorable tax and accounting treatments, an off-balance sheet fund would exist because any positive balance in the experience fund would not appear as an asset on ABC's balance sheet. However, a positive balance in the experience fund would be available to pay ABC's future losses.

4. An underwriting gain or loss is usually measured by comparing losses and premium only. For the purpose of analyzing a finite risk plan, this definition of underwriting risk includes expected investment income as well.

5. To offset the credit risk under a paid loss retrospective rating plan, insurers usually require financial security such as a letter of credit.

6. *Statement of Financial Accounting Standards No. 113* (Norwalk, CT: Financial Accounting Standards Board, 1992).

7. The cash flows arising from the premium and loss payments should be compared on a present-value basis.

8. Phyllis S. Myers and Etti G. Baranoff, "Non-Traditional Insurance Programs: The New Generation" (Washington, DC: National Association of Insurance Brokers, 1997), p. 33.

9. A maintenance deductible, which applies to each loss, usually comes into play before the stop loss coverage pays for losses.

References

"Alternative Risk Transfer (ART) for Corporations: A Passing Fashion or Risk Management for the 21st Century?" *Sigma*, no. 2 (1999), Zurich, Switzerland, Swiss Reinsurance Company.

Helbling, Carolyn P., and Georg Falleger. "Rethinking Risk Financing." Swiss Reinsurance Company, 1996.

International Risk Management Institute. Risk Financing: A Guide to Insurance Cash Flow. Dallas: International Risk Management Institute, Inc., 2000.

Monti, R. George, and Andrew Barile. A Practical Guide to Finite Risk Insurance and Reinsurance. New York: Executive Enterprises, 1994.

Myers, Phyllis S., and Etti G. Baranoff. "Non-Traditional Insurance Programs: The New Generation." Washington, DC: National Association of Insurance Brokers, 1997.

Chapter 11

Capital Market Products for Risk Financing

Introduction

This chapter provides an overview of recent product innovations that enable organizations to tap the **capital markets**[1] to finance risks traditionally covered by insurance (or reinsurance). In the past, the

> A **capital market** is a financial market in which financial assets having a maturity of more than one year are bought and sold.

capital markets' involvement in the financing of insurable risk was limited to providing capital to insurance (or reinsurance) companies, which have used this capital to underwrite their customers' risk. The capital market products described in this chapter provide an alternative to traditional insurance (or reinsurance).

Capital market products for risk financing that are currently in use can be grouped into insurance-linked securities, insurance derivatives, and contingent capital arrangements. Products in each of these categories are described throughout this chapter.

Capital Market Products for Risk Financing

Insurance-Linked Securities	Insurance Derivatives	Contingent Capital Arrangements

Insurance-linked securities are financial investments (usually in the form of bonds) that have insurable risk embedded in them. The investor receives a return higher than it would receive if the insurable risk were not embedded in the security. Any loss to the investor attributed to the embedded insurable risk benefits another organization, which is able to use the proceeds to offset its insurable losses.

Insurance derivatives are financial contracts that are valued based on the level of insurable losses that occur during a specific time period. An insurance derivative increases in value as specified insurable losses increase and, therefore, the purchaser of the derivative can use this gain to offset its insurable losses. The seller of an insurance derivative accepts insurable risk and receives a commensurate return for doing so.

A **contingent capital arrangement** is an agreement entered into before losses occur and enables an organization to raise cash by selling stock or issuing debt at prearranged terms following a loss that exceeds a certain threshold. The loss can arise from insurable risk, such as property damage resulting from an earthquake. The organization agreeing to provide the contingent capital receives a commitment fee.

These new capital market products involve a great deal of time and expense to implement, so only a small number of large organizations, mainly insurance and reinsurance companies, have used them to finance risk. Also, these new products have been used mostly to finance catastrophe risk, such as the risk of a large number of losses from an earthquake or a hurricane.

Conceptually, these new products can be used to finance any type of insurable risk for any type of organization. They will grow in importance as a source of risk financing if a large market of buyers and sellers develops for them. A well-developed market will reduce the cost and improve the accessibility of these products. If they prove superior to traditional insurance by efficiently deploying risk capital, their use will grow exponentially.

The convergence of insurance with other financial services is spurring the development of these capital market products. Noninsurance financial institutions, particularly investment banks, see opportunities to expand their traditional business by using the capital markets' capacity to finance losses arising from organizations' traditionally insurable risks, thereby entering the turf of insurance (and reinsurance) companies and insurance brokers. Likewise, insurance (and reinsurance) companies and insurance brokers see opportunities to expand their traditional business by using insurance policies and/or these new capital market products to cover not only losses from traditionally insurable risks but also losses from other types of risk, such as commodity price risk and interest rate risk.

Risk Management in Practice

Convergence of Insurance and Banking Services

Insurance companies and banks are entering each other's turf, resulting in a convergence of the insurance and banking businesses. For example, in 1999 Tokyo Disneyland arranged the transfer of its earthquake risk through Goldman Sachs, an investment bank. Goldman Sachs accomplished this transaction with an insurance-linked security, by which it arranged for $200 million worth of "earthquake-linked" bonds to be sold to investors.[2] Similarly, insurers are offering products that resemble those traditionally provided by bankers.

Securitization

Insurance-linked securities are the first major product category discussed in this chapter. However, in order to understand the mechanics of an insurance-linked security, one must understand the concept of securitization and how it can be applied to insurable risk. This section discusses securitization in general, and the next section discusses insurance securitization and insurance-linked securities.

Securitization means to create a marketable investment security based on the expected cash flows from a financial transaction. A financial institution can use securitization to transfer income-producing assets off of its balance sheet in exchange for cash. For example, a credit card issuer might securitize its credit card receivables, or a bank might securitize its mortgage receivables.

> **Securitization** means to create a marketable security based on the expected cash flows from a financial transaction.

As an example of a mortgage securitization, assume that a bank that loans money to individuals who purchase homes would like to transfer its mortgage receivables (an asset) off its balance sheet. The bank could sell the receivables for cash to an intermediary, usually called a special purpose vehicle (SPV). As a result of this transaction, the bank exchanges one asset for another—it takes the mortgage receivables off its balance sheet and boosts its available cash.

The SPV securitizes the mortgage receivables by using them to collateralize securities it sells to investors. The SPV uses the interest and principal repayments on the mortgage receivables to fund the interest and principal repayments to the security investors. The securities carry the risks of the mortgage receivables held by the SPV. These risks include the possibility of default by the mortgagors (the borrowers) and the risk that the mortgagors might cancel their mortgages because they are able to refinance them at lower interest rates elsewhere. Therefore, through the technique of securitization, the risk inherent in the mortgage receivables is transferred from the bank to the security investors.

Special Purpose Vehicles (SPVs)

In a securitization transaction, a **special purpose vehicle (SPV)** is a facility established for the purpose of purchasing income-producing assets from another organization and holding title to them. The SPV uses the income-producing assets to collateralize securities, which the SPV sells to investors.

A major benefit of involving an SPV in a securitization transaction is that investors can decide whether or not to invest in the securities based solely on the risk presented by the income-producing assets held as collateral by the SPV. If an organization directly securitized its income-producing assets without using an SPV as an intermediary, investors would need to consider not only the risks presented by the income-producing assets but also the overall credit risk of the organization. Analyzing overall credit risk is complex because an organization holds many different types of assets and incurs many different types of liabilities.

A generic securitization model is shown in Exhibit 11-1.

Exhibit 11-1
Generic Securitization Model

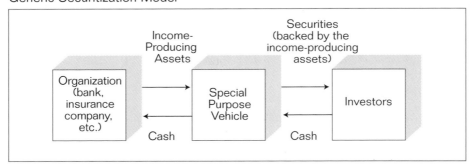

The organization sells income-producing assets to an SPV in exchange for cash. The income-producing assets are no longer on the organization's balance sheet but instead reside with the SPV to collateralize securities sold to investors. The investors purchase the securities for cash and receive a return commensurate with the risk inherent in the income-producing assets that back the securities.

Insurance companies can participate in a securitization transaction in a number of ways. For example, an insurance company can securitize its premium receivables by transferring them to an SPV in exchange for cash. The SPV could then use these premium receivables to collateralize securities it sells to investors. Another type of securitization transaction that an insurance company can participate in is an insurance securitization, which is discussed in the next section.

Insurance Securitization

Insurance securitization is a unique form of securitization. It is defined as creating a marketable insurance-linked security based on the cash flows that arise from the transfer of insurable risks. These cash flows are similar to premium and loss payments under an insurance policy. The insurance-linked securities issued to date are mainly in the form of bonds.

> *Insurance securitization* creates a marketable insurance-linked security based on the cash flows that arise from the transfer of insurable risks.

The concept of an insurance-linked security is best explained through an example. Imagine that an investor purchases a bond from an SPV that provides a premium rate of interest, meaning it is higher than that provided by a United States Treasury bond of comparable maturity. Assume that the bond is relatively free from credit risk because it is collateralized by liquid investments held by the SPV.

In exchange for receiving a premium interest rate, the investor's return on the bond is linked to the risk that a hurricane may or may not occur during the term of the bond. If a hurricane does occur, the investor's return on the bond is reduced if the hurricane causes total property losses that exceed a certain dollar threshold. When hurricane losses exceed the threshold, the investor's return falls in direct proportion to the size of the total losses from the hurricane. The losses that serve as the basis for adjusting the return could be those incurred by a specific insurance company or noninsurance organization, or they could be overall insurance industry losses.

If a hurricane does occur and total property losses are high enough to trigger a reduced return on the bond, the investor's (1) interest income or (2) interest income and principal repayments on the bond are lowered, depending on the terms of the bond and the extent of the losses. The SPV uses this savings in interest and principal repayments to pay cash to an insurance or a noninsurance organization, which uses the cash to offset its hurricane losses.

By purchasing the bond and receiving a premium interest rate, the bond investor underwrites hurricane risk, which is an insurable risk because it can also be underwritten with a traditional insurance policy. Therefore, the bond is an insurance-linked security. It is marketable because it is a financial instrument that can be sold to another investor. Therefore, through the process of insurance securitization, the risk of loss due to a hurricane has been "securitized" by linking it with the returns provided to investors in a marketable security.

Insurance-linked securities were originally designed by financial engineers as a way to apply the risk-taking capacity of the capital markets to insurers' catastrophe risks, helping to make up for a shortfall in traditional catastrophe reinsurance. However, in principle, this new type of security can be used to transfer any type of insurable risk for any type of organization, whether an insurance or a noninsurance company.

Exhibit 11-2 shows a generic insurance securitization model.

In the model shown in Exhibit 11-2, the SPV acts as an insurance (or a reinsurance) company. Cash is paid by an organization to the SPV in exchange for the promise to pay any losses that occur. The payments are analogous to the premium and loss payments under an insurance policy.

The Unique Role of an SPV in an Insurance Securitization

With an insurance securitization transaction, an SPV takes on a different role than it takes with other types of securitization transactions.

- The SPV transforms insurable risk into investment risk and vice versa.

- The SPV receives cash from both the investors and the organization transferring insurable risk. It holds the cash as collateral for its obligation to repay interest and principal on the insurance-linked securities and its obligation to pay any losses that occur.

- Depending on the jurisdiction involved, the SPV might qualify as an authorized insurer (or reinsurer), which enables the organization transferring its risk of loss to treat the transaction as insurance (or reinsurance) for tax and accounting purposes. The advantages of treating the transaction as insurance (or reinsurance) are discussed in the last section of this chapter.

Exhibit 11-2
Generic Insurance Securitization Model

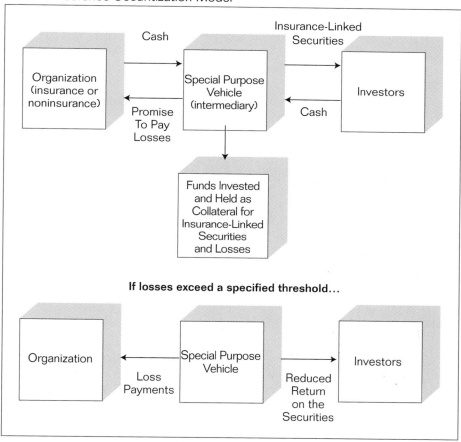

Insurance securitization differs from most other types of securitization because, instead of selling income-producing assets to an SPV and receiving cash, the organization engaging in an insurance securitization pays cash to the SPV and receives reimbursement for a potential liability, namely any losses that occur. The reimbursement for losses can be based on the organization's actual losses or on the level of an index of insured losses incurred by a group of insurance companies. When the reimbursement is based on the organization's actual losses, the insurance securitization transaction mimics a traditional insurance transaction.

Investors that purchase insurance-linked securities receive a return that compensates them for accepting the insurable risk embedded in the securities. The return approximates the amount they could earn on U.S. Treasury bonds of comparable maturity (the risk-free rate) plus an amount commensurate with the frequency and severity characteristics of the insurable risk they are accepting. If a loss occurs, the investors stand to lose interest payments, principal redemptions, or both depending on the terms of the security and the extent of any losses. The SPV holds liquid assets to collateralize both the promise to pay losses and the obligation to pay interest and principal to the investors in the insurance-linked securities.

U.S. Treasury Bonds and an Insurance-Linked Securities Comparison of Credit Risk

U.S. Treasury bonds, which are backed by the full faith and credit of the U.S. government, provide a risk-free rate of return because they are considered to be free from credit risk. Insurance-linked securities issued by an SPV are relatively free from credit risk because they are collateralized by liquid investments held by the SPV. The chance of default by the SPV (its credit risk) is minimal because the SPV does not engage in any business other than the insurance securitization transaction, and the SPV holds sufficient liquid assets (the collateral) to ensure that it can perform its obligations under that transaction. Therefore, investors in insurance-linked securities usually receive a return that equals the risk-free rate of return on U.S. Treasury bonds of comparable maturity plus an amount to compensate them for the frequency and severity characteristics of the insurable risk embedded in the securities.

Just as with an excess insurance policy, an insurance-linked security can be designed to cover an organization's losses either on a per occurrence or an aggregate basis. The definition of covered loss is specified in the contract between the investors and the SPV and in the contract between the SPV and the organization transferring its risk.

Insurance-linked securities can be organized into **tranches**, which are classes of securities that usually differ in terms of the risk taken by investors. For example, one tranche could be **principal protected**, meaning that investors in these securities stand to lose only interest and no principal. Another tranche could place both principal and interest at risk.

A **tranche** is a separate class of security that differs in terms of the risk taken by investors.

Principal protected refers to the fact that investors in a security stand to lose only interest and no principal.

Tranches can be organized so as to mimic layers of excess insurance (or reinsurance). For example, Tranche A could be a class of insurance-linked securities that puts investors' principal and interest at risk when losses from a hurricane fall between $10 million and $30 million. Tranche B could be a class of insurance-linked securities that puts only investors' interest at risk when losses from a hurricane fall between $30 million and $40 million. These relationships are illustrated in Exhibit 11-3.

Exhibit 11-3

Example of Tranches for an Insurance-Linked Security

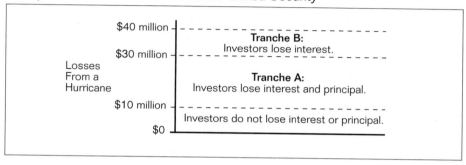

The Investor's Perspective

Insurance-linked securities provide an investor with a unique asset class and are an alternative to stocks, bonds, and other common financial investments. (An **asset class** is a distinct category of investments, such as high-yield bonds or large-company stocks.) Insurance-linked securities differ from most other types of investments because the investor takes only a specifically defined insurable risk and not the overall risks of an organization, as with investments in traditional stocks and bonds. This difference is illustrated in the following example, which compares the risk taken by an investor in insurance company stock with that taken by an investor in an insurance-linked security.

> **Asset class** is a distinct category of investments, such as high-yield bonds or large-company stocks.

Insurance Company Stock	Insurance-Linked Security
The investor's risk includes all of the risks on the insurer's balance sheet. These include the frequency-severity characteristics of the insurer's portfolio of insured loss exposures and the investment risks of the insurer's assets. The investor also takes "management risk," meaning that an insurer's management may or may not take appropriate actions to maintain or increase shareholder value.	The investor's risk is based on the frequency-severity characteristics of a specifically defined insurable risk.

The insurable risk embedded in insurance-linked securities provides a major benefit to most investors because it does not correlate with the other risks normally taken by them, such as the risk of interest rate or stock market movements. Therefore, by adding insurance-linked securities to its portfolio, an investor can increase its asset diversification and, therefore, its available risk-return options. For example, adding insurance-linked securities to a portfolio might increase an investor's return without increasing its overall risk, or its return might stay the same with a decrease in its overall risk. A combination of an increase in return and a decrease in overall risk is also possible.

Insurance-linked securities have gained acceptance by investors, and a small secondary market has developed for them.[3] Rating agencies, such as Standard & Poor's and Moody's, report on the creditworthiness of many insurance-linked securities. The information contained in these reports is essential for selling these securities to investors, which include pension funds, mutual funds, banks, hedge funds, property-casualty insurers, and life insurers.

Catastrophe Bonds

Catastrophe bonds, a type of insurance-linked security, are specifically designed to transfer insurable catastrophe risk to investors. Examples of losses from insurable catastrophe risk are those that arise from hurricanes or earthquakes. Virtually all of the insurance-linked securities issued to date are in the form of catastrophe bonds.[4]

The catastrophe losses that trigger payment under a catastrophe bond can be based on aggregate catastrophe losses over a defined period of time or on the occurrence of a single catastrophic event. Losses can be measured using an insurance industry loss index for catastrophes or the actual catastrophe losses of an organization, whether it is an insurance or a noninsurance organization. Losses can also be measured using a specific parameter, such as a hurricane that is a Category 4 or greater. Sophisticated computer models are used to measure the frequency and severity probabilities of the catastrophic risk that is embedded in the bonds.

Catastrophe bonds mimic traditional excess (catastrophe) insurance (and reinsurance). The following example compares these two types of financial instruments.

Catastrophe Bond	Excess (Catastrophe) Insurance
• An organization pays cash to an SPV, which issues catastrophe bonds to investors.	• The insured pays a premium to an excess insurer.

- A catastrophe loss triggers a default on the catastrophe bonds. Investors lose interest or interest and principal, with the investors' loss used by the SPV to reimburse the organization for catastrophic losses.

- The excess insurer indemnifies the insured for losses as defined in the excess (catastrophe) policy.

Catastrophe bonds can be issued for any type of catastrophic insurable risk. Examples are weather-related risks, directors and officers liability risks, and environmental risks.

Risk Management in Practice

United Services Automobile Association (USAA) Securitizes its Hurricane Risks

In June 1997, the United Services Automobile Association (USAA) used an SPV to issue $477 million in insurance-linked securities to reinsure its Gulf Coast and East Coast hurricane risks. The securities were in the form of catastrophe bonds. The bond investors lose (1) interest or (2) interest and principal, depending on the bond series, if a Category 3, 4, or 5 hurricane causes insured losses to USAA of between $1 billion and $1.5 billion. USAA receives reimbursement for any catastrophe losses from the SPV. The bond offering was reported to be highly successful, with investors unable to purchase as much of the issue as they would have liked.[5]

Advantages and Disadvantages of Insurance Securitization

Insurance securitization supplements existing risk-transfer capacity and provides organizations with an alternative to traditional insurance and reinsurance. The value of this advantage depends on the cost and supply of traditional insurance (and reinsurance), which varies over time. For example, in recent years insurance-linked securities have helped to alleviate a shortage of catastrophe reinsurance.

Another advantage of insurance securitization is that the obligation to pay losses to an organization and interest and principal to investors is fully collateralized with liquid investments held by the SPV. This feature provides an organization with dedicated risk capital equal to the loss limits provided by its contract with the SPV. One could argue that the financial security provided by a typical insurance securitization is higher than that provided by a traditional insurance (or reinsurance) transaction because, in general, insurance (and reinsurance) companies maintain capital that is only a fraction of the total policy limits they write.

The fact that an insurance-linked security is fully collateralized can be viewed as a disadvantage as well. This disadvantage arises because the funds held by the SPV are tied up in liquid assets and, therefore, earn a relatively low rate of return. If held in riskier investments, these funds, on average, would return a higher rate, potentially lowering the amount that must be paid by the organization transferring its risk of loss. Therefore, with an insurance securitization transaction, as with traditional insurance and reinsurance, the insured faces a tradeoff between cost and financial security.

Another possible disadvantage of an insurance securitization transaction is cost.[6] The cost depends on the return demanded by investors. The relationship between this return demanded by investors and premiums for traditional insurance (and reinsurance) varies depending on two factors: (1) the attractiveness of insurance-linked securities to investors when compared with their other investment opportunities and (2) the state of the insurance underwriting cycle, that is, whether it is "hard" or "soft." Insurance-linked securities are relatively new, so it will take time for investors to feel that they understand the risk involved. As investors feel more comfortable with the risk, the cost of insurance-linked securities will probably fall.

Other factors that contribute to the cost of an insurance securitization are legal expenses and the expenses of analyzing and modeling the risk involved. Legal opinions are necessary for dealing with complex issues, such as compliance with investment and insurance regulations, and they help satisfy investors, rating agencies, and government regulators. Analyzing and modeling risk involves gathering large amounts of data and using complex computer simulation programs, which project the probability of various loss scenarios. Investors use this information to help them decide whether or not the expected return from an insurance-linked security is commensurate with its risk.

Another disadvantage is that, depending on its design, an insurance securitization transaction can present basis risk to the organization transferring its risk of loss. **Basis risk**, in the context of an insurance securitization transaction, is the risk that the amount the organization receives to offset its losses

> **Basis risk**, in the context of an insurance securitization transaction, is the risk that the amount an organization receives to offset its losses might be greater than or less than its actual losses.

might be greater than or less than its actual losses. For example, an organization is subject to basis risk if it negotiates an insurance securitization transaction to cover its losses from hurricanes, but its contract with the SPV specifies that it will get paid based on the level of an insurance industry index of insured losses from hurricanes. In virtually all cases, the organization's actual losses suffered as a result of a hurricane will differ from the amount indicated by the insurance industry index of insured losses based on that hurricane. Although most organizations view basis risk in an insurance securitization to be a disadvantage, it is important to remember that basis risk also offers the possibility that the amount received by an organization will be greater than its actual losses.

Insurance Derivatives

Insurance derivatives are the second major category of capital market products discussed in this chapter. A *derivative* is a financial contract that derives its value from the value of another asset, such as a commodity. A derivative can also derive its value from the yields on another asset or the level of an index of yields or values, such as the Standard & Poor's 500 stock index.

> A *derivative* is a financial contract that derives its value from the value of another asset, the yields on another asset, or an index of yields or values.

An insurance derivative is a financial contract that derives its value from the level of insurable losses that occur during a specific time period. The value of an insurance derivative can be based on the level of insurable losses experienced by a single organization or on the level of an insurance industry index of insured losses.[7] An example of the latter is all insured hurricane losses that occur in the Southeastern United States during the third quarter of a particular year.

Two major categories of insurance derivatives are swaps and options. Organizations routinely use swaps and options to offset their financial risk. Examples are interest rate swaps to offset the risk that interest rates will rise or fall and foreign exchange options to offset the risk that the value of one currency will rise or fall in relation to another. This section explains how an organization can apply swaps and options to offset its insurable risk.

Swaps

A **swap** is an agreement between two organizations to exchange their cash flows based on movements in the value of an asset, yields on an asset, or an index of values or yields. Therefore, a swap is a derivative because it derives its value from the value of an underlying asset, yield, or index. The cash flows are exchanged back and forth between the organizations on a continuous basis throughout the term of the swap.

> A **swap** is an agreement between two organizations to exchange their cash flows based on movements in the value of another asset, yields on an asset, or an index of values or yields.

For example, assume that Organization A has a $1 million loan with a variable rate of interest and that Organization B has a $1 million loan with a fixed rate of interest. Further, assume that Organization A prefers a fixed rate of interest because it predicts interest rates will rise and that Organization B prefers a variable rate of interest because it predicts interest rates will fall.

To accommodate their preferences, the two organizations could enter into a swap agreement whereby, if interest rates rise, Organization B pays Organization A the difference between the higher interest rate and a fixed rate applied to a notional principal amount of $1 million. (The principal is notional because neither party owes it to the other. It is just used to calculate the differential cash flow due to differences in interest rates.) The opposite happens if interest rates fall, with Organization A paying Organization B the difference between the lower rate and a fixed rate applied to the same $1 million notional principal amount. Through a swap arrangement, Organization A, in effect, is able to transform its variable-rate loan into a fixed-rate loan, and Organization B is able to transform its fixed-rate loan into a variable rate loan.

An organization can use a swap to transfer its insurable risk, in which case the swap is an insurance derivative. Insurance companies can spread their risks through a swap arrangement. For example, one insurance company could exchange a portion of the cash flows (premium and losses) arising from its hurricane exposure in the Southeastern United States with a portion of the cash flows arising from another insurance company's tornado exposure in the Midwestern United States. A swap arrangement between two insurance companies is, in effect, a reinsurance arrangement.

Risk Management in Practice

Mitsui Marine Swap Transaction

In 1998, Mitsui Marine arranged a swap linked to earthquake risk in the Tokyo area. The swap has a value of $30 million in U.S. dollars and a term of three years.[8]

Although the majority of swaps have been arranged to mimic reinsurance transactions, the swap concept can be used to mimic an insurance transaction as well. Therefore, the cash flows that arise under a swap that applies to insurable risk are essentially the same as the cash flows that arise under an insurance policy.

A major advantage of swaps is that their cost is less than that for insurance-linked securities. A disadvantage of swaps is that the cash flows arising from them are not collateralized. Therefore, the issuer of a swap takes the risk that the other party (the counterparty) will not meet its financial obligations.

Insurance Options

Like a swap, an **insurance option** is a derivative because it derives its value from insurable losses, either an organization's actual insurable losses or an insurance industry index of losses. The value of an insurance option increases as the value of the

> An **insurance option** is a derivative that is valued based on insurable losses, either an organization's actual insurable losses or an index of losses covered by a group of insurance companies.

underlying insurable losses increases. Therefore, an organization can use a gain on an insurance option to offset its losses from insurable risk.

In order to understand insurance options, it is important to understand options in general. This section explains the mechanics of options as well as the specific characteristics of insurance options. It covers two categories of options: over-the-counter options and exchange-traded options. **Over-the-counter options** are customized

> An **over-the-counter option** is placed privately and is customized to meet an organization's specific needs.
>
> **Exchange-traded options** are options traded on an organized exchange, such as the Chicago Board of Trade.

to meet an organization's specific needs and are placed privately with investors. **Exchange-traded options** are traded on an organized exchange, such as the Chicago Board of Trade.

Options

An **option** is an agreement that gives the holder the right but not the obligation to buy or sell an asset at a specific price, called the **strike price**, over a period of time. A **call option** gives the holder the right to buy an asset. By contrast, a **put option** gives the holder the right to sell an asset.

A call option on a stock gives the holder the right but not the obligation to buy the stock at the strike price during a specified period of time. If the market price of the stock rises above the strike price during the period of time specified in the contract, the holder most likely will exercise the option because he or she can make a profit by purchasing the stock at the strike price and immediately selling it at the higher market price.[9] If the market price of the stock does not rise above the strike price by the end of the option period, the holder is not able to exercise the option, and it expires with no value.

As an example, assume you have an option to purchase 100 shares of AT&T stock at a strike price of $70 per share over the next year, and the current market price is $60 per share. If, during the year, the market price of AT&T rises to $80 per share, you are likely to exercise the option. By exercising the option you can purchase 100 shares at $70 for $7,000 and immediately turn

---

Continued on next page.

around and sell those shares in the market for $8,000 ($80 × 100). You would realize a $1,000 profit on the transaction.

The following graph illustrates the relationship between the value of a call option to the buyer and the value of the underlying asset.

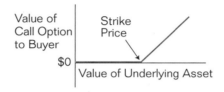

The preceding graph can be related to the example previously given. When the price of AT&T stock is above the strike price ($70 per share), the value of the call option to the buyer is positive. When the price of AT&T stock is below the strike price (less than $70 per share), the value of the call option to the buyer is $0.

The value of the call option to the seller is shown as a mirror image of the first graph.

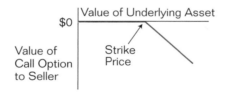

As illustrated by the above two graphs, when the value of the underlying asset exceeds the strike price, the option has a positive value to the buyer because it can exercise the option and realize a gain. If the buyer exercises the option, the seller realizes a loss equal to the buyer's gain, and the buyer receives cash from the seller. If the value of the underlying asset is below the strike price, the buyer is not able to exercise the option.

The seller of the option receives a premium from the buyer.[10] The premium compensates the seller for accepting the risk that it will have to pay cash if the value of the underlying asset exceeds the strike price and the buyer exercises the option.

Insurance options, as do swaps, have the same cash flow characteristics as insurance policies. For a call option, imagine that the underlying asset is individual insurable losses and that the **strike value** (similar in concept to a strike price but involving a value other than price) is set equal to the deductible or self-insured retention level under an insurance

> A **strike value** is the price (value) at which an option can be exercised.

policy. In this case, the call option is an insurance option that serves the same function as an insurance policy with a deductible or a self-insured retention. The buyer of the insurance option pays a premium and receives cash when the value of the insurable losses exceeds the strike value (deductible or self-insured retention level) during the period of the option (the policy period). The seller of the option is in the opposite position because he or she receives the premium and must pay cash if the value of the insurable loss exceeds the strike value.

The following summary compares an insurance policy with an insurance option.

Insurance Policy	**Insurance Option**
• Premium is paid by the purchaser.	• Premium is paid by the purchaser.
• Deductible or self-insured retention can apply to a single occurrence or to aggregate losses for the policy period.	• Strike value can apply to a single occurrence or to aggregate losses for the option period.
• Purchaser is indemnified by the insurer if the level of insured losses exceeds the deductible or self-insured retention.	• Option increases in value to the purchaser if the level of underlying insurable losses exceeds the strike value.
• Has a policy limit.	• Theoretically, has no limit.

Over-the-Counter Options

As previously mentioned, over-the-counter options are customized to meet an organization's specific needs and are privately placed with investors. As a result, over-the-counter options can be designed so that the organization purchasing the option has no basis risk. Because an insurance option has cash flow characteristics similar to an insurance policy, an over-the-counter insurance option can be custom designed so as to mimic an insurance policy by rising in value in concert with an organization's insurable losses.

Option Spreads

A **call option spread** is the simultaneous purchase and sale of call options, each option with a different strike price, with all other terms remaining the same. The net result is that the option spread increases in value within a

---

Continued on next page.

limited range of increasing values for the underlying asset. This is shown in the following series of graphs.

In the example that follows, the holder of the call option spread pays a premium to buy a call option with Strike Price 1 and receives a premium for selling a call option with Strike Price 2, all other terms being equal. Because Strike Price 1 is lower than Strike Price 2, the premium paid to buy a call option at Strike Price 1 is higher than the premium received for selling a call option at Strike Price 2. The difference between the premium paid and received is the net premium paid to purchase the call option spread, which increases in value when the value of the underlying asset increases between Strike Price 1 and Strike Price 2, as shown in the lower part of the graph below.

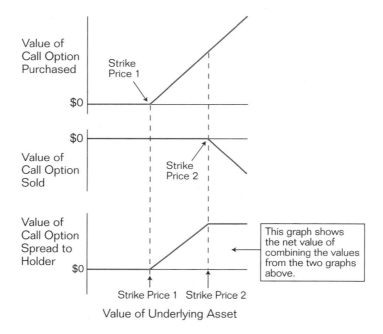

Using the example previously given, assume you purchase a call option that gives you the right but not the obligation to purchase 100 shares of AT&T stock over the next year at $70 per share. Further, assume that at the same time you sell a call option by which you agree to sell 100 shares of AT&T over the next year at $90 per share. (The buyer of the second option has the right but not the obligation to exercise it.) Therefore, you have purchased a call option spread with a lower strike price of $70 per share and an upper strike price of $90 per share.

If the price of AT&T stock rises above $70 per share, the value of the call option you purchased also rises. However, if the price of AT&T stock rises above $90 per share, the additional increase in value of the call option you purchased will be canceled out by the reduction in value of the call option you sold. The net effect is that the value of the call option spread will rise as the price of AT&T stock rises between $70 and $90 per share.

Using the concept of a call option spread, an organization could arrange an over-the-counter insurance option to offset its risk of loss for an excess liability layer. The value of the call option spread would increase if an organization's insurable losses increase between a lower and an upper strike value over the period of the option. These strike values are analogous to the lower and upper attachment points of an excess of loss insurance layer.

Exhibit 11-4 shows a call option spread that mimics a $25 million excess of $20 million loss layer. The underlying asset is a per occurrence insurable loss.

Exhibit 11-4
Call Option Spread That Mimics a $25 Million Excess of $20 Million Excess Insurance Layer

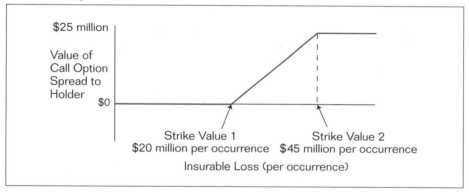

The holder of the call option spread purchases a call option with a strike value of $20 million per occurrence (Strike Value 1) and simultaneously sells a call option with a strike value of $45 million per occurrence (Strike Value 2), all other terms being equal. Therefore, the value of the call option spread to the buyer increases as the value of an insurable loss rises above $20 million per occurrence up to $45 million per occurrence. The buyer of the spread pays a net premium (difference between the premium paid to buy the first option and the premium received for selling the second option) and can use a gain in the value of the spread to offset its losses in the $25 million excess of $20 million layer. Therefore, the call option spread mimics an excess insurance layer.

The following summary compares an excess insurance layer with an insurance call option spread.

Excess Insurance Layer	**Insurance Call Option Spread**
• Premium is paid by the purchaser.	• Net premium is paid by the holder.
• Purchaser is indemnified by the insurer if an insured loss exceeds the attachment point of the excess layer.	• Rises in value to holder if the level of the underlying insurable loss exceeds the lower strike value.
• Has an upper limit for the layer.	• Has an upper strike value for the layer. The upper strike value limits the holder's recovery.

Weather Options

Weather options derive their value from a measurement of weather conditions, such as average temperature over a period of time. An organization can purchase these options to transfer its weather-related risk.

For example, a snowthrower manufacturer could purchase a weather option that is based on the average temperature during the winter season. The option could be designed so that for every degree for which the average temperature measurement exceeds a strike value, the option increases in value. If a warm winter occurs whereby the average temperature measurement exceeds the strike value, the snowthrower manufacturer could use the increase in the value of its option to help offset any lost profit from a reduction in sales of its snowthrowers, which is likely under warm-weather conditions.

Exchange-Traded Options

Exchange-traded options are traded on an organized exchange, such as the Chicago Board of Trade or the New York Mercantile Exchange. The exchange brings together buyers and sellers and guarantees the value of the options. Therefore, exchange-traded options differ from over-the-counter options, which are placed privately with investors.

The most common type of exchange-traded insurance option in use is a **catastrophe call option spread**. Its value is based on an index of insured catastrophe losses, such as insured losses that arise from hurricanes and earthquakes. A catastro-

> A **catastrophe call option spread** is a call option spread based on the value of catastrophe losses.

phe call option spread is usually designed to apply to aggregate catastrophe losses over a specific time period as opposed to losses from an individual catastrophic event.

Both insurance and noninsurance organizations can purchase a catastrophe call option spread to offset the risk of their catastrophic losses. However, because the value is based on an index of insured catastrophe losses, this type of option is best suited for an insurance company, which is likely to face less basis risk than a noninsurance organization that purchases one. The seller of an exchange-traded catastrophe call option spread is usually an insurance company or another type of financial institution.

An exchange-traded catastrophe call option spread gives the buyer the right but not the obligation to settle the contract for cash with the exchange when the value of an index of insured catastrophe losses exceeds a specified strike value. Because it is a call option spread, this type of option also has an upper strike value, which places a cap on the amount of cash that the buyer can recover. Exchange-traded catastrophe call option spreads differ from most types of options because they can only be exercised at the end of the contract period (called a "European option") rather than at any time throughout the life of the contract.

Exhibit 11-5 illustrates the relationships between an organization transferring its risk of loss and the sellers (investors) of an exchange-traded catastrophe call option spread.

Exhibit 11-5
Exchange-Traded Catastrophe Call Option Spread Arrangement

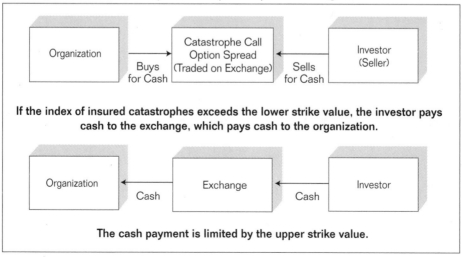

A catastrophe call option spread is similar in nature to a catastrophe insurance (or reinsurance) agreement. The buyer of a catastrophe call option spread pays cash (similar to a premium) and receives money at the expiration of the option if the level of the insured catastrophe loss index is above the strike value specified in the option (similar to a loss recovery). The seller (investor) of a catastrophe call option spread receives cash (similar to a premium) and pays money at the expiration of the option if the level of the insured catastrophe loss index is above the strike value. An upper strike value limits the buyer's recovery and the seller's obligation in the event of a catastrophic loss.

PCS Call Option Spreads

The Chicago Board of Trade (CBOT) is an organized exchange that makes a market in catastrophe call option spreads. The value of the call option spreads traded is based on national, regional, and state indices, which are based on insured losses arising from catastrophic events. The indices are compiled by Property Claims Services (PCS), a division of Insurance Services Office (ISO). Therefore, these spreads are called **PCS Call Option Spreads**, or **PCS Options** for short.

The loss period under a PCS Option is the period during which catastrophe losses that occur are included in the index that underlies the option. The loss period can be from three months in length to a year. For example, the loss period could be the third quarter of a calendar year. Included in the option agreement is a development period, which is a length of time after the end of the loss period during which information about paid catastrophe losses can be accumulated and loss reserves can be estimated. Development periods are either for six or twelve months. A PCS Option settles for cash on the last day of the development period.

For example, assume an insurer writes a large number of U.S. East Coast homeowners policies and is concerned about the potential of a hurricane causing catastrophic losses to its book of business during the July 1 to September 30 quarter. The CBOT makes a market in PCS Options based on the level of the PCS catastrophe loss index for the Eastern United States over the third quarter of the year. Early in the year, the insurer could purchase a quantity of these PCS Options on the CBOT. The insurer selects the quantity of options based on its exposure to catastrophic loss. Assume that the options have a six-month development period. If, on March 30 of the next year (at the end of the loss development period), the PCS catastrophe loss index for the Eastern United States is above the strike value contained in the PCS Options, the insurer would receive cash from the exchange. The amount is based on the difference between the level of the PCS index and the strike value of the options. The insurer uses the cash to offset the catastrophe losses it has suffered on its book of business.[11] Because the PCS Option is a spread, the amount of cash received on the options is limited by the upper strike value. If on March 30 of that next year the PCS loss ratio index were below the lower strike value because the Eastern United States has little or no hurricane activity during the third quarter of the year, the PCS Options would expire and be worthless.

Advantages and Disadvantages of Insurance Derivatives

An advantage of insurance derivatives is that they supplement existing risk-transfer capacity and provide an alternative to traditional insurance (and re-insurance). The importance of this advantage depends on the cost and supply of traditional insurance (and reinsurance).

A disadvantage of insurance derivatives is that the market for them is not well developed. Therefore, an organization might not be able to purchase the amount of protection it requires.

As with insurance securitization transactions, another possible disadvantage with an insurance derivative, depending on its design, is basis risk. For example, an organization that purchases PCS Options is subject to basis risk because the cash value of the options is based on the PCS catastrophe loss index. In virtually all cases, the value of the PCS catastrophe loss index will not be equal to the organization's (the buyer's) actual catastrophe losses for the option period.

Another disadvantage of insurance derivatives is that they present credit risk. Over-the-counter options and swaps are not collateralized, so the degree of credit risk involved depends on the financial security of the other party to the transaction (the counterparty). Exchange-traded options are guaranteed by the exchange, so the credit risk involved with them depends on the credit-worthiness of the exchange.

Contingent Capital Arrangements

Contingent capital arrangements are the last major category of capital market products discussed in this chapter. A contingent capital arrangement is an agreement entered into before any losses occur and enables an organization to raise cash by selling stock or issuing debt at prearranged terms following a loss that exceeds a certain threshold. The organization pays a capital commitment fee to the party that agrees in advance to purchase debt or equity following a loss.

With a contingent capital arrangement, the organization does not transfer its risk of loss to investors. Instead, after a loss occurs, it receives a capital injection in the form of debt or equity to help it pay for the loss. Because the terms of the capital injection are preagreed to, the organization generally receives more favorable terms than it would receive if it were to raise capital after a large loss, when it is likely to be in a weakened financial condition.

Investors in a contingent capital arrangement become creditors of, or equity investors in, the organization following a loss. A contingent capital arrangement is usually set up as an option, so the organization that purchases a contingent capital arrangement is not obligated to exercise the option even if losses exceed the threshold specified in the agreement.

Contingent capital can be provided in the form of a loan, surplus notes, or equity. Exhibit 11-6 shows the types of contingent capital arrangements that are discussed in this section.

Exhibit 11-6

Contingent Capital Arrangements

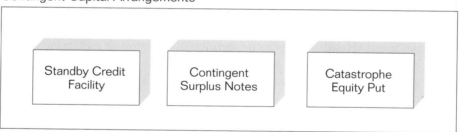

Standby Credit Facility

A **standby credit facility** is an arrangement whereby a bank or another financial institution agrees to provide a loan to an organization in the event of a loss. The credit is prearranged so that the terms, such as the interest rate and principal repayment schedule, are known in advance of a loss. In exchange for this credit commitment, the organization taking out the line of credit pays a commitment fee.

A **standby credit facility** is an arrangement whereby a bank or another financial institution agrees to provide a loan to an organization in the event of a loss.

Risk Management in Practice
Lloyd's Contingent Credit Coverage[12]
In early 1999, Lloyd's of London purchased contingent credit coverage to protect its Central Fund. The coverage, which has an aggregate limit of 500 million British pounds, helps reinforce the security provided by Lloyd's.

Contingent Surplus Notes

In the United States, statutory accounting rules allow insurance companies to issue **surplus notes**, which are notes sold to investors that are counted as policyholders' surplus rather than as a liability on an insurer's statutory balance sheet. A benefit of surplus notes is that they increase an insurer's assets without increasing its liabilities. (Regular debt increases both assets and liabilities.) Although surplus notes have many of the characteristics of debt, their treatment as equity (policyholders' surplus) on an insurer's statutory balance sheet allows an insurer to increase its capacity to write business.

> **Surplus notes** are notes sold to investors by an insurance company and counted as policyholders' surplus on the insurance company's statutory balance sheet.

Contingent surplus notes are prearranged so that an insurer, at its option, can immediately obtain funds by issuing surplus notes at a preagreed-to rate of interest. An insurer can use the funds to bolster its surplus following a loss. Both Nationwide Mutual Insurance Company and Arkwright Mutual Insurance Company have used contingent surplus notes as part of their strategic risk financing for catastrophic losses.[13]

> A **contingent surplus note** is an agreement that allows an insurer, at its option, to immediately issue surplus notes and obtain funds.

Contingent surplus notes are made available to an insurer through a trust, known as a **contingent surplus note (CSN) trust**. The trust receives funds from investors and places them in liquid investments, such as U.S. Treasury securities. In exchange, the investors receive trust notes from the CSN trust. For a specified period of time, the insurer, at its option, can receive the cash value of the investments in the trust in exchange for surplus notes that it issues to the trust. Therefore, the insurer has a standby source of cash that it can use to help itself recover from large losses.

> A **contingent surplus note (CSN) trust** is a trust that is established for the purpose of purchasing surplus notes from an insurer, at the insurer's option, at preagreed-to terms.

As compensation, investors in the CSN trust receive a return higher than that available from other liquid investments of comparable maturity because the investors (1) provide standby funds to the insurer and (2) take the credit risk involved with any surplus notes that are issued. The cost to the insurer for the option to issue surplus notes is the difference between what the investors receive and the return on liquid securities purchased by the CSN trust.

If it exercises its right to issue the surplus notes, the insurer must repay interest and principal to the CSN trust over time so that funds are available to provide interest and principal repayments on the trust notes to the investors. Exhibit 11-7 illustrates the relationships among the investors (capital providers), the trust, and insurers for contingent surplus notes.

Exhibit 11-7
Contingent Surplus Note Arrangement

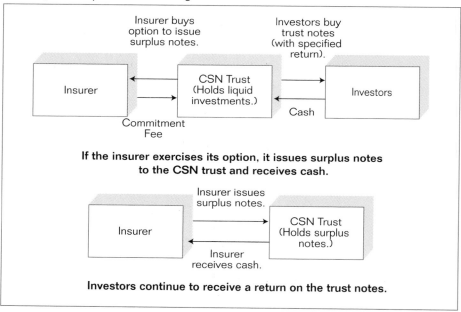

A major benefit of contingent surplus notes is that funds are available to the insurer at a preagreed-to rate of interest after a loss. Without this arrangement, after a large loss the insurer might find it difficult to issue surplus notes on favorable terms.

Catastrophe Equity Put Options

Catastrophe equity put options (also called catastrophe equity puts) are another way for an insurer or a noninsurance organization to raise funds in the event of a catastrophic loss. As previously mentioned, a put option is a right to sell an asset at a predetermined price. A **catastrophe equity put option** is a right to sell equity (stock) at a predetermined price in the event of a catastrophic loss. The purchaser of a catastrophe equity put option pays a commitment fee to the seller, which agrees to purchase the equity at a preagreed-to price in the event of a catastrophic loss, as defined in the put agreement.

> A **catastrophe equity put option** is the right to sell equity at a predetermined price in the event of a catastrophic loss.

Exhibit 11-8 illustrates the relationship between an insurance or a noninsurance organization (the buyer) and an investor (the seller) in a catastrophe equity put.

Exhibit 11-8
Catastrophe Equity Put Arrangement

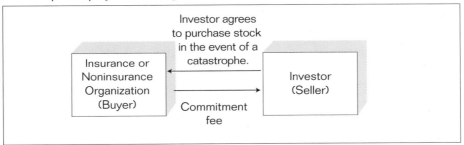

A major advantage of catastrophe equity puts is that they make equity funds available at a preagreed-to price when an organization needs them the most: immediately following a catastrophe. If an organization suffers a loss of capital due to a catastrophe, its stock price is likely to fall, lowering the amount it would receive for newly issued stock. Catastrophe equity puts provide instant equity at a predetermined price to help an organization regain its capital following a catastrophe.

A disadvantage of catastrophe equity puts is that they dilute ownership in the organization following a loss. The amount of equity increases when the put option is exercised, thereby reducing the existing shareholders' percentage of ownership.

Risk Management in Practice
RLI Corp. Catastrophe Equity Put[14]
In 1996, RLI Corp. and Centre Re entered into a catastrophe equity put agreement. If RLI's losses from a California earthquake exceed the limit of its catastrophe reinsurance program, then Centre Re buys up to $50 million of newly issued nonvoting preferred shares in RLI. This gives RLI an injection of up to $50 million in capital if a California earthquake reduces its surplus. RLI reportedly paid Centre Re a commitment fee of about $1 million per year for this put option.

Analyzing the Concerns of Organizations Transferring Risk and Investors Supplying Capital

The capital market products for risk financing described in this chapter can be analyzed in terms of various characteristics that determine their attractiveness to (1) the organizations that use them to transfer risk and (2) the investors that supply the risk capital.

Organizations Transferring Risk

The organizations that use insurance-linked securities and insurance derivatives to transfer risk are concerned with cost, the financial security (credit risk) of the parties supplying the risk capital, and the risk that the amount received might not match the amount of their loss (basis risk). Exhibit 11-9 compares traditional insurance (and reinsurance), insurance-linked securities, and various types of insurance derivatives in terms of financial security (credit risk) and basis risk.

Insurance-linked securities, traditional insurance (and reinsurance), and exchange-traded options are shown as providing a high level of financial security. Insurance-linked securities fall into this category because they are usually fully collateralized. The financial security of traditional insurance (and reinsurance) varies, depending on the strength of the balance sheet of the insurer (or reinsurer). The value of exchange-traded options is guaranteed by the exchange on which they are traded. The financial security of over-the-counter options and swaps varies depending on the financial strength of the other party (the counterparty) to the transaction, so these financial instruments are shown as having a lower level of financial security.

Over-the-counter options and traditional insurance (and reinsurance) are shown as having a low level of basis risk. Over-the-counter options, like traditional insurance and reinsurance, are usually custom-tailored to the organization, providing indemnification for its actual losses. Exchange-traded options tend to have high basis risk because their value is based on an insurance industry loss index. Insurance-linked securities and swaps can be designed to have high or low basis risk, depending on whether their value is based on an index or an organization's actual losses.

When using insurance-linked securities and insurance derivatives (swaps and options) to offset its losses, an organization must decide on the relative importance it places on financial security and basis risk. As previously mentioned, there is a tradeoff between cost and financial security. Products that provide high financial security tend to cost more than those that provide low financial security. There is also a tradeoff between cost and basis risk. Products that provide a perfect hedge (no basis risk) against an organization's losses tend to cost more than those that do not.

Exhibit 11-9
Insurance (Reinsurance), Insurance-Linked Securities, and Insurance Derivatives[15]: Financial Security and Basis Risk

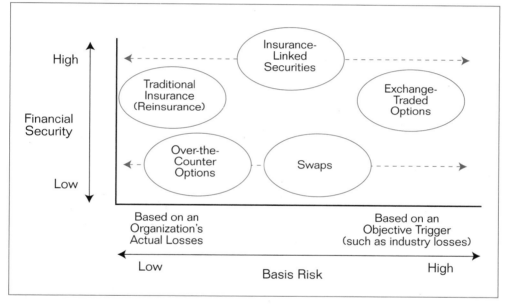

The purchasers of contingent capital arrangements have similar concerns to those mentioned previously. These concerns include cost, the creditworthiness of the party supplying the risk capital, and the adequacy of the prearranged capital injection for recovering from a loss.

Investors Supplying Capital

The investors that supply risk capital for these new capital market products are concerned with **moral hazard**, which is the degree to which an organization can influence the level of its insurable losses that occur. For example, an organization could decide that, because it has transferred or otherwise financed its risk, it will not be diligent in preventing or settling its losses.

> A **moral hazard** exists when an organization can influence the level of its insurable losses.

Capital market products that are based on objective triggers, such as loss indices or earthquake parameters, eliminate moral hazard. However, these objective triggers introduce basis risk to the transaction. By contrast, when a transaction is based on an organization's own losses so that there is little or no basis risk, a degree of moral hazard could be involved. Therefore, a tradeoff

> An **objective trigger** is a measurement that determines the value of an insurance-related capital market product based on a parameter that is not within the control of the organization transferring its risk. Examples are an insurance industry loss index or an earthquake parameter, such as a Category 4.

exists between basis risk and moral hazard. In general, the lower the degree of basis risk, the higher the degree of moral hazard. This relationship helps explain why capital market products that have little or no basis risk tend to cost more than those that do not.

Regulatory and Accounting Issues

A major issue with regard to insurance-linked securities and insurance derivatives is whether they are "insurance" and should be regulated as such. It can be argued that "insurance" is a contract that indemnifies an organization for its actual losses and that an insured organization must have an insurable interest that is the subject of an insurance contract. Based on these requirements, one could argue that insurance-linked securities and insurance derivatives (swaps and options) that are valued based on an organization's actual losses are insurance and should be regulated as such. Using the same logic, one could argue that insurance-linked securities and insurance derivatives that are valued based on an objective trigger, such as an index of insurance industry losses, are not insurance and, therefore, should not be regulated as such. This regulatory issue is still evolving and will test the current definitions of insurance.

If insurance-linked securities and insurance derivatives are determined to be insurance, then the organizations that use them to transfer risk as well as the investors that supply risk capital must comply with insurance regulations. State premium taxes would need to be paid. The amount paid (premiums) to transfer risk would probably be tax-deductible to the insured organization, which would not be required to record outstanding losses that are covered by the insurance on the liability section of its balance sheet.

If insurance-linked securities and insurance derivatives are determined not to be insurance, then the investors must comply with the requirements of the various regulators of securities and derivatives, such as the Securities and Exchange Commission and the Commodities Futures Trading Commission in the United States. Also, an organization probably cannot deduct for tax purposes the amount it pays to transfer risk because that amount would be considered an investment in an asset rather than an insurance premium expense. In addition, the organization must record on its balance sheet outstanding losses that are meant to be covered by the proceeds from the insurance-linked security or insurance derivative. However, the organization can show a corresponding asset on its balance sheet for the fair value of the insurance-linked security or insurance derivative.

FAS 133 in the United States

In 1998, the Financial Accounting Standards Board (FASB) of the United States issued *FAS 133* titled *Accounting for Derivative Instruments and Hedging Activities*. **FAS 133** requires that derivative instruments, except those that qualify for hedge accounting, be valued on an organization's balance sheet at fair value. Therefore, changes in the value of investments in speculative derivatives will show up immediately in the company's net worth.[16]

Statutory Accounting Practices In the United States

In most U.S. states, statutory accounting practices for insurance and reinsurance companies do not allow premium- and loss-offset benefits for insurance-linked securities and insurance derivatives. Cash paid by an insurer (or a reinsurer) for an insurance-linked security or an insurance derivative is not subtracted from the insurer's (or reinsurer's) direct written premium on its statutory financial statements. Also, the insurer (or reinsurer) is not allowed to subtract ("net out") from its loss reserves the portion of loss reserves meant to be covered by insurance-linked securities or insurance derivatives. Instead, both the value of the losses (a liability) and the value of the insurance-linked securities and insurance derivatives (an asset) are recorded on the insurer's (or reinsurer's) balance sheet.

Therefore, with the use of insurance-linked securities and insurance derivatives, an insurer's (or reinsurer's) reported ratio of net written premium to policyholders' surplus is higher (a disadvantage) than it would be using traditional reinsurance to offset the same losses. Also, its net loss reserves are higher than they would otherwise be. The accounting practices that produce these disadvantages may be eliminated by regulators over time as capital market products for risk financing become more common.[17] As explained below, these accounting disadvantages can be avoided by using an SPV that qualifies as a reinsurer under U.S. statutory accounting practices.

Tax and Accounting Advantages to Using an SPV With an Insurance-Linked Security

As previously mentioned, with insurance-linked securities, the insurance securitization transaction usually involves an SPV. For a transaction involving a U.S. organization, the SPV usually qualifies as an insurer or a reinsurer under U.S. state insurance regulations. In this case, the organization transferring its risk of loss benefits from having the transaction treated as insurance (or reinsurance) because the organization overcomes the previously mentioned tax and accounting disadvantages. Although most SPVs to date have been formed in jurisdictions with limited regulation such as Bermuda, U.S. insurance regulators are encouraging the formation of onshore SPVs in various states.

Risk Management in Practice
INEX Insurance Exchange Allowed To Establish Special Purpose Vehicles

In 1999, the Illinois Insurance Department allowed the INEX Insurance Exchange to set up special purpose vehicles (SPVs) for the purpose of conducting insurance securitization transactions. Shortly thereafter, Kemper Insurance Companies purchased $100 million of Midwest earthquake coverage from an SPV named Domestic Re, which through its parent company, Domestic, Inc., issued notes and bonds to investors. Domestic Re was established on the INEX Insurance Exchange.[18]

Summary

- This chapter provides an overview of recent product innovations that enable organizations to tap the capital markets to hedge, or offset, the risks that insurance (or reinsurance) policies have traditionally covered. These products include insurance-linked securities, insurance derivatives, and contingent capital arrangements. The convergence of insurance with other financial services is spurring the development of these new capital market products, and their future growth depends on their ability to deploy capital efficiently.

- Securitization means to create a marketable security based on the expected cash flows from a financial transaction. Insurance securitization is a unique form of securitization because it involves creating a marketable insurance-linked security based on the cash flows that arise from the transfer of insurable risks. The insurance-linked securities issued to date are mainly in the form of catastrophe bonds, which can be designed to mimic an excess insurance (or reinsurance) layer. Investors are attracted to insurance-linked securities because they constitute a distinct asset class with risk that does not correlate with that of other asset classes, such as traditional stocks and bonds. Therefore, by adding insurance-linked securities to its portfolio, an investor can improve its asset diversification and, therefore, its available risk-return options.

- Insurance-linked securities created through insurance securitization supplement existing risk-transfer capacity and provide an alternative to traditional insurance and reinsurance. Another advantage of insurance-linked securities is that the obligation to pay losses is usually fully collateralized. A disadvantage is that funds are tied up in liquid investments, and they could be earning a higher return, on average, if invested elsewhere in riskier securities. Another disadvantage is high cost (at present) and the possibility of basis risk.

- An insurance derivative is a contract that derives its value from the level of insurable losses that occur during a specific time period. The two major categories of insurance derivatives are swaps and options.

- A swap is an agreement between two organizations to exchange their cash flows based on movements in the value of another asset, yields on an asset, or an index of values or yields. Interest rate swaps are common. An organization can use a swap that mimics an insurance policy to transfer its insurable risk. In general, the cost of a swap is less than the cost of an insurance-linked security. However, a disadvantage of swaps is that they present credit risk because the obligation to pay losses is not collateralized.

- An option is an agreement that gives the holder the right but not the obligation to buy or sell an asset at a specific price, called the strike price, over a period of time. A call option specifically gives the holder the right to buy an asset according to the terms of the option. For a call option, imagine that the underlying asset is individual insurable losses and that the strike value (similar in concept to a strike price) is set equal to the deductible or self-insured retention under an insurance policy. In this case, the call option is an insurance option that serves the same function as an insurance policy with a deductible or a self-insured retention.

- A call option spread is the simultaneous purchase and sale of call options, each option with a different strike price, with all other terms remaining the same. The net result of buying and selling the call options is that the option spread increases in value within a limited range of increasing values for the underlying asset. If the underlying asset is insurable losses, the call option spread can be designed to mimic an excess (catastrophe) layer of insurance (or reinsurance) with lower and upper attachment points.

- Insurance options can be traded over-the-counter or on an exchange (exchange-traded). Over-the-counter insurance options are customized to meet an organization's specific loss-offset needs and are privately placed with investors. Exchange-traded insurance options are traded on an organized exchange, the most common in the United States being PCS Options traded on the Chicago Board of Trade.

- A contingent capital arrangement is an agreement entered into before losses occur that enables an organization to raise cash by selling stock or issuing debt at prearranged terms following a loss that exceeds a certain threshold. The major types of contingent capital arrangements are standby credit, contingent surplus notes, and catastrophe equity puts. A standby credit facility is an arrangement whereby a bank or another financial institution agrees to provide a loan to an organization in the event of a loss. The credit is prearranged so that the terms are known in advance of a loss. Contingent surplus notes are prearranged so that an insurer, at its option, can immediately obtain funds by issuing surplus notes that carry a predetermined rate of interest. A catastrophe equity put gives an organization the right to immediately place equity (stock) at a preagreed-to price in the event of a catastrophic loss. The purchaser of a contingent capital arrangement pays a capital commitment fee.

- The capital market products for risk financing described in this chapter can be analyzed in terms of various characteristics that determine their attractiveness to (1) the organizations that purchase them and (2) the investors that supply the risk capital.

- Purchasers are concerned with cost, the creditworthiness (financial security) of the parties supplying the risk capital, and basis risk or, in the case of contingent capital arrangements, the adequacy of the capital infusion for recovering from a loss. Insurance (and reinsurance) can be compared with insurance-linked securities and insurance derivatives by placing it alongside them on a matrix with two dimensions: financial security and basis risk. There is a tradeoff between (1) cost and financial security and (2) cost and basis risk. The purchaser of insurance (or reinsurance) or a capital market product must determine the relative importance it places in cost, financial security, and basis risk. From the investor's (the capital provider's) perspective, a tradeoff exists between moral hazard and basis risk. In general, the lower the basis risk, the higher the moral hazard. However, the lower the basis risk, the higher the return received by the investor. The investor must decide whether it is willing to accept moral hazard in exchange for a higher return.

- A major issue with regard to insurance-linked securities and insurance derivatives is whether they are "insurance" and should be regulated as such. If they are determined to be insurance, then the organizations that use them to transfer risk as well as the investors that supply risk capital must comply with insurance regulations. State premium taxes must be paid. Also, the cash paid (premium) to transfer risk is probably tax-deductible when it is paid. If insurance-linked securities and insurance derivatives are not determined to be insurance, then the investors must comply with the requirements of the various regulators of securities and derivatives. Also, the cash paid to transfer risk is probably not tax-deductible when it is paid.

- For an insurance (or a reinsurance) company, there are disadvantages to using insurance-linked securities or insurance derivatives in place of traditional reinsurance. In most U.S. states, statutory accounting practices do not allow net accounting when using these instruments, as they do with traditional reinsurance transactions. Therefore, by using an insurance-linked security or an insurance derivative to offset losses, an insurer's (or a reinsurer's) statutory financial ratios are not as favorable as they are when traditional reinsurance is used to offset the same losses. However, with insurance-linked securities, the insurance securitization transaction usually involves an SPV that qualifies as an insurer or a reinsurer for U.S. state regulatory purposes, which enables the insured or reinsured to overcome the above-mentioned statutory accounting limitation.

Chapter Notes

1. A capital market is a financial market in which financial assets having a maturity of more than one year are bought and sold. This definition is taken from David C. Colander, *Economics*, 3d ed. (Burr Ridge, IL: Irwin/McGraw-Hill, 1998), p. 232.
2. "Tokyo Disney Securitizes $200 M Cat Risk," *National Underwriter*, May 24, 1999, p. 3.
3. An example of a development in this area is that Swiss Re New Markets, in association with Bloomberg LP, provides a pricing service for insurance-linked securities. See the Web site at www.swissre.com.
4. To date, insurers have been the main users of catastrophe bonds. These catastrophe bonds serve a similar function as reinsurance.
5. Rodd Zolkos, "Hurricane Bond Issue Takes Market by Storm," *Business Insurance*, June 23, 1997.

6. As of this writing, investors in insurance-linked securities demand a higher premium for taking property-casualty risk than do traditional insurers (and reinsurers).

7. An insurance policy can be considered a derivative.

8. "ART 101: The Basics of Alternative Risk Transfer," *Emap Business Communications Ltd.*, London, March 1999, Appendix 1.

9. The owner of the option may also sell the option to another person.

10. The use of the term "premium" in this context should not be confused with an insurance premium.

11. The insurer is subject to basis risk, the size of which depends on how well its exposures are correlated with those of the group of insurance companies that make up the PCS catastrophe loss index.

12. "Lloyd's Boosts Central Fund With $600 Million Policy," *Business Insurance*, April 26, 1999, p. 1.

13. Richard E. Smith, Emily A. Canelo, and Anthony M. DiDio, "Reinventing Reinsurance Using the Capital Markets," *The Geneva Papers on Risk and Insurance*, January 1997, p. 33.

14. Gavin Souter, "New Product Trades Cat Cover for Stock," *Business Insurance*, October 14, 1996.

15. This exhibit is inspired by an exhibit presented during a lecture on April 28, 1999, given by Neil A. Doherty, Ph.D., Professor of Insurance and Risk Management, The Wharton School of the University of Pennsylvania.

16. At the current time, the application of *FAS 113* to insurance-linked securities and insurance derivatives is unclear.

17. Derivatives also increase an insurer or a reinsurer's required risk-based capital because these instruments are classified as assets against which capital must be held.

18. "Kemper Transaction May Drive More Cat Bonds Onshore," *Business Insurance*, April 5, 1999, p. 1.

References

"Alternative Risk Transfer (ART) for Corporations: A Passing Fashion or Risk Management for the 21st Century?" *Sigma*, no. 2 (1999), Zurich, Switzerland, Swiss Reinsurance Company.

Chicago Board of Trade. *PCS Options: A User's Guide*, 1995.

Doherty, Neil A. "Hedging and Securitizing Catastrophe Risk." The Wharton School of the University of Pennsylvania. October 1996.

"Financing Catastrophe Risk: Capital Market Solutions." New York: Insurance Services Office, Inc. 1999.

Helbling, Carolyn P., and Georg Fallegger. "Rethinking Risk Financing." Swiss Reinsurance Company, 1996.

International Risk Management Institute. *Risk Financing: A Guide to Insurance Cash Flow*. Dallas: International Risk Management Institute, Inc., 2000.

Latza, William D. "Securitization of Insurance Risk." The College of Insurance, Financial Reinsurance Seminar. April 8, 1999.

Riggin, Donald J., ed. "Financing Risk and Reinsurance." Dallas: International Risk Management Institute, 1999.

Skipper, Harold D., Jr. *International Risk and Insurance*. Burr Ridge, IL: Irwin/McGraw-Hill, 1998.

Spudek, Ray. "Securitization and Insurance: Could This Be Big?" *NAIC Research Quarterly*, V, no. 31 (July 1999).

Glossary

Accidental risk—See **Hazard risk.**

Acid-test ratio ("quick ratio")

> (Cash + Marketable securities + Accounts receivable)/Current liabilities. [Chapter 2]

Aggregate excess policy (stop-loss excess policy)

> An excess policy that requires the insured to retain a specified amount of total loss from the first dollar during a specified period of time, usually one year. [Chapter 5]

Aggregate limit

> Maximum amount that the insurer will pay for all losses over the policy period. [Chapter 4]

Allocated loss adjustment expenses

> Expenses that relate directly to the adjustment of an individual loss; for example, legal defense costs, litigation management expenses, court fees, and premiums for bonds. [Chapter 8]

Asset class

> A distinct category of investments, such as high-yield bonds or large-company stocks. [Chapter 11]

Association captive

> A group captive sponsored by an association. [Chapters 3 and 9]

Assumption certificate—See **Cut-through endorsement.**

Bailees' customer insurance

> Purchased to cover customers' goods in an organization's custody. The insurance applies regardless of fault. [Chapter 4]

Basic premium

A component of the retrospective premium formula that covers insurer acquisition expenses, administrative costs, overhead, and profit. It also includes the insurance charge. The basic premium is expressed as a percentage of the standard premium. [Chapter 8]

Basis risk

In the context of an insurance securitization transaction, the risk that the amount an organization receives to offset its losses might be greater than or less than its actual losses. [Chapter 11]

Basket aggregate retention

A large aggregate retention spanning multiple types of risk exposure. [Chapter 10]

Brand-name risk—See Reputation risk.

Brother-sister relationship

Relationship between one subsidiary and another subsidiary of the same parent. (In the Humana case, this concept was used as the basis for allowing a tax deduction of premium to a captive.) [Chapter 9]

Buffer layer

A layer of excess insurance between a primary layer and an umbrella policy. [Chapter 5]

Business income coverage—See Loss of income coverage.

Business risk

The possibility of loss or gain due to economic variables, such as product demand and market competition. [Chapter 1]

Call option

Gives the holder the right but not the obligation to buy an asset according to the terms of the option. [Chapter 11]

Call option spread

The simultaneous purchase and sale of call options, each with a different strike price. [Chapter 11]

Capital market

Financial market in which financial assets having a maturity of more than one year are bought and sold. [Chapter 11]

Captive insurance company

A subsidiary formed to insure the risks of its parent and affiliates, although a captive is sometimes owned by and insures more than one parent. [Chapters 3 and 9]

Case reserves

The estimated amount to be paid on losses that are known (or reported). [Chapter 1]

Cash flow

Cash inflow minus cash outflow. [Chapter 2]

Catastrophe bond

An insurance-linked security specifically designed to transfer catastrophe risk. [Chapter 11]

Catastrophe call option spread

A call option spread based on the value of catastrophe losses. [Chapter 11]

Catastrophe equity put option

The right to sell equity at a predetermined price in the event of a catastrophic loss. [Chapter 11]

Catastrophe reinsurance

A specific form of excess of loss reinsurance that reimburses an insurer for losses from a single catastrophic event that, in total, exceed a specific amount. Catastrophic events include hurricanes, tornadoes, and earthquakes. [Chapter 6]

Cede

Transferring premiums and losses to a reinsurer. [Chapter 6]

Ceding commission

A percentage of a reinsurance premium that reimburses an insurer for its policy-acquisition costs and other expenses. It can also include a profit-sharing component. Usually applies only to pro rata reinsurance. [Chapter 6]

Ceding company

An insurance company that cedes, or transfers, premiums and losses to a reinsurer. [Chapter 6]

Combination excess policy

Combines the following-form and self-contained approaches for excess policies. [Chapter 5]

Commodity price risk

The possibility that the price of a commodity, such as crude oil, will rise or fall. [Chapter 1]

Commutation

An agreement to extinguish all liabilities between the parties to an insurance or a reinsurance contract. Commutation usually involves a payment from the insurer to the insured (or from the reinsurer to the reinsured). [Chapter 10]

Conditions

Qualifications that an insurer attaches to its promises. [Chapter 4]

Contingent capital arrangement

An agreement entered into before losses occur and enabling an organization to raise cash by selling stock or issuing debt at prearranged terms following a loss that exceeds a certain threshold. [Chapter 11]

Contingent surplus note

An agreement that allows an insurer, at its option, to immediately issue surplus notes and obtain funds. [Chapter 11]

Contingent surplus note (CSN) trust

A trust that is established for the purpose of purchasing surplus notes from an insurer, at the insurer's option, at preagreed-to terms. [Chapter 11]

Converted losses

A component of the retrospective premium formula that consists of retained incurred losses times the applicable loss conversion factor. [Chapter 8]

Cost of risk

Administrative expenses, risk control expenses, retained losses, and transfer costs. [Chapter 2]

"Cost of risk"

A concept that was developed in 1962 by the Risk and Insurance Management Society (RIMS) to measure the cost of hazard risk. It consists of administrative expenses, risk control expenses, retained losses, and insurance premiums. [Chapter 2]

Credit risk

(1) The possibility of loss due to a borrower's failure to fulfill its contractual obligation to pay back funds [Chapter 1]; (2) under an insurance contract,

credit risk is the risk that an insurer will not collect premium owed by its insured. [Chapter 10]

Current assets

Cash and other items that can or will be converted into cash within one year. [Chapter 2]

Current liabilities

Obligations that will be paid in cash within one year. [Chapter 2]

Current ratio

Current assets divided by current liabilities. [Chapter 2]

Cut-through endorsement (assumption certificate)

An endorsement to an insurance policy that states that reinsurance proceeds will be paid directly to a named payee in the event of the insurer's insolvency. [Chapter 6]

Declarations

Section of a policy that contains information that is "declared" by both the insured and the insurer. [Chapter 4]

Depressed pay-in

A feature of an incurred loss retrospective rating plan whereby the insured is allowed to pay the standard premium over a period that extends beyond the actual policy period. [Chapter 8]

Derivative

A financial contract that derives its value from the value of another asset, the yields on another asset, or an index of yields or values. [Chapters 1, 3, and 11]

Direct writer (captive)

A captive that issues policies directly to its parent(s) and affiliates and does not use a fronting company. [Chapter 9]

Direct writer (reinsurer)

Reinsurers that usually do not use intermediaries and, therefore, deal directly with insurers. [Chapter 6]

Discount rate

The rate used to discount cash flows back to the present value. Usually the rate is equal to the firm's cost of capital. [Chapter 2]

Diversifiable risk—See Unsystematic risk.

Drop-down coverage

An umbrella policy provision that states the policy takes the place of the underlying insurance when underlying aggregate limits are exhausted and also states the policy covers some claims that the underlying policies do not cover. [Chapter 5]

Dual-trigger cover

A type of integrated risk plan whereby the retention and limit are tied to two different types of risk. The distinguishing characteristic of a dual-trigger cover is that a loss above a certain retention threshold must occur under each of the two types of risk during the same time period in order to "trigger" coverage under the policy. [Chapter 10]

Efficient frontier

A series of portfolios that maximizes an organization's return for each level of risk. [Chapter 2]

EITF 93-6 and EITF 93-14

Two opinions issued by the Emerging Issues Task Force of the Financial Accounting Standards Board (FASB). Taken together, they require that, under a finite risk plan, an insured should recognize for financial accounting purposes the retained portion of losses as they are incurred. [Chapter 10]

Enterprise risk management

A comprehensive approach to managing all of an organization's risks. [Chapter 1]

Excess insurance

Covers losses above an attachment point, below which there is usually another insurance policy or a self-insured retention. [Chapter 4]

Excess liability policy

A policy designed to provide coverage above, or in excess of, underlying coverage. [Chapter 5]

Excess loss premium

A component of the retrospective premium formula that compensates the insurer for the risk that an individual loss will exceed the loss limit. Expressed as a percentage of the standard premium. [Chapter 8]

Excess of loss reinsurance agreement

A reinsurer agrees to reimburse an insurer for the portion of each loss that exceeds a specific attachment point. [Chapter 6]

Exchange-traded options

Options traded on an organized exchange, such as the Chicago Board of Trade. [Chapter 11]

Experience fund

A fund under a finite risk plan that an insurer uses to share profit with the insured. The premium less the margin, which equals net premium, is added to the experience fund each year along with investment income, and paid losses are subtracted. [Chapter 10]

Experience rating

Adjustment upward or downward of a guaranteed cost premium based on an organization's past loss experience. [Chapter 3]

Externality

Benefits are transferred to parties that do not incur any of the associated costs, or costs are transferred to parties that do not receive any of the associated benefits. [Chapter 2]

Facultative reinsurance

An insurer and a reinsurer agree to share all or part of the losses arising from one of the insurer's policies. [Chapter 6]

FAS 113

A standard issued by the Financial Accounting Standards Board (FASB) that requires the following two conditions for a transaction to be accounted for as reinsurance: (1) The reinsurer assumes significant insurance risk under the reinsured portions of the underlying insurance contracts and (2) it is reasonably possible that the reinsurer may realize a significant loss from the transaction. Although the provisions of FAS 113 refer to reinsurance, they may be applied to finite risk insurance as well. [Chapter 10]

FAS 133

Requires that derivative instruments, except those that qualify for hedge accounting, be valued on an organization's balance sheet at fair value. Therefore, changes in the value of investments in speculative derivatives will show up immediately in the company's net worth. [Chapter 11]

Financial leverage

Borrowing money with the expectation that it can earn a return higher than the interest paid to the lender, resulting in an increased return to a firm's shareholders. [Chapter 2]

Financial risk

The risk that a firm will not be able to meet fixed financial obligations, such as the principal and interest payments on its debt. [Chapter 1]

Financial/market risk

(Not to be confused with "financial" risk above.) The possibility of loss or gain in the value of financial instruments caused by a change in market prices or rates. Includes changes in interest rates, foreign exchange rates, securities prices, and commodities prices. [Chapter 1]

Finite/integrated risk plan

An integrated risk plan written on a finite risk basis. It transfers a limited amount of risk to an insurer and usually includes a profit-sharing arrangement. Finite/integrated risk insurance agreements are usually written over several lines of coverage and over multiple years. [Chapter 10]

Finite risk insurance plan

Transfers a limited amount of risk of loss to an insurer and usually includes a profit-sharing arrangement. [Chapter 3]

Finite risk reinsurance

A nontraditional type of reinsurance whereby the insurer transfers a limited amount of risk to the reinsurer. Finite risk reinsurance is similar to finite risk insurance. [Chapter 6]

Following-form excess policy

An excess policy that covers a loss only if it is covered by the underlying insurance. [Chapter 5]

Foreign exchange rate risk

The chance that the value of the currency of one country will change relative to the currency of another country. [Chapter 1]

Frequency

The number of occurrences of a loss over a specific time period, such as a year. [Chapter 1]

Fronting company

(1) An insurance company that issues policies and reinsures all of the risk to another insurance company [Chapter 3]; (2) (for captive) a licensed insurer that issues an insurance policy and reinsures the risk to a captive insurer owned by the insured. [Chapter 9]

Funded loss retention plan

Any retention plan whereby assets are set aside specifically to pay for retained losses. [Chapter 2]

Group captive

A captive insurer owned by multiple parents, usually from the same industry. [Chapters 3 and 9]

Group self-insurance plan

Organizations band together to self-insure their workers compensation exposures as a group. Applies to a single state. Similar in operation to a pool. [Chapter 7]

Guaranteed cost insurance

"Guarantees," or fixes, the amount of premium the insured will pay for a policy, regardless of the amount of losses that fall under the policy. [Chapter 3]

Hazard risk (accidental risk)

The possibility of loss arising from property, liability, net income, and human resource loss exposures. [Chapter 1]

Holistic risk management—See Enterprise risk management.

Hybrid plans

Combine elements of both loss retention and loss transfer. [Chapter 3]

Incurred loss retrospective rating plan

A retrospective rating plan whereby the insured pays a deposit premium during the policy period. After the end of the policy period, the insurer adjusts the premium based on the insured's actual incurred losses. [Chapters 3 and 8]

Incurred losses

Paid losses plus loss reserves. [Chapter 1]

Incurred-but-not-reported (IBNR) loss reserves

The estimated amount to be paid on losses that have occurred but have yet to be discovered by (or reported to) the organization suffering the loss. [Chapter 1]

Informal retention

An organization pays for losses with its cash flow and/or current assets. Generally, no record is kept of losses. [Chapter 3]

Insurance charge

Included in the basic premium to provide the insurer with premium to compensate it for the risk that the calculated retrospective premium might be higher than the maximum premium or lower than the minimum premium. The insurance charge is a net charge because the insurer will benefit if the calculated retrospective premium is lower than the minimum premium. [Chapter 8]

Insurance derivative

A financial contract that derives its value from the level of insurable losses that occur during a specific time period. [Chapters 3 and 11]

Insurance-linked securities

Debt instruments (usually in the form of bonds) that have insurable risk embedded in them. [Chapter 11]

Insurance option

A derivative that is valued based on insurable losses, either an organization's actual insurable losses or an index of losses covered by a group of insurance companies. [Chapter 11]

Insurance securitization

A recent phenomenon whereby marketable insurance-linked securities are created based on the cash flow that arises from the transfer of insurable risks. [Chapters 3 and 11]

Insuring agreement

Any policy statement in which the insurer agrees to make a payment or provide a service under certain circumstances. [Chapter 4]

Integrated risk plan

An insurance plan that provides an insured with a single block of risk-transfer capacity over several types of risk exposures, which can include financial/market risk (for example, risk related to interest rates and foreign exchange) along with hazard risk exposures. [Chapter 10]

Interest rate risk

(1) The chance that interest rates will rise or fall [Chapter 1]; (2) (finite risk insurance plans) the chance that interest rates will be above or below the expected rate. [Chapter 10]

Internal fund

Current assets segregated in a fund to pay for retained losses. [Chapter 2]

Investment risk

Under an insurance contract, the risk that an insurer's investment income will be higher or lower than it expects. Investment risk includes timing risk and interest rate risk. [Chapter 10]

Large deductible insurance plan

A deductible plan for workers compensation, automobile liability, or general liability, in which the per accident/occurrence deductible amount is $100,000 or greater. [Chapter 3]

Large-line capacity

An insurer's ability to provide a high limit of insurance for a single risk exposure. [Chapter 6]

Law of large numbers

The larger the number of loss exposures, the more predictable the loss outcomes resulting from those loss exposures taken as a whole. [Chapter 3]

Limit

Maximum amount that the insurer will pay for each loss. [Chapter 4]

Liquid asset

An asset that can easily be converted into cash. [Chapter 2]

Litigation management

Controlling the cost of legal expenses for claims that are litigated. It involves tasks such as evaluating and selecting defense lawyers, auditing legal bills, and experimenting with alternative fee-billing strategies. [Chapter 7]

Loss

An outcome that reduces an organization's financial value. [Chapter 1]

Loss conversion factor

A factor applied to incurred losses to account for the unallocated portion of loss adjustment expenses. [Chapter 8]

Loss development

The tendency for incurred losses to increase over time (1) due to the late reporting of unanticipated losses and (2) the upward revision of case loss reserves. [Chapter 1]

Loss exposure

Anything that presents a possibility of a loss. [Chapter 1]

Loss of income coverage (business income coverage)

Reimburses the organization for the loss of its net income plus expenses that continue during a period that a business is shut down. [Chapter 4]

Loss limit

The level at which each individual accident/occurrence is limited for the purpose of calculating a retrospectively rated premium. In other words, a maximum amount of each loss (from ground-up) that is used to adjust the retrospective premium. [Chapters 3 and 8]

Loss portfolio transfer

A retroactive plan that applies to an entire portfolio of losses. [Chapter 10]

Loss reserves

Estimates of amounts to be paid in the future for losses that have occurred. [Chapter 1]

Manuscript policy

A policy with provisions that are specifically drafted or selected for that one contract. It is the product of negotiations between the insurer and the insured. [Chapter 4]

Margin

An amount charged under a finite risk plan to cover the insurer's underwriting risk, investment risk, and credit risk, as well as its administrative expenses. [Chapter 10]

Maximum premium

An amount that the retrospective rating plan premium will not exceed so as to limit the amount of premium paid by the insured. [Chapter 8]

Minimum premium

A minimum amount that the retrospective rating plan premium will not fall below. [Chapter 8]

Moral hazard

(1) Any condition that increases the chance that some insureds or other persons will intentionally cause a loss [Chapter 4]; (2) exists when an organization can influence the level of its insurable losses. [Chapter 11]

Morale hazard

Any condition that causes insureds to be less careful than they would otherwise be. [Chapter 4]

Nondiversifiable risk—See Systematic risk.

Objective trigger

A measurement that determines the value of an insurance-related capital market product based on a parameter that is not within the control of the organization transferring its risk. Examples are an insurance industry loss index or an earthquake parameter, such as a Category 4. [Chapter 11]

Obligee

Under a surety contract, the individual or organization for whose benefit the principal is obligated to perform in some way. [Chapter 4]

Obligor—See Principal.

Off-balance sheet fund

A fund in which an outside organization, such as an insurance company, holds money to pay for an organization's retained losses. [Chapter 2]

Operating risk

The possibility of loss due to the malfunction or breakdown of existing technology or support systems. [Chapter 1]

Operational risk

Specific to a business and defined by the types of risks it includes, such as business, financial, operating, credit, hazard, and reputation risks. [Chapter 1]

Opportunity cost

A forgone benefit from an alternative use of resources. [Chapter 2]

Option

An agreement that gives the holder the right but not the obligation to buy or sell an asset at a specific price during a specified period. [Chapter 11]

Over-the-counter option

An option placed privately and customized to meet an organization's specific needs. [Chapter 11]

Paid loss retrospective rating plan

A retrospective rating plan whereby the insured pays a small deposit premium at the beginning of the policy period and reimburses the insurer for its losses as the insurer pays for them. The total amount paid is subject to minimum and maximum amounts. [Chapters 3 and 8]

Paid losses

The amount of loss that has already been paid to claimants. [Chapter 1]

PCS Options (PCS Call Option Spreads)

Catastrophe call option spreads based on indices compiled by Property Claims Services, a division of Insurance Services Office. These spreads are traded on the Chicago Board of Trade. [Chapter 11]

Perils

Causes, such as fire, windstorm, or explosion, that might lead to loss, damage, or destruction of property. [Chapter 4]

Planned loss retention

The organization has identified and measured its loss exposures and has decided on a retention plan. [Chapter 2]

Policy provisions

Components of an insurance policy that constitute the distinctive agreements that collectively make up an insurance contract. [Chapter 4]

Policy-acquisition costs

Upfront costs, such as state premium taxes and agents' commissions, incurred by an insurer at the time of policy issuance. [Chapter 6]

Pool

A group of insureds that band together to insure each other's risk. [Chapter 3]

Portfolio reinsurance

An arrangement whereby an insurer stops writing a particular line of insurance and transfers the book of business to a reinsurer. [Chapter 6]

Premium capacity

The aggregate premium volume that an insurer can write. [Chapter 6]

Present value

The amount that must be set aside today to equal the amounts that must be paid in future periods if invested at the discount rate, or the rate of return expected on the funds. [Chapter 2]

Present value factors

Factors that are multiplied by future dollar amounts to calculate the present values of those amounts. [Chapter 2]

Primary insurance (underlying insurance)

Insurance that falls below excess insurance and covers from the first dollar. [Chapter 4]

Principal (obligor)

Under a surety contract, the party that is obligated to perform in some way for the obligee's benefit. [Chapter 4]

Principal protected

Investors in a security stand to lose only interest and no principal. [Chapter 11]

Pro rata reinsurance agreement (proportional reinsurance agreement)

An insurer and a reinsurer share premiums in the same proportion as they share losses. For example, if a reinsurer receives 80 percent of the premium, it pays 80 percent of each covered loss. [Chapter 6]

Proportional reinsurance agreement—See Pro rata reinsurance agreement.

Prospective plan

An insurance plan arranged to cover losses from events that have not yet occurred. [Chapter 10]

Protected cell company (PCC)

Similar to a rent-a-captive in which an organization pays premium and receives reimbursement for its losses as well as credit for underwriting profits and investment income. Each member is assured that the other members cannot access its capital and surplus and that third parties cannot access its assets. [Chapter 9]

Pure captive—See **Single-parent captive.**

Pure risk

A risk that can result only in a loss and no gain. [Chapter 1]

Put option

Gives the holder the right but not the obligation to sell an asset according to the terms of the option. [Chapter 11]

Reinsurance

The transaction whereby the reinsurer, for a consideration, agrees to indemnify the reinsured company against all or part of the loss that the company may sustain under the policy or policies that it has issued. [This definition is from Robert W. Strain, CPCU, CLU, *Reinsurance Contract Wording* (Athens, TX: Strain Publishing and Seminars, 1996), p. 776. Quoted with permission from Robert W. Strain Publishing & Seminars Incorporated, P.O. Box 1520, Athens, TX 75751.] In other words, a transaction in which one insurance company transfers insured risk to another insurance company. [Chapters 3 and 6]

Reinsurance intermediary

An organization that provides services to both insurers and reinsurers in a reinsurance transaction by providing coverage and premium negotiation, claim handling, accounting, and underwriting advice. It also investigates, on the insurer's behalf, the financial strength of reinsurers. [Chapter 6]

Rent-a-captive

An arrangement whereby an organization rents capital from a rent-a-captive facility, to which it pays premium and receives reimbursement for its losses. The organization also receives credit for underwriting profits and investment income. Each insured keeps its own premium and loss account, so no risk shifting or distribution occurs among the members of the rent-a-captive. The rent-a-captive facility receives a fee for its services. [Chapter 9]

Reputation risk (brand-name risk)

A real or perceived loss of reputation or tarnishing of a brand name. [Chapter 1]

Retention

A risk financing technique whereby an organization uses its own resources to pay for or offset the cost of its losses. [Chapter 1]

Retention by default

The result of not identifying and measuring loss exposures and/or not deciding on a plan to retain or transfer them. It also can occur when risk transfer is not available or a third-party payer is unable to or unwilling to pay for losses. [Chapter 2]

Retention plan

A plan by which an organization uses its own resources to pay for its losses. [Chapter 3]

Retroactive plan

An insurance plan arranged to cover losses from events that have already occurred. [Chapter 10]

Retrocession

An arrangement to share risk between two reinsurers.

Retrocessionaire

The reinsurer that receives premium and pays losses under a retrocession. [Chapter 6]

Retrospective premium formula

(Basic premium + Converted losses + Excess loss premium) × Tax multiplier. [Chapter 8]

Retrospectively rated insurance plan

A plan in which the premium rate is adjusted after the end of the policy period based on a portion of the insured's actual losses during the policy period. [Chapter 3]

Risk

Potential variation in outcomes. [Chapter 1]

Risk averse

Given the choice, preferring to take a certain amount that is less than the expected value of outcomes that vary. [Chapter 2]

Risk charge

A charge over and above the expected loss component of the premium to compensate the insurer for taking the risk that losses might be higher than expected. [Chapter 1]

Risk distribution

The sharing of risk by an insurer among its insureds. Risk distribution and risk shifting are required for an insured to take a tax deduction for an insurance premium. [Chapter 10]

Risk financing

To obtain funds to pay for or offset an organization's losses that occur. [Chapter 1]

Risk neutral

Being indifferent to giving up an amount equal to expected value of outcomes that vary or taking a chance of gaining or losing on those outcomes. [Chapter 2]

Risk retention group

A group captive formed under the requirements of the U.S. Liability Risk Retention Act of 1986. A major benefit to a risk retention group is that it needs to be licensed in only one state in the U.S. in order to write liability coverages in all fifty states. [Chapter 9]

Risk shifting

The transfer of the risk of loss to an insurer. Risk shifting and risk distribution are required for an insured to take a tax deduction for an insurance premium. [Chapter 10]

Risk taker

Being willing to give up more than the expected value of outcomes that vary for the chance to gain from a favorable outcome. [Chapter 2]

Securitization

To create a marketable security based on the expected cash flows from a financial transaction. [Chapter 11]

Self-contained excess policy

An excess policy subject to its own specific provisions. It does not depend on the provisions of the underlying policies for determining the scope of the coverage. [Chapter 5]

Self-insurance

A loss retention plan for which an organization keeps records of its losses and maintains a formal system to pay for them. [Chapters 3 and 7]

Self-insured retention

(1) A formal retention that sits below the attachment point of an insurance policy [Chapter 3]; (2) in an umbrella policy, the amount of loss that the insured retains when claims are covered by the umbrella policy but not by the underlying policies. [Chapter 5]

Severity

The size of losses in terms of the dollar amount that must be paid to recover from the losses. [Chapter 1]

Single-parent captive (pure captive)

A captive insurer that is owned by one parent. [Chapters 3 and 9]

Special purpose vehicle (SPV)

A facility established for the purpose of purchasing income-producing assets from another organization and holding title to them. An SPV uses the income-producing assets to collateralize securities, which the SPV sells to investors. In an insurance securitization, an SPV plays a different role: it transforms insurable risk into investment risk and vice versa. [Chapter 11]

Specific excess policy

An excess policy that requires the insured to self-insure a stipulated amount of loss from the first dollar for all losses resulting from a single occurrence. [Chapter 5]

Speculative risk

A risk that can result in either a loss or a gain. [Chapter 1]

Standard premium

Calculated by using state rating classifications and rates and applying them to an insured's exposures, allowing for various adjustments. [Chapter 8]

Standby credit facility

An arrangement whereby a bank or another financial institution agrees to provide a loan to an organization in the event of a loss. [Chapter 11]

Stop-loss excess policy—*See* **Aggregate excess policy.**

Strike price

The price at which an option can be exercised. [Chapter 11]

Strike value

The value at which an option can be exercised. [Chapter 11]

Surety

Under a surety contract, the party that guarantees that the principal will fulfill its obligations to the obligee. [Chapter 4]

Surplus notes

Notes sold to investors by an insurance company and counted as policyholders' surplus on the insurance company's statutory balance sheet. [Chapter 11]

Surplus relief

A function of pro rata reinsurance whereby a reinsurer pays a ceding commission to an insurer. The ceding commission offsets the insurer's policy-acquisition costs. This payment relieves the insurer from the temporary reduction of its surplus due to the fact that, under statutory accounting practices, policy-acquisition costs must be immediately charged as expenses. [Chapter 6]

Swap

An agreement between two organizations to exchange their cash flows based on movements in the value of another asset, yields on an asset, or an index of values or yields. [Chapter 11]

Systematic risk (nondiversifiable risk)

Gains or losses on a portfolio of risks that tend to occur at the same time, rather than randomly. [Chapter 1]

Tax multiplier

A component of the retrospective premium formula that adds an amount for state premium taxes, license fees, service bureau charges, and residual market loadings. Expressed as a factor that is applied to the other components of the retrospective premium formula. [Chapter 8]

Third-party administrator

An outside organization that administers claims for a fee. [Chapter 7]

Third-party business

Business written by a captive that is not directly related to the business of its parent(s) and affiliates. [Chapter 9]

Timing risk

Under an insurance contract, the risk that an insured's losses will be paid out faster or slower than expected. [Chapters 4 and 10]

Tranche

A separate class of security that differs in terms of the risk taken by investors. [Chapter 11]

Transfer

An organization (the transferor) uses another organization's (the transferee's) resources to pay for or offset its losses. [Chapter 1]

Transfer plan

A plan whereby an organization uses another organization's (the transferee's) resources to pay for or offset its losses. [Chapter 3]

Treaty reinsurance

An insurer and a reinsurer agree to share losses arising from more than one policy, usually a whole line or book of the insurer's business. The ceding of losses arising from a policy is usually automatic and does not require the reinsurer to specifically accept the policy as long as it falls within the categories of policies covered by the treaty. [Chapter 6]

Umbrella liability policy

A policy that provides coverage above underlying policies but also offers coverage not available in the underlying policies, subject to a self-insured retention (retained limit). [Chapter 5]

Unallocated loss adjustment expenses

Loss adjustment expenses not attributable to an individual loss. [Chapter 8]

Underlying asset

The asset from which a financial derivative derives its value. [Chapter 3]

Underlying insurance—*See* **Primary insurance.**

Underwriting risk

For the purpose of analyzing a finite risk plan, the risk that an insurer's losses and expenses will be greater or less than its premium plus the investment income it expects to earn under the insurance contract. [Chapter 10]

Unfunded loss retention plan

Any retention plan whereby assets are not set aside in order to pay for losses. [Chapter 2]

Unsystematic risk (diversifiable risk)

Gains or losses on a portfolio of risks tend to occur randomly. [Chapter 1]

Weather options
   Options that derive their value from a measurement of weather condition, such as average temperature over a period of time. [Chapter 11]

Working capital
   Current assets minus current liabilities. [Chapter 2]

Working layer
   The layer of insurance most often called on to pay losses. [Chapter 5]

Index

Page numbers in italics refer to exhibits.
For Key Words and Phrases, *See also* Glossary pages.

retrospective rating plans and, 3-14–3-18,
3-26
deposit premium and, 3-14
risk financing plans combination with,
3-27–3-28
Hybrid risk financing plan, captive insurer
plan combination with, 9-4–9-5

I

IBNR (incurred but not reported) loss
reserves, 1-12
Ideal characteristics, insurable exposure.
See Insurable exposure, ideal characteristics of.
Income
investment, contingent sharing of,
finite risk plans and, 10-11
net, over-reserving and, example of, 7-14
Income taxes, captive insurer plans
advantages and, 9-16–9-18
Incurred but not reported (IBNR) loss
reserves, 1-12
Incurred loss retrospective rating plan, 3-17–
3-18, 8-6–8-7, *8-17*
definition of, 3-17, 8-6
paid loss retrospective rating plan
comparison with, 8-20–8-21
Incurred losses, 1-12
Independent risk exposures, 1-19
INEX Insurance Exchange, special
purpose vehicles (SPVs) and, 11-32
Informal retention, 3-3–3-4, *3-26*
definition of, 3-3
Inland marine insurance, 4-13–4-15
Insurable exposure, ideal characteristics
of, 4-5–4-10
definite cost, 4-7–4-8
definite happening, 4-7–4-8
definite time, 4-7–4-8
large number of insured exposures, 4-8
loss not simultaneously affecting
many insureds, 4-8–4-9
loss occurrence uncertainty, 4-6

loss uncertainty, 4-5–4-6
time of loss uncertainty, 4-6–4-7
Insurance
banking services and, 11-3
definition of, 3-7–3-8, 4-2–4-3
risk financing objectives and, 5-14–5-15
risk financing program through, 4-3–4-5
transfer plans through, 3-6–3-7, *3-26*
Insurance charge, 8-13
Insurance company stock, insurance
securitization comparison with, 11-9
Insurance derivatives, 11-13–11-24
accounting issues and, 11-30–11-32
advantages of, 11-23
definition of, 3-9, 11-2
disadvantages of, 11-23
example of, 3-10
insurance-linked securities and,
investors and, 11-29–11-30
organizations transferring risk and,
11-28–11-29
insurance options. *See* Insurance options.
regulatory issues and, 11-30–11-32
swaps, 11-13–11-14
definition of, 11-13
transfer plans through, 3-9–3-10, *3-26*
Insurance-linked securities. *See also*
Insurance securitization.
accounting issues and, 11-30–11-32
definition of, 11-2
insurance derivatives and, investors
and, 11-29–11-30
organizations transferring risk and,
11-28–11-29
regulatory issues and, 11-30–11-32
Insurance options, 11-15–11-23
definition of, 11-15
exchange-traded options, 11-20–11-23
definition of, 11-15
PCS Options (PCS Call Option
Spreads) and, 11-22–11-23
insurance policies comparison with,
11-17
over-the-counter options, 11-17, 11-19–
11-20

M